EPILOGUE

ALSO BY WILL BOAST

Power Ballads (fiction)

EPILOGUE

■ **A MEMOIR** ■

WILL BOAST

B10
Boast
10/14

LIVERIGHT PUBLISHING CORPORATION
a Division of **W. W. NORTON & COMPANY**
NEW YORK ■ LONDON

Author's Note
Epilogue is a work of nonfiction. Certain names and
identifying characteristics of the people who appear in
these pages have been changed.

For information about permission to reproduce
selections from this book, write to Permissions,
Liveright Publishing Corporation,
a division of W. W. Norton & Company, Inc.,
500 Fifth Avenue, New York, NY 10110

For information about special discounts for bulk
purchases, please contact W. W. Norton Special Sales at
specialsales@wwnorton.com or 800-233-4830

Manufacturing by Quad Graphics, Fairfield
Book design by Brooke Koven
Production manager: Julia Druskin

ISBN 978-0-87140-381-0

Liveright Publishing Corporation
500 Fifth Avenue, New York, N.Y. 10110
www.wwnorton.com

W. W. Norton & Company Ltd.
Castle House, 75/76 Wells Street, London W1T 3QT

1 2 3 4 5 6 7 8 9 0

For my family

Contents

EPILOGUE

Prologue

PAIN

M y father was never one to complain. On the morning of the day he died, an ulcer he'd suffered from for years, and left untreated, ruptured and began to bleed. Two days later I met with the town coroner. He told me the end had been painless, that, as his life leached away, my father would only have felt increasingly weak and light-headed. The coroner, trying to make me feel better, was lying. By any other account, when an ulcer perforates and blood, bile, bacteria, and partially digested food begin to spill into the abdominal cavity, you feel as if a knife has just been buried in your guts. You might faint. You might vomit blood or something that looks like coffee grounds: blood oxidized black by stomach acid. Or your body shuts down completely, total collapse its only remaining response to the shock and agony.

But my father, on the day he died, carried his burning, pleading stomach with him on his morning commute and worked his usual day, seven in the morning till seven at night. He told one of the other engineers he wasn't feeling well and then, schematics piled on his desk, worked straight through his lunch. I don't imagine he would've felt like eating. On the way home, a twenty-minute drive, no longer able to endure his pain—or finally, in privacy, willing to succumb to it—he pulled to a soft shoulder and came to a stop.

Six months earlier he'd leased a brand-new Chevy Impala. He loved that car. It was one of the few indulgences he allowed himself, and on my last visit home to Wisconsin, he'd been proud to show it off, especially the built-in car phone, which could be activated simply by saying, "Dial." Another feature of the system: It could instantly connect you to emergency assistance. You only had to push a red button and say, "Help."

But my father sat behind the wheel of his car—pale, sweating, aching, losing his vision—and did nothing. A passerby found him hours later, slumped back in the driver's seat.

GROWING UP, I thought he was unbreakable. My younger brother, Rory, and I wrestled with him on the grape-juice-stained shag carpet of the living room. Kick him, punch him, jump on his back, pull his hair (what little he had left)—we could never hurt him. In the backyard, sawing old railway ties to make raised flower beds for Mom, he cut himself with his ripsaw, and looked down impassively at his meaty, callused hand, now torn open and bloody, as if it were a thing unconnected to him. In the kitchen, he picked up hot saucepans by their bare handles. When I tried, my hand shot back. On the coldest Wisconsin winter days, he went out gloveless and hatless, his face and fingers gone angry red in the frigid, prickling wind. Never bothered him. Freeze him, burn him, cut him, kiss him—he wouldn't even flinch.

* * *

HIS STORIES about his schoolboy days back in England were litanies of brutality. His English master at Bishop Wordsworth's Church of England Grammar School for Boys, to give it its full name, was the author William Golding. Golding would later use his dreary tenure at Bishop Wordsworth's as inspiration and research for *Lord of the Flies*, in his boredom conducting social experiments on the boys, pitting them against each other in schoolyard battles. My father and his classmates—who had nicknames like "Knocker" Nokes, "Taff" Thomas, and "Tarzan" Taylor—not so affectionately referred to Golding as "Scruff," because of his scraggly beard. In the island-tight schoolyard hierarchy, my father didn't fare badly. He wasn't Ralph or Jack—and he definitely wasn't Piggy—but I have little doubt that he ran with the choir boys and the hunters. He was on the boxing team and fought bare-knuckle. By age thirteen, he was beating even the fifth-form boys; he knew how to take a blow. As for a nickname, his classmates called him "Beastie."

Through his late teens, my father played rugby for club teams around Wiltshire, often taking the pitch with men twice his age, men who could only hope to compete by playing dirty. In a scrum, just as the ball was put in, they'd reach out and grab your balls ("goolies," my dad would say at this point in the story, his eyes lit with mischief), leaving you howling while they plucked the ball from the fray.

Dirtiest of all was Doc Mitchell, who played for my dad's club. If a player on the other team went down, however minor the injury, Doc Mitchell would dash across the pitch, do a quick examination, then send him off, saying, "Have that looked at straight away, lad." Club teams struggled to field a full side, never mind substitutes. With an injured player, the opposition would have to play one man short; they'd almost certainly lose.

Once, my dad was sent sprawling by a rough tackle. He went to the touchline, clutching his leg, gasping from the pain. Doc Mitchell huffed his way over and fingered a few bones as if he were testing fruit at the market. "Oh, you're all right. Stop whinging and get back in." Only after they'd won and my father was hobbling off the pitch did Doc say a confidential word in his ear: "Get to hospital, Andrew. You've a broken shin."

A broken shin, a broken foot, a broken ankle—the injury sometimes changed with the retelling. Yet I knew Dad wasn't exaggerating. He'd played out that game with an excruciating injury and done so with pride.

The point of the story, I understood, was not that winners could suffer through and losers could not. The point was that showing your pain was a choice, and the choice not to show it required only an exercise of will. How joyous to laugh and play on in the face of pain! Dad thought the story was hilarious, just another in an endless series of boyhood larks. He cracked up whenever he told it, and so did Rory and I. Even my mother had a thin smile for him.

But now I don't laugh. I think of his refusal, throughout his life, to see any doctor, not Dr. Almgren, our family GP, not a specialist for his rotten stomach, and certainly not a therapist or a psychologist for his grief-stricken heart. Too proud, too stubborn, too tough, too ashamed to be seen sidelined or entrust anyone else with his suffering.

MY FATHER'S FATHER, Alfred J. Boast, captain in the Welsh Guards, set an impossible bar for discipline and hardiness. As a young man, he worked long, dangerous, suffocating days in the coal mines of southern Wales. As soon as World War II broke out, he joined up, and in the last years of the war, he commanded a POW camp in occupied Italy. Back home, he played rugby for both the army and Wales. I barely remember the man—he died when I was four—but in photos I see all I need to know. On his wedding day, black busby hat in one arm, bride in the other, he stands bolt upright in his dress uniform, still tanned from the Italian sun, looking like a statue chipped from one massive block of shale. This was the man who taught my dad how to throw a punch and how to take one, how to lower a shoulder on the rugby pitch and lay the other man flat. The man who beat him when he trampled flowers in the garden, the man whose army memen-tos formed a little shrine in our house, the man he hardly ever talked about, neither fond nor sad memories of Captain Boast, whose mammoth shadow looms over the lives of all the men in my family.

DAD LIKED to play a game when we roughhoused on the carpet: Fraggles and Gorgs. He chased Rory and me around the living room, rumbling after us like one of the giants in the garden in *Fraggle Rock*. When he caught us, he'd give us Indian burns or pinches on the arm he called "Smurf bites" (he could never keep our Saturday morning TV shows straight). I remember how terri-fied I was of him and, at the same time, how much I wanted him to catch me, to pull me close. I was enthralled by my dad's body—the sharp stubble on his chin, his broad chest covered in delicate curls, his yellowed feet that reeked like Stilton cheese—and even when he exacted these reminders of his physical dominion over us, I'd cry out as much in pleasure as in pain. "That didn't hurt," he'd murmur in my ear as he twisted my arm just that little bit harder, "that didn't hurt, did it?"—and I could only shake my head as I clenched my teeth and my eyes began to water, and then I broke out into frantic giggles. And when he released me, I'd rush right back to him.

Once, he went too far, and I struck out at him. He let me go, rumbling, "Fraggles! Fraggles! I'll get you, Fraggles!" in his belly-shaking imitation of a Gorg (with his hairy, pendulous belly he looked like one, too). I fled across the room, picked up his slipper where he'd kicked it off on the carpet, and winged it at him. It hit him, heel first, square in the eye. I was surprised, as surprised as he was, to see him recoil from the blow.

When he caught me, he thrashed me with the same slipper, the only time I remember him really beating me. I can still see the shine in his eyes as he let himself go. He was, for a moment, enjoying himself, relishing pain and giving pain in a way he hadn't since his boxing and rugby days. I crawled away, sobbing, locked myself in the upstairs bathroom, stripped off all my clothes, and sat naked in the bath without turning the water on. I resolved to kill myself just to punish him. But the sting of the spanking had already faded. I got out of the tub feeling like I wanted to retch. What caused that terrible, devouring ache in my stomach? It wasn't that I'd been cast out forever (as I thought then) from my father's good graces but the shock of the realization: I'd wounded him. This unbreakable man—I'd put the first chip in him.

THE OLD WISDOM tells us the longer we suffer, physically and otherwise, the more indifferent we become to pain: We cry out at the first lash, but the tenth is bearable, and the hundredth we hardly notice. Actually, the opposite may be true. During a long ordeal or a long depression, we begin to feel pain *more* acutely; we only learn to show it less. The stoic's creed, the stoic's prayer— what doesn't kill you makes you stronger; bear down and take it, you'll get through; keep calm and carry on—it all turns out to be nonsense. Only years later do I see that my father's upbringing and my own—midwestern *and* English, fuck me—left us uniquely, pathetically unequipped for the course my family's life in America would take.

AT THE END of my senior year of high school, my mother started having bad headaches. She and I were on a road trip together, scouting colleges, when the first big one hit. She couldn't drive; she couldn't even stand. We cut the trip short, and I drove us from Iowa City back to Wisconsin while she lay curled in the backseat, her eyes squeezed tightly shut, unable to speak for the thumping and hammering in her skull. The next day, while Dad was at work, Rory and I took her to Dr. Almgren, then to the county clinic in Elkhorn, then to St. Mary's in Madison. The diagnosis came that evening—a tumor in her brain the size of a jawbreaker. Glioblastoma, terminal cancer. Over the next six months of surgery, chemo, and radiation, my mother knew pain like none of us could imagine. Two days before Christmas, she died, a withered husk of the woman who, as the illness chewed up first her mind and then her body, grew harder and harder for me to remember.

In the same awful week, my father's own mother also died, of old age. These two deaths hardly seemed to affect him; he kept calm, steady, and mostly sober, organizing two sets of funeral arrangements with the same frightening rigor he brought to his work at the plant. I followed his example. I felt I should cry, but I couldn't. I came up with a list of chores and went at them every day until I was too exhausted to do anything but crawl into bed. When I went back to college, I bore down, filling my schedule with as many career-torpedoing courses (Early

Baroque Music, Postmodern American Poetry, Existentialism) as I could, writing arts reviews and fluff pieces for the student newspaper, playing in five different bands, practicing trombone and tuba, practicing drum set, timbales, congas, bongos, laboring to do anything but grieve.

The day my mother died, Rory went up to his room and didn't come out, except for meals, until Christmas morning. When I passed his door, I could hear him sobbing. My father could never seem to compel my younger brother toward the application of discipline, delayed gratification, and tireless work as an antidote for grief. No doubt because Dad, as a young man, had run just as wild as Rory did. (Just how wild and how reckless my dad was at that age I wouldn't find out until later.) Rory started partying harder than ever, veering as far as he could from the straight-arrow path I'd taken. He ditched school, quit doing homework, passed out in study hall after hotboxing a blunt in his friend's Jeep at lunch, tripped on shrooms and acid at Phish concerts, ran the second family car off the road and crashed it into a Cadillac parked in someone's driveway. And my father, who downed seven or eight whiskies a night, tried to cajole, lecture, and bully him out of it. They went to war with each another, Dad threatening Rory with perpetual grounding, military academy, and expulsion from the house if he didn't shape up and fly right. Then, the following winter, every fear my dad ever had came true: Rory was killed in a car accident, driving with his buddies, slamming beers and smoking joints, on their way to a party in the Chicago suburbs.

My father, with no other means of understanding or coping with the pain of Rory's death, turned to the only medicine he knew. Broken by grief, unable to suffer more than he had already, he set to the business of drinking himself to death.

* * *

MOST OF HIS LIFE he'd suffered from a shitty stomach. Hardly a day went by when he didn't bear some discomfort. Now, on ten or twelve whiskies a night, every night, the stomachaches got worse. When he tossed and turned in his sleep, groaning and calling out in the night, I tried not to hear. Some days his guts were so twisted up all he could do was sit in his easy chair in silent agony, his face going pink, then blister white, sweat pouring down his face. But this spectacle could only be seen on the weekends. In thirty years at the same company, he missed only a handful of days of work, even when Mom was sick, even after Rory's accident. We needed to eat, after all. Still, one fact seems cruel to me now: The company gave him an award for his attendance.

TOWARD THE END, he softened. After college I moved down to Chicago and then, two years later, fled farther away to go to grad school. I told myself he wasn't hurt that I drove home only once every couple of months and always arrived hours later than I'd promised. I'd find him in his easy chair holding vigil, staring out the window, down the length of the driveway, drink in hand, his eyes as dull and watery as the ice-thinned whisky. I knew he'd been sitting there as many hours as I was late, waiting for my car, the car Rory had once driven, to pull in. Over the course of an evening, he'd get so stewed he couldn't even hold a conversation, let alone finish cooking the elaborate dishes he'd labored over in advance of my arrival. (Now, he burned himself at the stove, too clumsy, too anesthetized to handle the saucepans trembling under the boil.) In this state, he would sometimes talk about Mom and Rory, halting, apologetic, fumbling for words, as if he didn't speak this language of regret, guilt, and loss. "You and me," he said, "we've got to stick together. We've got to keep the family going." He cried in front of me, and I felt ashamed for him.

ON THE MORNING of the day he died, he called me. He seemed to be in a cheerful mood. "Rise and shine, guy," he said. "Hands off cocks, on with socks!" He used to shout this up the stairs to Rory and me when it was time to get ready for school. Over the years his accent had faded, but his voice still had a musicality, a gruff singsong.

I was hungover and pissy about being woken early. At twenty-four, I was already well on my way to my own midwestern, ten-beer-a-night-every-night drinking problem.

He asked if I'd taken my car in for a tune-up like he'd told me to last week. I lied and said I had. Was I doing okay on cash? "Yeah, fine." We had the same conversation two or three times a week. Sometimes we talked about music—Bill Evans, Modern Jazz Quartet, Van Morrison—but mostly practical stuff: car, money, news from Wisconsin, news from "across the pond."

He told me he'd added me to his AAA policy. He gave me the number, asked me to repeat it back to him, twice. He fretted paranoiacally about my safety and health, even as he seemed to care almost nothing for his own.

"Dad, quit worrying. I've got it, okay?"

"Have you rung your grandmother?"

"I'll call her this weekend."

"Guy, tell me you'll ring your grandmother."

"Christ, I'll call her," I said. "Anything else?"

Nothing else, Dad said, but then he went on about a Dilbert comic I'd torn out of the paper and mailed to him, what he'd had for dinner the night before, a few projects he was thinking of doing

around the house but would have to put on hold, just wasn't feeling up to them at the moment. And then he asked me—a merry,
almost giddy note coming into his voice—how things were going
with my love life, if I'd had "any romance" the last few weeks.

It was an odd thing for him to ask me. We never talked about
those things. I never imagined he would *want* to talk about them.
I'd recently broken up with Claire, my college sweetheart, whom
I'd been dating for three years. I hadn't even had the guts to do it
in person. She lived a block away, and I'd done it on the phone,
coldly but not cruelly (I thought) informing her that whatever
we'd had was over. I believed the breakup wouldn't hurt me—
after all, *I* wasn't in love anymore. That night, and into the early
morning, I found myself roaming the streets of Bloomington,
bawling and tearing my hair. When I told Dad that Claire and
I had split up, that I wanted to "see what else was out there," I
could tell he was disappointed. I knew he'd always been taken
with her. She had a great smile, a bright, quick laugh, and a
pouncing interest in pretty much anything to do with England.
He used to light up whenever she and I came home together—
he'd been hoping for a daughter-in-law. But when I told him we
were through, he hardly said a word, only that I should make
sure I knew what I was doing. Probably he was heartbroken.

"No one special at the moment," I told him on the phone.
"Yeah, nothing much happening. Keeping busy."

"That's fine," he said. "That's fine. Concentrate on your studies." Then he said something else about the car.

Did he know he was going to die that day? When he felt that
first stab to his guts, he must have known something was wrong,
seriously wrong. My God, the self-control! Before calling me, no
doubt, he'd already had to rush to the bathroom and cough up
blood. In less than nine hours, he'd take his last breath.

"Got a couple things I need to finish before class," I said, wanting to wrap up our conversation. "A couple response papers." Actually, I was going to put all that off and work on a story I'd dreamed up the night before: a boy who buries his father alive in the back garden only to be terrorized by a demon plant that grows out of the very same spot.

"All right, guy. Don't forget to call your nanny."

"I'll try her this weekend."

"They say it's going to snow."

"Yeah, that's what they say."

"Drive careful, please."

"Dad, you don't have to say please. I'll be careful. I'll be fine."

That was the end, small talk and my impatient protests. All that pain we shared between us, and we were talking about the goddamn weather. If I sensed—or Dad was trying to tell me—this would be the last conversation we'd have, I was too distracted or too hungover to notice.

THAT EVENING my father pulled to the side of County Road B, halfway between work and home. He stopped the car on the gravel shoulder, parked neatly, turned off the engine. The Wisconsin winter stretched out on both sides of him, the gray dark, the endless, flat fields stubbled with chewed-up stalks of corn. He sat sweating and hurting, staring up at the red button. All these years later, I'm still struggling to understand why he didn't just reach up, press it, and speak that single word: "Help."

He taught me that the worst, the weakest, the most shameful thing you could do was indulge your pain—swallow it down, don't say a word. You didn't talk about it; you certainly didn't *write* about it. His methods killed him, but he did with his pain only what he'd been taught to do, all he knew how to do.

Now the question remains: What will I do with mine?

1

COMEDIANS

Two days before the funeral, Nanny, Aunty Sarah, and Aunty Janet arrived from England, unpacking their floral print canvas suitcases, bringing out their crochet hooks and Alan Titchmarsh gardening/antiquing/romance novels. Nanny had even packed a small tin of Typhoo tea bags: "You just can't get a good cup in the States." They sat in the back room of the house, chatting about the state of their gardens, the ghastly weather back home, all the dreadful rubbish on telly. This was the third trip they'd made to America for a funeral; the bleary confusion of jet lag and shock must almost have felt familiar. When my dad's name came up, they'd fall silent. Aunty Sarah, my father's sister, would sigh, make a tutting sound, and say how often she'd nagged him about his health and his weight. "But he never would listen, would he?"

Whether she'd nagged him about his drinking, I didn't know. (Perforated ulcer: the death of such champion alcoholics as

James Joyce and Charlie Parker.) I, for one, never said a thing about the cabinet continuously stocked with jugs of Seagram's Canadian. It wasn't a son's place to tell his father his business.

"Once you get past the funeral," Nanny told me, "everything feels a bit easier."

It helped having her there. When she said those words, I heard her saying that loss is ordinary, a common injury that must be patiently endured. Just grit your teeth and wait for the bone to be reset.

For all that, I couldn't help thinking I'd been singled out for special punishment.

A CALL CAME for me from Pastor Dan. At my mother's and brother's funerals, Dad had arranged for him to handle the ceremonies. Pastor Dan led a booming Lutheran congregation over in Lynn Township. He lived in one of the lakeside condo developments, drove a convertible (its vanity plate read BAYREV), and before taking up his vocation had worked, semiprofessionally, as a comedian in the area resorts. My family was nominally—very nominally—Church of England. Religion was just something weird that Americans did. Only my mother had any belief, and that came near the end, after a chunk of her brain had been cut out and the morphine started blurring the line between her sleeping and waking.

In his murmuring, magnetic voice, Pastor Dan was telling me how sorry he was for my losses—my mother, my brother, and now my dad. "It's been a difficult few years for you," he said. "You must be facing some tough questions right now."

"I'd prefer a nondenominational funeral."

Let's cut to the chase, I was thinking.

"The service needn't adhere to any one denomination," Pastor Dan suggested. "I could make some general remarks."

But I remembered the churchy things he'd said standing up in front of my mother's and brother's coffins, and I wanted none of it.

"You know what?" I said, losing patience. "I think we'll be okay. I think we'll be just fine. I'll get Tom Solheim to officiate."

The truth was Pastor Dan had done a fine job for Rory and Mom. He brought comfort, perspective, and the proper amount of ceremony to the proceedings. Relating a few stories about Mom and Rory told to him by family friends, he'd even gotten a few laughs.

DOWN IN Solheim's basement showroom, I perused the gleaming, brass-handled coffins, their hinged top halves lolling open to reveal plush, cream-colored, velveteen interiors. (Even in death, it seemed, the body needed its comforts.) I had my eye on a mahogany model, lacquered black with elegant scrollwork, that or the next model up, a hulking slab of teak. Then Tom Solheim showed me his price list.

I asked which coffin my dad had chosen for Mom and Rory. The pine, he said, pointing to the second-to-least-expensive option, just above the cloth and pressboard model. All his life my father kept up a tortured courtship with money. He railed against anyone who had it, especially Americans, who "lived on credit." Of course, we'd come to America for just that sort of life. Dad worked feverishly to get ahead and could hardly bring himself to spend a dime. In almost everything, he'd imposed his own private austerity. Even here in the funeral parlor he'd scrimped. But I didn't fault him. What did I do that night he spanked me with his slipper, after I dried my tears and climbed out of the tub? I went to my dresser and, from the top drawer, where it sat in a little nest of socks, took out my prize possession: a twelve-tool Victorinox Swiss Army knife. I carried it downstairs in my hot little hand and found my dad in the bathroom, where he was inspecting his already purpling eye. At eight years old, I'd already become his acolyte to the profane sanctity of money, the dread importance of how much everything cost. "Here, Dad," I said, offering up my knife for him to sell, "to fix your eye."

A coffin was a purely functional purchase, I told myself. After the funeral, it was just going to be burned to cinders, along with my father's body. Still, I hesitated. "Let's go one up from there." Tom Solheim brought in the paperwork. There would be a slight up-charge for the oversize casket, he explained. My father, after all, was a large man.

AS I STOOD in the lobby of Solheim's shaking hands, I had to fight it down. Family friends and neighbors were filing in, giving me, my nanny, and my aunts their best wishes, their sympathy, their condolences. Was I doing all right? they wanted to know. Was I holding up okay? "Doing okay," I kept saying, "doing okay," nodding manfully to confirm it. The whole time the corners of my lips were twitching. It was all I could do to keep it in.

A succession of men with bristly mustaches, looking uncomfortable in sport coats either too big or too small, came up to introduce themselves. They told me how much they'd respected my father, how much they'd learned from him. He'd expected a lot, they said. He always made sure they gave a hundred and ten percent. This was company-speak, but I understood. For my dad, the job always came first. If the transmission department, which he'd headed for the last fifteen years, made up a fair slice of the company's business, he hadn't made many buddies on the shop floor along the way. He spoke about people the way he spoke about engineering, always in terms of problems.

Next came the sales reps, tanned and wearing gold watches. One of them, Bob, the company rep to GM, I knew well. Whenever he came in from Detroit, Dad took him out for dinner, and I went along and got us into long, vague arguments about politics. Bob was the very portrait of a heartland Republican (he listened to Reagan's recorded speeches in his car), but I liked him. He was the closest my dad had to a best friend.

My friends started to file in. They came into the lobby wide-eyed, cautious, as if intruding on the adults. Now the urge was almost irresistible. Why couldn't I smile, kid around, crack them up? It was like I'd thrown a party, and everyone had come.

"I wish there was something I could do," my friend Kerry told me. "Anything. I wish I could change all of this." She seemed angry she couldn't help. I'd always considered my friends second family, but at that moment I felt like I'd passed some barrier and they couldn't follow—like they'd come to see me off on some ill-timed voyage and none of us could work up the words appropriate to the occasion. If this was a party, it was a going-away.

TOM SOLHEIM had his thinning hair plastered high up his forehead. In a dull, chloroformed voice, he recited a few factual things about my father and then invited anyone else who felt so moved to say a few words in remembrance of Andrew James Boast. Without a proper MC, the whole thing felt queasily tenuous, like bad improv theater.

Bob was first to speak. He told a story, which I can't recall, about the first time he met my dad, assuming in imitation of him an accent more Scottish than English. Still, he handled it smoothly and got some laughs. Two more men Dad had worked with said a few words. His boss spoke about "Andy's" contributions to the business. I'd thought Aunty Sarah might want to say something, but she made no sign. Unexpectedly, my best friend growing up, Cal, got up, marched to the podium, and tried to relate a scene from our childhoods: my dad at a barbecue, serving up exotic Anglo-Indian fare—tandoori chicken, lamb kofta, lime pickle—while the other families were chowing down on burgers and dogs. I was now grinning openly at the memory. Cal could hardly speak. He was more choked up than I was.

Standing before my father's casket, I heard myself faintly, as if from the other end of a tin can phone, talking about West Gomeldon, his birthplace, about his parents, and his roughhouse tales of his school days at Bishop Wordsworth's. I told the one about the time Dad and his friends grabbed Titch, the smallest boy in their form, at the beginning of tumbling class, stuffed him inside the hollow vaulting horse, and spent the rest of the period performing various florid, hilarious acrobatics off and over him. Or the time they rolled Knocker Nokes up in the coconut-hair wrestling mat and left him itching and howling for help until the headmaster, hours later, finally discovered him. And then there were the rugby stories, aka the drinking stories. The club used to celebrate a victory by piling on one of their own, stripping off his clothes, pushing him out of the bus, and leaving him to walk the mile or two to the pub naked ("stark nackers," my dad would've said). Once he arrived, they made up for it by buying him pint after pint, and the night usually ended with everyone wearing their jock straps over their heads and Doc Mitchell swinging from a chandelier trying to piss into a beer mug.

The faces in that half-full room looked up at me, smiling and nodding thoughtfully. Maybe my timing was off. Or I wasn't telling the stories as well as Dad had. He had a dry, anarchic sense of humor, loved Monty Python, *Fawlty Towers*, *The Secret Policeman's Balls*, and *Hancock's Half Hour.* Mom, Rory, and I had loved them, too, or anyway we loved seeing the way Dad spluttered and gagged every time "The Dead Parrot Sketch" came on or Prunella Scales screeched down the hotel stairs at John Cleese, "Oh, *Basil!*" Maybe it was just that so few people in the room had known this side of my father. Maybe they just didn't get British comedy.

My father was a fiercely intelligent man, I went on. Fierce, obsessive, and exacting. Building the flower beds for Mom or a towering backyard playhouse on stilts for Rory and me, he drew up detailed scale designs, hand-selected the lumber, broke out his spirit level and plumb line. When I entered the Space Derby in Cub Scouts, he took my balsawood rocket to work and bored it out on the computer-controlled lathe, for speed and maximum torque of the rubber-band motor. With only a few night school certificates to his name, he'd patented more than forty inventions. Including, I said (bringing out my best line), his greatest triumph, the gas release valve on colostomy bags—otherwise known as the "fart valve." A few laughs, but they quickly died out.

I glanced at the notes I'd scribbled down the night before. This was my father; I knew him better than I knew anyone else, maybe even better than he knew himself. I was sure I wouldn't need more than a sketch to get through the funeral. Yet here we were, already coming to the "but seriously" part of the speech.

Though he was a practical man, I said, relentlessly devoted to his job, he indulged me in every one of my own dorky obsessions. In fifth grade, I started playing tuba in school band; he took me to polka bars in the area, so I could see the tubist up there oom-pahing and study his technique. When I started informing everyone that I was going to be an aeronautical engineer, he bought me books on aviation and gave me design tips on the drawings I made of experimental fighters, their wings laden with heavy ordnance, all scrupulously researched and labeled in colored pencil. In high school, I suddenly shed all this militaristic precision, became a pacifist and a class warrior, and decided to be either a journalist or a jazz drummer (tuba was starting to seem, perhaps, uncool). For most immigrant parents who slave day in, day out for a better life for the family, I told the funeral guests, the moment the kid gets into the arts is the beginning of the nightmare. But my dad never said a discouraging word. He helped me buy my first good drum set and hoarded every one of my clippings from the student newspaper in a fat manila folder.

Telling my father's story, I'd somehow ended up telling my own as well, as if the eulogy were for both of us.

"He taught me to always do the right thing, the responsible thing, to never cheat or cut corners. What he was . . . ," I said, coming now to the rhapsodic part. My father had never really inspired rhapsody, and I wasn't partial to it either. The principles that ruled his life—hard work, caution, an almost physical aversion to strong feeling—had leached into mine like the sloe berries my relations back home pick from wild hedges and use to infuse gin and vodka. Only over the last year had I come to realize that I loved him. And that I was desperate to escape him. "What he was," I said, "he was honorable."

I looked down at my notes. I'd thought I'd need twenty or thirty minutes to rattle through them. It hadn't taken more than five. I looked out at the guests, and they looked back at me, smiling and nodding. I stood there, a manic grin stretched across my face.

The guests began to file out. Abruptly, my laughter drained out of me, and I felt headachy and sore, hungover even though I wasn't. I sat next to Aunty Sarah, staring at the casket, that glorified packing crate with its tacked-on brass fittings, now looking so gaudy and impermanent. The waxy, tight-lipped figure inside wasn't how I wanted to remember him, but there it was anyway, the last image of my father.

Tom Solheim came over and closed the casket. Aunty Sarah and I got up and made to leave, but then something strange happened. I turned and threw myself at the coffin, flinging my arms around it. It was only a touch on the shoulder from Aunty Sarah that woke me from my fever.

"William," she said. "Come on. Time to go."

But I could only stand there. There were photos arranged on either side of the casket, some in frames, some taped carefully to a poster board. Dad with his arm around my shoulders at my college graduation. Mom, Dad, and me gathered around Rory's bassinet just after he was born. Rory and me in our school uniforms in Ireland. The whole lot of us at Christmas, posing in front of the tree, wearing paper crowns. Who were those smiling people? They seemed so foolishly, giddily happy. Couldn't they see what was coming?

2

THE QUEEN ON
THE FROZEN TUNDRA

orest Drive to Hillcrest to Arrowhead to Sauganash—half the streets had these odd, yawping Indian names—to Shabonna, looping down to the lake, frozen three feet deep, dusted with snow, a giant cataract eye in the middle of town: All the hills and hairpin turns on Lakeshore, she took them, attacked them, in high gear and at speed. In snowstorms—the locals called them "whiteouts"—she drove with high beams up, leaning over the wheel to squint into the tunnel of reflected light that kept rushing up to meet her. The wipers kept swiping away the condensation, which kept filling back up, the world reduced to two portholes. Tailgating the village plows and the big yellow trucks out salting the roads, she'd honk and curse under her breath— "Streuth, get a move on"—so Rory and I wouldn't hear, then buzz past in a spray of slush. Well, it was better than Ireland, where you'd get caught behind tractors for miles on the narrow lanes. That really was the countryside, another world. She'd gotten stuck once for twenty, thirty minutes—God, at least—staring at a cart full of hay, until she finally passed and realized it was a donkey pulling the cart.

One clear bright morning, when she was taking Rory and me to school, a patch of black ice sent the Buick spinning. The world slipped out from underneath us; for a vast moment we hung suspended. Then the Buick—the ugly, turd brown Buick Century Dad had *just* leased—hit the high snowbank with a teeth-grinding thump. She shook her head once, twice, the world slid back in again, then leapt out to look. No dings, no dents, no mirrors missing. She pulled off a glove, squeaked the fender with her finger, and what looked like a scratch rubbed off. She leaned against the cold fender, took out her cigs, lit a B&H, closed her eyes, and mouthed a silent *thank you* between drags. For weeks afterward she drove so cautiously it was the locals lined up behind, honking and flashing their brights.

MY PARENTS met in Dreamland.

So went the joke in our family. Dreamland was a light industrial concern on Southampton Water manufacturing electric blankets. Mom worked in personnel. Dad was a foreman on the line, and the dreamiest thing about him, in my mother's eyes anyway, was that he always forgot to take off his hairnet when he came into the office to chat her up. Soon, he was taking her for drinks in town or to the Concorde Club to see the giants (munchkins anywhere else) of British jazz: Ken Colyer, George Shearing, Acker Bilk. She never cared for the music but liked seeing my dad dressed up in his camel hair coat and Yves Saint Laurent shirts.

England in the late seventies: the Three-Day Week, rolling blackouts, rubbish piling up on the high street. Miners' strikes, hospital strikes, rail strikes, gravediggers' strikes—in Liverpool and Tameside, they refused to bury the dead. I'd like to believe that my parents sided with the unions, but there are snapshots of them grinning in the audience as Thatcher addresses a Tory rally in Southampton. Maybe they thought they were primed to enter the managerial classes: Dad's colostomy valve had gotten him some attention. He was headhunted by a plastics company. Chasing cheap labor and low taxes, Filtertek already had plants in Brazil and Puerto Rico. Dad would help open a new plant in Ireland, in Newcastle West, a backwater town in County Limerick touted as "one of the fastest growing in Europe."

I remember trips to the ruins of Bunratty Castle, to Adare Manor, to the seaside, where the surf boomed against the craggy cliffs and huge mysterious caves stretched down into the blackness at the very center of the earth. Even in town, there was the grassy, ripe smell of manure, the flocks of sheep clogging the main road as the farmers drove them to pen, the Travelers' caravans parked in lay-bys. At the Convent of Mercy National School of Limerick, Sister Attracta (the kids called her Sister O'Tractor) taught us Irish. Every morning started with vocab lessons in our Young Ireland exercise books: "*Dia dhuit' a dúirt an pearóid le Barry.* 'Hello,' the parrot said to Barry." We were taken outside one day on a nature lesson. I managed to lose the group and wandered the school grounds for what seemed like hours, terrified I'd never be heard from again, when I came into a clearing and stood there, transfixed by the mild gaze of the Virgin. Spanking was still part of Irish schooling then. When Sister O'Tractor finally found me staring mutely, raptly into the middle distance, she made me take down my scratchy school uniform trousers and set to work.

We'd been in Ireland four years when Filtertek decided it required Dad's skills—he'd gotten the plant up and running in less than six months—at "international headquarters." Dad was going off to work in Illinois, an exotic-sounding place none of us knew much about, except that it was close to Chicago, where Al Capone and Michael Jordan were from. While Dad settled into the job and looked for a house for the four of us (he found one just over the state line, in Wisconsin, which, as we all knew, was famous for its . . . its . . .), Mom, Rory, and I returned to Southampton, where for half a year we lived again in our old house on Clarendon Road.

I don't remember Dad leaving or how often he called or wrote home. I seem not to have missed him much. Now Rory and I went to what Mom called a "proper school," no Irish lessons and no nuns. One night in Newcastle West I'd started saying a prayer. Mom wouldn't have minded (she didn't mind religion, unless they came knocking on your door) except that I kept on and on, listing names—*Declan Meaney, Stephen Casey*—she'd never heard before. "What's that all about?" I told her it was a prayer for the dead—*Tim O'Neill, Michael Casey, Helen O'Shay*—and the names were all of the village dead.

Dad described Fontana to Rory and me over the phone: the clear blue lake, the sandy beaches, white sailboats dotting the water, the huge stone mansions tucked away in the trees. The Playboy Mansion, he said, sat on the shores of Lake Geneva (Mom groaned when we repeated this to her), and Capone and Dillinger once had hideouts just down the road from where we'd be living. Acres and acres of forest, bright green lawns, baseball diamonds, tennis courts, endless fields of corn, red barns, swimming pools—he made it all sound like something out of a storybook. We were escaping the drab, rainy confines of the British Isles and lighting out for the vast plenty of America. A storybook vision, yes, but a persuasive one. In fourth grade I was cast as a little immigrant boy in the class musical, and every time I sang out my line from the deck of our cardboard prop ship—"The Lady of Liberty, I see her! I see her!"—I couldn't help my heart booming in my chest.

SNOWSUITS, heavy coats, woolly hats, earmuffs, insulated gloves, ski masks, moon boots, sometimes two sweaters on the coldest days, ChapStick, ice scrapers for the car, antifreeze, snow shovels, snow tires, salt to sprinkle on the walk, long sheets of clear plastic to tack over the windows, space heaters, hot water bottles, thermal underwear . . . It wasn't just the numbing depth of the cold that came as a shock, or the flat blank Wisconsin landscape, or the minor mountain of snow that could fall in a single day— though these things impressed us deeply—but the sheer amount of *stuff* needed to survive in this new place. At night we lay shivering under our Dreamland blankets, thriftily rewired by Dad for North American voltage. A few of the local mothers had warned Mom that we'd need to be well equipped for winter. They'd given her lists. "Well, really," Mom said on the phone with Nanny, "I can't believe we'd *need* all of that."

DURING THE DAY, with Rory and me at school, she set about putting the house in order. The moldering shag carpet, a brownish-purplish morass of dust and grape juice stains left behind by the previous owners—summer people from the Chicago suburbs— seemed somehow immune to the vacuum. We'd also inherited the Desmonds' old furniture, a mishmash of colonial-themed kitsch: lamps with bases shaped like the Liberty Bell, woodcut scenes of hardy pioneers pounding out wagon wheels, a dark oil painting depicting the Horn of Plenty spilling forth various gourds. There was also a broken telescope, tilted optimistically to the night sky, a broken dishwasher, and several hulking air conditioners, also broken. Dad wouldn't let her throw any of it away. He considered these items part of the great deal he'd gotten on the property.

No matter how hard she cleaned, the house never seemed to yield, remaining sunk and slumbering under an air of stillness and seasonal use. By midmorning she'd be writing yet another letter home—to Nanny, my Aunty Jan, her aunties, her best friends Colleen and Vanessa. Rory and I were curiosities at Fontana Elementary. At the end of our first day, I called out "Cheerio!" to my classmates. A month later, it was still the first grade's pet joke to shout out, at any provocation, "Cheerio, everyone! Cheerio!" I took it hard and quickly shelved my accent, laboring to mimic the other kids' twangs. Rory followed my example. Mom wrote to Nanny saying she didn't know where she was sometimes. One day she was "Mummy," then "Mammy" (as they said in Ireland), and now suddenly she was "Mom."

When she couldn't find the words to write another letter, she'd work on her stamp collection, carefully steaming profiles of the queen or portraits of Lord Mountbatten off powder blue RoyalAir envelopes and patiently fixing them in her album with little adhesive hinges. By midafternoon she'd find herself staring out the window, sipping her umpteenth cup of tea, waiting for the big yellow bus to grind its way by and deposit Rory and me across the street.

But the first thing Rory and I wanted to do when we got home was rush back outside. The novelty of snow, inches of it, feet of it, hadn't worn off—the way it crunched and squeaked under our moon boots and humped over the barbecue grill and patio chairs, the way it erased the world. We'd wade waist-deep into a blizzard just to pelt each other with little puffs of snowballs. We'd dig out caves from the snowbanks piled up by the plows and build forts out of huge snow boulders we could hardly roll by the time they were finished. There was something hypnotic about the way a snowfall would drift and float in the wind, or dart down out of the sky like bullets, or even seem to fall up, swirling and curtaining. Mom would stand at the window, cup of tea going cold in her hands, and watch us playing, listening to our muffled shouts and laughter through the single-pane glass, which trembled whenever the wind came up.

When we finally came inside, she'd take a towel and rub the blood back into our faces, fingers, and toes. She tousled our hair, which stood up from the static in the dry air. (She loved our hair, could hardly stand to have it cut, and so took up the scissors herself and sent us to school looking like haystacks.) She had us strip out of our clothes, sat us at the kitchen table in our underwear, and gave us hot cocoa while our shirts and trousers clattered in the dryer. To this day, I still put my trousers in the dryer before I pull them on, just to remember those afternoons, my mother's hands in my hair.

THE SCREEN DOOR hissing open—a sudden slab of cold air shoving into the house—the door banging shut, the floor shaking as he stomped the snow off his boots on the hall mat—"Dad's home!" Rory or I shouted. She startled at the sound, as she always did, though she'd been waiting for him all afternoon and evening. She cast around her, straightening anything in reach; it was all straightened already, had been hours ago. "All right, you lot," Dad called out, "who's ready for grub?" Yawning and sighing and shaking out his shoulders, he'd change out of his work clothes and into sweats, fix himself a 7&7, and start dinner, clanging pots and pans around and tasting sauces off the wooden spoon. He had a flair for cooking offal—kidneys, oxtails, pigs' trotters, pigs' knuckles—and his egg curries, beef casseroles, and "stump" (carrots and swede—rutabaga—mashed together with butter) were miracles of economy. There was a show on TV, *The Frugal Gourmet*, that he watched devoutly, but I'm not sure it's possible to make a meal for four cheaper than egg curry.

Dad enjoyed his own cooking immensely and at the table encouraged us to laud him. "You like your brussels sprouts, don't you, William?" he'd say as I shoveled them in. He'd assign a topic of conversation—travel or sport—or quiz Rory and me on astronomy, geography, and familiar quotations. Education, or trivia, anyway, was important to him. He liked to affect a kind of colonial gentility—Americans, he pointed out, ate in front of the TV—as if these exercises in self-improvement were our bulwarks against the savagery all around.

"'Genius is one percent inspiration and ninety-nine percent perspiration.'"

"Thomas Edison!" I knew that one by heart.

"'Sarcasm is the lowest form of wit.' Who said that?"

"I don't know, Dad," Rory said. "Maybe you did."

"Oh, very clever, clever clogs. It's Oscar Wilde. Now answer this one . . ."

In the middle of his lecture, the gaseous power of the rich, heavy food building, Rory or I would—

"Disgusting," Mom would say, wrinkling her nose and trying to rearrange her features into scolding. "Absolutely disgusting. You wouldn't do that if we were having dinner with the queen, would you?"

She and Dad were always saying this, as if Lizzie, out here on the frozen tundra on an American tour, might happen to pop in on some of her loyal subjects.

Mom waved her hand to break up the smell.

"The Arabs consider it a compliment to the chef," Dad informed us.

"Don't you go encouraging them."

Then she'd let one slip herself, a succinct, melodious fart—God, egg curry, how could you not?—and we'd all break up laughing.

Rory and I did the dishes, making beards out of the soap bubbles. "Look, I'm Honest Abe!" (My first-grade teacher, Mrs. Churchill, had been banging on for weeks about Lincoln.) With the table cleared, Dad brought out his briefcase. He took from it a wedge of plastic the size of a thin book. A transmission filter, he told us. Every car had one inside, but this filter was different— it lasted longer, worked better, and was cheaper to make. He launched into a rather poetic description of how they joined the two halves of the filter by rubbing them together, at very high speed, until the plastic heated up and the halves fused. It became one solid part, the weld as strong as the rest. "Your dad came up with that," he said proudly. "That was Daddy's idea." He'd pass the filter to me, then draw another from his briefcase for Rory, then four mint green hairnets, which he had each of us put on, Mom and Dad grinning at each other while Rory and I maneuvered the filters through the air, making whooshing spaceship noises.

God knows it wasn't the filters themselves that fascinated us but their connection with what Dad went off to do ten, eleven hours of the day, among the big humming machines, the computers, the clean rooms, and the men in hairnets. I liked seeing him display his expertise, his technical mind, his dogged need never to let a problem get the better of him. Over those dark winter evenings, he was in full flight.

After dinner, we huddled under Dreamland blankets in the living room and watched *Wheel of Fortune, Yan Can Cook,* and

Murder, She Wrote on our thirteen-inch Zenith. During commercials, Dad roughhoused with Rory and me on the shag carpet. But then, exhausted from working overtime, he'd fall asleep even as we tried to play with him, making sputtering sounds as he dropped off, the remote control resting on his belly rising and falling. Then he'd startle himself awake with his own snoring, and we'd try to explain what he'd missed, how the murderer turned out to be the lighthouse keeper, the ship's captain, the vindictive heiress, the ventriloquist and his dummy . . .

BEFORE SHE PUT Rory and me to bed, she'd go out on the back step for a last cigarette. The nights were so still and silent. No leaves to rattle on the trees, no traffic, no voices from the empty houses on Forest Drive, nearly all of them summerhouses. When the wind came up, she didn't hear its progress, only felt the prickling of her cheeks. She lit a B&H, watched the tendrils of her breath twining with the smoke as it rose up to be carried away, across the prairie and the corn and mustard fields blanketed in dirty snow.

In Ireland, going home, on the ferry, was easy and cheap. Flights from O'Hare to Heathrow were a different matter. Four thousand miles. She could hardly imagine the distance. She hadn't been thrilled about Ireland, but Dad was so determined to get away from Southampton he would've taken Rory and me whether she liked it or not. So she'd made the best of it, the nuns and the rain and the smell of sheep shit. All for a better life—he really seemed to believe it. And now here we were, in America, and she'd agreed to this as well.

She stood on the back step, fingers gone numb, teeth chattering, watching the wind blow snow off the roof, dancing the fine particles in the floodlight shining above the patio. Inside, Rory and I would be clinging to each other under our electric blanket, falling in and out of sleep despite our excitement at staying up late. Dad would be snoring. She'd get Rory and me off to bed, teeth brushed, faces washed, read us A *Bear Called Paddington* or *The Lion, the Witch, and the Wardrobe,* then go back down and rouse Dad and drag him to bed. By the time she was finished brushing her teeth, he'd already be asleep again, his alarm set for five so he could get into the plant early and make his overseas calls. She'd lie awake, trying to get to sleep next to his sputtering, his tossing and turning and sitting up suddenly in the middle of the night to rough out diagrams on the yellow graphing paper he kept on the bedside table. Or maybe she'd just keep herself awake, thinking of home, her mother, her sister, her friends, her aunties and uncles, and the four thousand miles between her and them.

She sighed, and her breath, made visible, drifted up into the night. The light, powdery snow whirled up, and when the wind died, a curtain of tiny lanterns floated slowly back down. Perhaps the sight was beautiful—perhaps. She lifted the bin lid, flicked the butt in, took out her cigs and lit another.

3

EPILOGUE

'd already found the will tucked in a pocket of his briefcase, in with his draftsman's tools and a set of precision gauges. He kept the rest of his papers filed neatly in manila folders, each one labeled in his tight, angular script. I sat back on my hands, the folders spread out around me, listening to Nanny cooking breakfast, bacon sizzling and popping, the kettle heaving up to a boil, my aunties in the back room discussing the latest Titchmarsh opus, *Animal Instincts*. Strange, all that bustle in our house. It had once been filled with music: Mom ironing along to *Camelot* and Phil Collins, Dad and I bopping to Miles and the MJQ, the ecstatic squall of Rory's jam bands. Over the last year and a half, the only thing to break the silence of those rooms was the blare of the TV, which Dad left on to fill the house with voices and only watched with whisky-eyed uninterest.

The night the police knocked on my door and told me my father was dead (it felt like years ago; it had only been a week) it had seemed that everything would change, that everything *must* change. Death in its enormity tells us exactly how much of our lives we waste in idleness, worrying, putting things off. I told myself that night that I would take *my* life by the neck. I would live for all four of us now, do everything I humanly could to honor my family's memory. Such grand feelings! A week later, I already wanted to flee back to my old, bookish routine. But what came next for me? Finish grad school, travel maybe, or move back to England, back home where I could be close to Nanny and my aunties, find a job, any kind of job, it didn't matter what. Poverty, art, music, books—all I wanted was that simple, pure life. All I wanted was for Dad to be proud of me. Now he was gone, nothing could matter. The story of my family had come to an end. It was just me left, some kind of tacked-on epilogue that went pointlessly on and on.

In an hour, I had an appointment at the law firm that had drawn up my dad's will. Wills, estates, trustees, personal representatives—I cared nothing for all this business. Still, it gave me something to do, and for the time being that was a comfort.

I reached into the drawer and felt around, one last OCD check to see I'd gotten everything the lawyer might need. My fingertips brushed something. Those last two folders, I might easily have missed them—perhaps I was *supposed* to have missed them, they were jammed so far back in there. The first was unmarked. I opened it and found a second copy of my dad's will. A melodramatic hidden-will scenario flashed through my mind, but it was identical to what I'd found in my dad's briefcase.

The second folder was smaller than the others. It was labeled, in my dad's handwriting, *Marriage/Div*. Marriage, divorce. I registered this with dull surprise. My first thought was that it had to do with my parents' marriage, that in their sexless, loveless middle age they must actually have started on the legal process of separation. Maybe things hadn't gone further than what was in this slim folder. My parents were not impulsive people; they would've waited till Rory and I were old enough to move out before finalizing anything. But then Mom got sick— glioblastoma, the survival rate next to zero—and it became clear that death would separate them, not the law. Yes, all that made sense. In a few sleepy moments, I'd pieced this notion together, and it seemed not only plausible but likely to me.

The documents inside had gone a gray-yellow, their corners curled with age. Each page was stamped in red with the symbol of the crown and the words *Southampton County Court*. In the bottom right corner were two signatures and the date—1 July 1975. I only recognized one of the signatures. My eyes ran over the form again, searching for the names. One was my father's, "Andrew Boast." The other read, "Sara Boast."

The next thought that came to me—my dad had once been married to his own sister—spun my head around. How could that be? I read over the form again, understanding little else, except that "Sara" was printed without an *h*. I didn't have any more time to think it through. Nanny was calling me. "Come on, Will! Get a move on." I still had to shave and get dressed before my meeting. Breakfast was a full English: sausages, bacon, eggs, baked beans, stewed tomatoes, and fried toast.

THE LAW FIRM was in the next town over, a squat brick building between a gas station and a clock factory. "Don't worry when you meet our junior partner," the senior partner in the practice had told me on the phone. "He might *look* like he's fourteen years old, but he's a fine lawyer. Perfectly competent." More to the point, he was cheap, his rate half what the other attorneys in the practice charged.

The junior partner didn't look fourteen, but he certainly didn't seem much older than me. He was in his midthirties, I hoped, but his baggy suit looked like a hand-me-down, and he smiled so much and so eagerly it made me nervous. He breezily informed me that executing the will wouldn't take more than a few weeks, nothing more than a formality. My brother and I were the only beneficiaries named, and because Rory had passed, there'd be even less for me to worry about. He skimmed the documents I'd brought, tabulating dollar amounts in the margin of his legal pad. He turned the pad so I could see, a satisfied smile on his face. I couldn't speak. The number he'd come up with . . . there were more zeroes behind it than my notions about my class status could contain. The bulk of the money, I saw as I scanned the calculations, came from an insurance settlement over Rory's accident, a wrongful death suit. Dad hadn't told me about that. "When I'm gone, guy," he sometimes said, when he was drunk enough to talk about such things, "you'll be taken care of." But I hadn't thought he meant all *this*.

The junior partner watched me taking it all in. People in my situation, he told me, often took some of their inheritance and used it as "fun money." They might buy a new car, redecorate their house, maybe go on a cruise. I must have turned a look of utter confusion, or horror, on him then, because he apologized immediately. Of course, he said, there's the grieving process to work through. He ducked out to make some copies. "Let's end there for now," he said, coming back in. "Next time, I'll have some forms for you to sign. We'll shuttle them through the county courthouse by the end of the week." He brushed his hands together as if he'd just finished chopping wood or something.

"There's one other thing," I said, still hesitant to share what I'd discovered that morning, not sure it was relevant, not convinced it wasn't some hoax. I gave him the divorce papers. He looked them over quickly, then sat down and read through them again. His smile drooped. His body began to tilt to the side like a sinking ship. By the time he finished, his head was in his hands.

THE CAR chunking along the potholed road, the heater roaring against my face, WXRT out of Chicago exploding into static every five seconds, my scarf, my fucking wool scarf itching, prickling, burning my neck where I'd just shaved—the drive from Delevan to Fontana, I must have made it a hundred times. That day I took three wrong turns.

At home, Nanny, Aunty Sarah, and Aunty Jan were sitting down for their late-morning cup of tea. Mechanically, I poured myself a cup. How did things go with the solicitor? Nanny asked. Okay, I said. I took a few swallows of tea, a bite of my chocolate digestive, and then suddenly I couldn't wait any longer. I had to know.

They reacted in a gentle way, smiling shyly and looking down at the carpet. I don't remember now who responded to my question first, or what exactly was said, but the short of it was that, yes, my dad had been married once before, years before he met my mother, when he was only nineteen, and the fact that he'd been so young had a good deal to do with the marriage ending as quickly as it did. His first wife, Sara—yes, her name was spelled without an *h*—had been a good deal older than him. Older and quite difficult, it turned out. Quite a difficult woman.

"We were going to tell you," Nanny said. "We thought it best to give it a few months, let things settle down first. We thought it might be a bit confusing for you."

I could only nod yes to what they told me—yes, yes, that seemed right, that seemed sensible—and finish my tea and biscuit. "What a surprise," I said, trying to be cheery about it. "I really can't believe it."

I helped Aunty Sarah take the cups and saucers out and started on the dishes. I washed, Aunty Sarah dried. When we finished, we sat back down in the living room, where Nanny was working on her crochet and Aunty Jan reading *Pruning and Training*.

Aunty Sarah stared out the window, then sighed and tutted. "Will," she said, "there is one other thing we should tell you. Now it's come up."

4

EXES

A week after the funeral, Nanny, Aunty Sarah, and Aunty Janet flew back to England. Would I be all right on my own? they asked. Of course, of course, I said. I had plenty of friends to look after me. I promised I'd come over to England that summer, as soon as I'd finished my courses. When they were gone, I locked up the house and drove the eight hours down to my apartment in Indiana in my dad's Impala, feeling gut-sick sitting in the same seat where the last of his life drained away. Coming into town, past the tire yard and trailer parks, past the bowling alley, the Video Saloon and Boxcar Books, down First Street and onto Grant, pulling up in front of my junky duplex, empty beer cans castellating the snow-covered porch railing, I felt the momentary thrill of arriving home. Bowed ceilings, humped floors, balsa-thin walls, a backyard rioting over with burs, mildewed kitchen linoleum that gave off the same bitter-sour odor as the skunk cabbage Rory and I used to thrash ragged with sticks playing in the back forty, a shower with a shallow, perpetually clogging drain that once a week at least hatched a new colony of fruit flies, which then covered the place with the little black dots of newborn flies, which looked a lot like mouse shit and some-times were, in fact, mouse shit, because mice were a problem, too, in the winter anyway—still, it was *my* apartment, *my* squalor, and I was even kind of proud of it. I shook the feeling off. I knew even then that, as comfortable as I felt there, Bloomington would be one more place I'd just be passing through.

"What's wrong?" Claire said when I showed up at her door.

Though we'd talked on the phone a couple of times before the funeral (Claire couldn't come, or else she'd sensed it would be better, less stressful or less confusing for both of us if she didn't), we'd spoken little over the last three months. She'd started seeing someone new, how seriously I didn't know, and I'd been obsessed with a lesbian girl (or was she bi?) who'd recently graduated from Smith, lived most of the year in Brooklyn, and was (or was not) still dating someone there. Still, three years didn't just evaporate in as many months, and Claire didn't need a long look at me to know something was up.

"Nothing's wrong. I'm fine," I said reflexively, then took a deep breath and in a rush told her what had happened—finding the divorce papers, learning about my dad's first wife. I could see her face bunching up with worry; this was a lot to take in as it was. "There's something else." Half-consciously, I let a little dramatic pause hang in the air. "I also have two brothers. Two half broth-ers, I mean."

Arthur, the older brother, forty or forty-one—Aunty Sarah wasn't sure exactly—and living in Brighton. Harry, the younger, thirty-eight or thirty-nine, living in Southampton. After the secret was out, fully out, I'd asked myself, Was it possible I *had* been told about them, that Mom or Dad had once sat Rory and me down and given us a talk—*the* talk? Maybe it had all been divulged years ago, but we'd been too young to understand or had simply forgotten. It was almost easier to believe this. But no, I'd been racking my brains, and there was nothing, not even a passing mention. At first I'd thought Aunty Sarah was joking. Arthur and Harry—they sounded like joke names to me. Not like Will and Rory, names as real as the ground beneath my feet.

I told Claire all of this. We were sitting now in her bright, clean living room, drinking frothy cappuccinos from her Krups machine. (Why exactly had I thought it was such a great idea for us not to live together when I moved to town?) She reached over, took my hand.

"Jesus, this must be really weird. I mean, how did it feel when they told you?"

"I was pretty surprised," I said blandly. "It was kind of a shock, I guess."

She crooked her head to one side, the look on her face concern or bewilderment, I couldn't tell. Finally, she smiled. She laughed. I couldn't help laughing, too, though it was the same giddy yelp of a laugh I'd held back all through my dad's funeral. This was more or less how it would go, for the next week, month, year, whenever I told someone new (though I didn't tell more than a handful of close friends) about my half brothers. Each of these was a test case. In the faces of my friends I was looking for how *I* should be responding to the news. It was wonderful or awful, comic or absurd, poetic or grotesque—to lose one family, then find out you had another—but no one seemed to be able to say which, least of all me.

I LAID LOW, tinkering with a few story ideas: a flaming dog that burns up a garage sale; a house full of old women who grow babies in their garden; two guys, ex-fiancés of the same woman, who break into her apartment to steal back their engagement rings. I practiced drums, unleashed napalm waves of Lysol (cheaper than bug spray) on my fruit flies, spent whole mornings and afternoons in bed with the sheets pulled over my head. One morning I woke to the phone ringing. The dial tone droned. It took me several sleep-thick moments to realize I'd been imagining things.

Rise and shine, guy. Hands off cocks, on with socks.

People kept stopping by to check on me, bringing food, magazines, videos, as if I were an invalid. The older guy living in the other half of my duplex, a tenured professor of German slumming with his grad-student mistress, invited me over for a drink. I coolly declined. I wasn't going to license some home-wrecking affair by accepting his craft beer and sympathy.

Anyway, I didn't need help. At that point, I considered myself something of an old hand at grief. Things didn't get better overnight. Whinging wouldn't help—you just had to wait it out. Therapy? Forget it, waste of money. I was a Boast. We didn't make a big show of our feelings or lumber others with our troubles.

But that was just a pose. The truth was, even if I made little outward display of feeling, I still wanted everyone to understand how direly I suffered. I wanted to be seen as the sturdy, stoic figure I'd long imagined myself to be. It is very possible to be proud of grief. I believed that storing it up somehow made me strong, that I was slowly filling a huge reservoir of emotional fortitude and authenticity, lying there in my apartment, alone and under the covers.

THE TWO YEARS I'd spent in Chicago after college had been a frantic exercise in dabbling. Wanting to play jazz, I'd quickly found there wasn't a chance in hell of me hanging with the big-city cats. Instead, I joined a honky-tonk band—the Cold, Cold Hearts. I bought a used pair of cowboy boots, and Claire got me a beaver fur Stetson for my twenty-second birthday. The Cold, Cold Hearts played every Tuesday at the Red Line Tap, a dive bar and supposed Communist hangout in Rogers Park. We got paid in beer. Instead of launching a career in journalism, I interned at a lit journal based in one of the ritzy North Shore suburbs, licking envelopes and hauling the slush pile back from the post office. On top of that, I put in fifty, sixty hours a week selling drums at a musical instrument store, listening to teenagers pounding away on "Wipe Out" all day long. The only relief for that torture was drinking. The bartenders all knew my name, and they didn't get too worked up if I passed out at the bar or puked in the bathroom. It was fun. Hell, it was a blast. After a long night playing shuffles and train beats, my bass player and I would throw down shots of Jack, load up the gear, and cannonball our way down Ashland at three in the morning, whooping and yowling along to Dwight Yoakam and Steve Earle.

After the funeral, I was back in the bars again before I was back in classes. It was easier to venture out at night, and I felt safe and hidden in those cavernous midwestern dives. You could get through a whole night with five bucks in your pocket, and some-times they played old movies on VHS on the TV behind the bar. Most nights my main drinking buddy, Zach, and I killed two pitchers apiece before weaving our way home along the snowy roads.

One night I stumbled back from the bar and called Claire. It was late, but she was still up studying. I told her to come over.

"What is it?" she said. "Everything okay?"

"No, it's . . . Can you just come over, please?"

I sat on the couch waiting, the room pirouetting around me.

A knock on the door woke me up. Claire came in wearing her heavy coat and snow boots over pajamas.

"I came as quick as I could. You okay? I couldn't tell on the phone."

I got up, big grin on my face, tightrope-walked to the fridge, and came back with a couple of High Lifes. Claire looked at me skeptically. "Not for me, thanks."

"They let me and Z stay past closing," I bragged. "That's what happens when you know all the bartenders. So, how's your raunchy eighteenth-century novel going?"

She'd been reading *The Monk*.

"We discussed it last week. It trailed off at the end, got kind of boring."

"Hot stuff." I cracked my beer and took a swig. "Z and I stopped for pizza at Rhino's the other night. We were loaded. I put *way* too much hot pepper on my slice. I was walking back, and my mouth was fucking burning, so I stopped at that church—you know, that big one on Kirkwood?—and ate snow off the lawn, crammed a big handful in my mouth." I paused to let her laugh. She didn't. "I puked like hell the next morning."

"I'll bet."

"I'm sorry, I—" I closed my eyes, tried to still my thoughts. "I didn't mean to disturb you. I just wanted to hang out with someone for a while. Here." I cracked the other beer. "Don't let it get warm. Then you might actually have to taste it."

She took a sip. "I was thinking about your dad tonight. I was thinking that when you pack up the house, I'd like to have one of his cameras."

At one time, my dad had been a keen photographer. He'd loved taking portraits of Rory and me when we were boys, series after series of the two of us in meticulously designed poses. Later, he amused himself driving out into the country to shoot old, abandoned gas stations and tumbledown grain silos. But he'd given it up for collecting old cameras, his engineer's mind treasuring the mechanics of the things more than what they were made for.

"One of the old Kodaks," Claire said. "If it's okay with you? It'd be a nice way to remember him."

"Of course," I said grandly, raising my beer in a toast, "all yours." I went over to the stereo. "I got the new Sigur Rós album." Make-out music.

"Won't it wake the guy next door?"

"Fuck him. The number of times I've heard him and his little grad student over there, moaning and groaning all night . . ."

I brought back another couple of beers and settled down on the couch, closer to Claire this time, our legs touching. Her feet were always so cold in bed, I remembered. I liked it when she told me to rub them with my feet. We sat there, neither of us moving. Then I found myself down on the floor, kneeling before Claire, fumbling at the laces of her snow boots.

"Will, what are you—?"

"Claire," I began, "please, Claire, take them off—"

She looked away. She was doing all she could not to look at me.

"Stay here tonight," I said. "Please, I want you. I want to sleep with you tonight. I'm still attracted to you. You should know that."

"I already know how you feel," she said. "You made it pretty clear."

Three years was a long time, I'd said the night I broke up with her, and we'd both changed a lot in the time we'd been apart. I wanted to "experience the world," as I put it then. Just as I'd done with my dad, I'd come to resent Claire. I somehow made her the enemy of all that was new and exciting in life.

I'd gotten one of her boots off. I'd expected her to laugh at my antics, give me a playful little kick. Finally, she looked at me, and I saw the pain in her eyes. I knew then the devastation I'd caused. Claire and I started dating not long after Rory died. I'd needed her then, and she'd wanted me. It was young love—pure, sentimental, fierce, and blind. We'd wake each other up in the middle of the night to fuck. Living apart, when it was time to say good-bye, we stood out in the street sobbing. I'd owed her better than a brusque phone call to cancel that love. I could at least have told her *any* part of what I was feeling over that long year in Chicago when I felt my attraction to her unraveling. Instead I grew aloof and secretive. I hedged my bets, moving to the same town as Claire but maintaining it was better we didn't live together at first, so we could ease back into things. Then, the weekend her mom came to visit, specifically to help me to decorate my new apartment, I freaked out. I turned off all the lights and hid until Claire and her mom drove away, puzzled why I wasn't at home. Over the years, something had frozen up in me. I'd convinced myself that because I'd suffered more than most people my age, I was somehow absolved of guilt and responsibility, that it wasn't really *me* perpetrating these petty, lowdown, pointless deceptions. I didn't know how to thaw myself out. Along the way Claire had certainly tried to help me—she'd tried and tried.

"I think I'll always love you," I said, holding her dripping boot in my hands.

Claire shook her head. "Don't say that. Just don't." She started to cry.

I might well have felt suddenly very sober then. Instead I felt more drunk, plummeting drunk.

"I can stay over if you want." She rubbed her eyes. "But I can't sleep with you. I'll crash here on the couch if it helps."

"No, go home. Please. I'll be fine."

She put her boot back on, her coat, her gloves. We went outside and said good night. Once, I'd been there for her, helped her come to grips with her parents' divorce, which had been tearing up her life for years. Later, she came with me to Wisconsin to help pack up the house in Fontana after I sold it. She was the first person I thought to ask, and she said yes without hesitation. But this was where we started drifting out of each other's lives. I stood in my socks on my concrete slab of a porch and watched her go up the street, her shadow trailing her, her breath uncoiling in the cold air, the streetlights ringing off the frost-skinned asphalt.

5

KISMET

We're trudging out across the golf course, pulling our sled behind us. We're whipping down the hill, faster and faster, tumbling out at the bottom, arms and legs a tangle, eating snow. We're thunking snowballs against the front of the house, trying to knock off icicles, till Dad comes out and yells at us. We're crawling through the crawlspace behind the two upstairs bedrooms, picking a path between the huge old air conditioners, old paint tins, busted picture frames. We're leaving Autumn Cornflower footprints on the carpet as a yellow paint tin oozes across the crawlspace floor. We're waiting for the bus, stomping stars into the ice on top of the ditch water, stomping as hard as we can, jumping up and down, then running home to Mom, soaking wet, shivering. We're riding the bus in a blizzard, bouncing on the sprung leatherette seats while Mrs. Laugen, the bus driver, screams at the kids, "Sit down and shut up!" We're building a fort out of couch cushions, peering out into the room, where dust hangs in the sunlight. We're playing Nerf basket-ball, leaping off the bed for slam-dunks, thundering the ceiling downstairs, till Mom comes up and yells at us. We're bursting into Mom and Dad's room, Sunday morning, worming in under their Dreamland Pure Luxury; we all fall back into warm, lazy sleep. We're playing hide-and-seek at the JCPenney, hiding in the center of a circular rack, breathing in the zingy, cardboard smell of the new clothes, peering out at Mom filling out forms at the counter. We're wrestling on the shag carpet in the living room, rolling back and forth in the dusty sunlight, burning our elbows and knees. I'm grinding my knuckles into Rory's skull, giving him a noogie. He's got my head squeezed in a sleeper hold. I get his arm behind him and twist till he starts to cry. He gives me a Smurf bite. I get him in a leg lock. My elbows are pinned under his knees, and he's clearing his throat, working up a loogie. I'm flailing, punching and kicking him. A heat is boiling up in me, my cheeks burning, I'm prickling all over, every hair on my scalp feels on fire, I can hardly breathe, and I don't just want to make him cry—I want to kill him, I'm going to kill him. Then he eases up, letting me get free, and it all dissolves into play again, gig-gling, not crying, and there doesn't seem a moment, not one, when I couldn't be my younger brother and he couldn't be me.

SNOW TURNED to mud, uncovering the patchy brown grass and orphaned mittens lost during snowball fights. A pickup truck parked out on what an ice fisherman thought was solid ice fell into the lake (this happened to some fool every year in Fontana). Dad starting building the raised flower beds for Mom to plant her bulbs in, sawdust from the cut-down railway ties settling softly on damp topsoil. Forest Drive swooped and swarmed and crawled: bats, owls, woodchucks, blue jays, cardinals, woodpeckers, raccoons that outsmarted Dad's attempts to engineer them out of the bins. We'd seen whitetail deer through the winter, quick flashes among the skeletal woods. Now the deer lingered, stepping daintily into the yard in the early morning light, then, sensing our gazes at the window, dissolving back into the quivering yellow-green trees.

FEWER THAN a thousand people lived in Fontana year round. Mom found some of the locals very American—brash, loud, nosy—but there was a part of the village, the part that worked on the dairy farms and in the fields, so taciturn you had a job getting more than "hello," "good-bye," and "stay warm" out of them. She had to get used to all of the German, Polish, and Swiss names—Pobursky, Magolski, Schnitke, Quist—the women with their high, hollow voices, the men with their bad mustaches, and their blond-haired, blue-eyed, aggressively charming kids.

At the beginning of each week, Dad wrote her a check for cash—$125 for the entire week, just barely enough—and pinned it underneath the pickle magnet on the fridge. He kept the checking account in his name alone. It was his salary that paid the mortgage, he said, and he would make damn well sure it got spent wisely. She was used to his stinginess. It was just that there were always little extra expenses: Rory and I needed new trainers for PE; Rory's grade was taking a trip to the observatory and lunch was five dollars; an elderly gentleman had come to a school assembly to give a "concert" on the Hohner brand mouth harp, and I'd gotten excited and handed in the form that said "Bill me later!" And each time she had to go to Dad and ask, and he'd write her another check, and make her feel that she was bankrupting the family.

He did, however, relent on buying a second car, a sporty little

Renault Fuego. She got her hair cut short and spiked it up with gel, and driving around town with her sunglasses on she felt foreign and exotic. In the countryside, you could go for miles into the muddy fields and see nothing but red barns, old grain silos, abandoned gas stations, and sleazy little strip clubs. But near the lake, which was set in a little valley scooped out by the Ice Age glaciers, everything was in bud and in bloom, the hostas and snapdragons and red sumacs exploding in the ditches. Back in England or Ireland a year could feel like one dreary, damp blear. Here spring came on like a riot. Suddenly people were friendly. They waved to you over their steering wheels (that odd midwestern wave, a quick flip of the wrist, like brushing away a fly). They nattered away to her in the grocery line. They kept coming up, without even introducing themselves, saying, "Hon, I just *love* your accent!"

At one point, she was asked by some enthusiastic stranger to record a radio ad for Fit for a Queen, a women's clothing store on the square. She was the queen, and Dad was drafted in to play her butler, informing Her Royal Majesty of an upcoming sale on spring wear. They took Rory and me along to the studio to watch them record the ad. Mom had a great time delivering her lines with hammy ad libs—"Yes, I certainly *do* approve!"—but Dad was monotonic, and the ad never aired.

After Memorial Day tourists flocked to the lake. Rory and I had made friends with Cal and Bree Meyer on the next block over, and then Mom made friends with their mother, and soon we were all streaming back and forth to the lake. Mom had Rory and me strip down and change into our trunks on the beach— who was bothered about seeing little boys' backsides?—until her new friend Julia told her, "Nance, that's not how we do things here." She felt embarrassed and neglectful. Every time she had to correct herself, to readjust, part of her was being chipped away.

And sometimes, out in the country, when she turned the Renault onto an empty street and without thinking started driving on the left-hand side, she didn't even startle but just kept going, waiting for something to correct her.

WE'RE SPRAWLED on a blanket on the sand. Everywhere around us, people sweating in lawn chairs, sitting on coolers, using half-deflated inner tubes as cushions, everyone talking at once—"Yeah, here, we're over here," "Friggin' skeeters are biting," "Give me a pop, yeah, the Mello Yello"—while the willow down by the water shushes us, shaking its head no, no. We pass around a big jug of ice water, so cold it's metallic, drink from the spout, drenching our shirts, so cold our throats go numb. Mom and Dad are smoking, tipping their heads back to exhale, elegant, not like Americans, sending up trails of smoke, and we can already see the bright trails up in the sky, the pinwheels, the starbursts, the big flashes followed by booms echoing across the lake. We slap at our arms; mosquitoes buzz near our ears like little thoughts. The air, thick and restless, might burst into light any minute. Past the end of the pier, the no-wake buoy keeps slapping against the water then gulping back up. Dad leans back on his elbows. We clamber over him and his big belly, but he doesn't want to play. We pull our baggy T-shirts down over our knock-off Umbro shorts, down over our knees—it isn't cold, but the nervous air makes us shiver—and Mom says, "Stop it, you'll ruin those shirts." We kick off our flip-flops and dig our toes into the beach, flicking sand onto the family next to us. "Boys," Mom warns. We feel everyone waiting. It's been dark for hours, and we can't see our arms and legs, can't see Mom and Dad, and it's hard to tell where someone ends and someone else begins; we're all one big thing, waiting, while the willow keeps whispering no.

The wind rushes up, dies off, rushes up, the waves washing against the beach then skirling back. People start leaving. We wrap ourselves in the blanket, huddle close to Mom—and wake to her shaking us gently. "Time to go, sweethearts." A storm coming; the fireworks have been canceled. But all up and down the shore, people are firing off their own private displays, sparks shooting off, then fizzling in the shallows, men hooting and clinking bottles. Ghostly sulfur trails hang over the water— Mom, can we stay and watch? Mom?—but, no, it's too late now, time for bed, time to go.

THE CICADAS made their slow pulsing sound in the August heat. The noon siren ran wearily up and down its wail. The low drone of the village truck out spraying for mosquitoes slowly circled the neighborhood. Mom put the sprinkler out on the lawn, leaving Rory and me to run and leap and do karate kicks through the arcing jets of water while she sat on the step, writing letters home, beads of sweat from her forehead dripping onto the paper. None of us could sleep at night. We couldn't afford new AC units, Dad said, and he refused to go into debt to have them put in: "We're not going to live on goddamn credit." He started working even longer hours and came home looking drawn and exasperated. At dinner, he let Mom serve up salami sandwiches, frozen Red Baron pizza, or Jennie-O turkey loaf. Afterward, he said almost nothing about his day or what projects he'd been working on at the plant.

On the weekends, we went to the Houstons'—Gary and Cindy's—down near the lake. Gary and my dad had more or less the same position at the plant, yet Gary and Cindy could some-how afford a huge A-frame on a private road with its own pier. We ate dinner on the screened-in porch, and then Gary mixed drinks at a little bar in the living room—7&7s for Dad, rosé spritzers for Mom, kiddie cocktails for Rory and me. Cindy was glamorous and sportive in short jean shorts, shirt knotted above her belly button, bright white socks, and bright white sneakers. Gary and Cindy didn't have kids and didn't care if Rory and I tore around their house, getting into all the closets and drawers. Mom might have scolded us, but she'd usually had a few spritzers at this point and was luxuriating in the silent chill of the central air. Dad and Gary talked shop, tolerances and thresholds and quality control. Dad's vibration welding process kept coming up, with Gary saying, Hell, Andy, you invented the goddamn system, shouldn't you see a little of the profits? Gary was suggesting he and Dad go out on their own. Dad stayed evasive. Filtertek had brought him here. Though he wanted nothing more than to be an inventor, run his own business, be anything other than a company man, he was loyal to the bosses who paid his salary. They dangled their lifestyles in front of him, having us over for afternoons on their thirty-passenger boats or picnics at their five-car-garage homes, which all made Gary and Cindy's A-frame look cramped, outdated, not worth taking the risk to do what he'd always dreamed of doing.

LATE THAT SUMMER Mom and Dad had a big fight. She thought Rory and I were starting to look shabby in our church-sale clothes and wanted to buy us a couple of smart new outfits for back-to-school. She went to Dad to ask for the money.

"School isn't a fashion show," he said—something he always said, and she always said, to Rory and me. But she was upset and told him, "This isn't bleeding wartime."

At which point they started shouting at each other all the refrains they shouted when the humidity went over 90 percent:

"How would *you* know what our finances are?"

"I bloody would if you'd bloody let me."

"I slave away, every day, every day of the week I slave."

"Streuth almighty, you're a lamb, a sacrificial lamb."

"Don't think I won't go. I'll go, right now, I'll go."

And it usually ended with Dad stomping back and forth across the kitchen linoleum and clattering pots and pans, cooking his way out of the argument, filling the freezer with Tupperware containers of curry or split pea soup. For a couple of weeks, sometimes longer, the house would settle back into an uneasy calm.

But a few days after this particular fight, Mom, Rory, and I came home from the Janesville mall with two full shopping bags: a Dockers button-up and a pair of blue corduroys for me; khakis and a toothpaste green polo for Rory. She'd taken out a store credit card at the JCPenney to pay for them. When the bill came in the mail, Dad pinned it to the fridge with the pickle magnet and then went into the bedroom without saying a word, without even coming out for dinner. That Monday, and then the Monday following, there was no check. The food in the fridge and then the freezer dwindled. Dad stayed out late, till eleven or midnight, putting in extra hours supervising the night shift or maybe just driving around town in the Buick. When he came home, he went straight to his room and didn't come out again until the next morning. The few times I saw him, his eyes were so hollow and uncertain, I couldn't speak. Not even he seemed to understand what he was doing. On the third week, there was still no check. What had been left in the cupboards and freezer was already gone.

She got us invited to dinner at the Meyers' or the homes of retired couples she knew from the village gardening club. Her friends, if they didn't know what was happening, sensed something was wrong. They were circumspect and gentle, but she took on a manic, garrulous charm, chain-smoking and telling stories about England and Ireland, a glass of rosé poured from the box waggling in her hand.

It ended as quietly and coldly as it began. A few days before the end of the month, Dad came home from work at five thirty with two sacks of groceries under his arms. He put water on the boil and then started to fry up kidneys and liver. The rich, sour smell filled the house. We sat down to kidneys, liver and onions, and cabbage and potatoes mashed together and fried—what Granddad Boast, Dad told us in the middle of that silent meal, used to call Army Fritters. Captain Boast used to season them with a pinch of snuff, the way they did in the barracks. We were damned lucky, Dad said, we'd never had to live on rations. The new clothes hung in the closet in my room—I don't think either Rory or I ever wore them—until finally Mom donated them to the church sale.

I'D LIKE to say that, back then, I took Mom's side in the fight. But no, I took my father's. When the food was dwindling but not yet gone, four or five days went by without a glimpse of him. When he finally came home, continuing the battle by disappearing into his room, I felt only relief. I wanted to run to him, grab hold, and never let go. Because for a minute there, I'd thought Mom had really messed up this time, and now he was gone for good.

IT CAME as a surprise when we woke to the first frost, the grass crunched underfoot as Rory and I trudged down to the bus stop, and winter wasn't months away but weeks. We lost our playroom downstairs. Dad forked out for another bed, and the playroom became Mom's bedroom. With a wall between her and his snoring, at least she could finally get a night's sleep.

Then came that long, strange, ambiguous feeling—settling in. Most Brits who work abroad eventually return. Bahrain, the UAE, Europe, Australia, Canada—the English are spread across the globe, saving for the day they can go home and actually afford to *live* in Great Britain. But Dad was no longer talking about going back.

"No use moping about!" Mom kept repeating to herself (something I've heard Nanny say again and again). She started volunteering, taking on the job of treasurer at the village gardening club and joining the PTA. She ran the school's bulk food subscription service and got a 10 percent discount. She put Rory and me in Scouts and became a den mother. Then she started working, watering plants and cleaning houses for summer people. Later, she got a part-time job at the village library. There were library patrons who came in just to chat with her. When she opened her mouth and that canorous voice came pouring out, there wasn't a soul in the village who could resist her.

She opened a savings account, in her own name, and used it for little indulgences: taking Rory and me out to lunch at Diamond Dave's Tacos in the mall, taking us to movies, buying us new shoes. Perhaps Dad wouldn't have made a fuss, but, then, she was just glad not to have to ask him.

She was writing two or three letters home a day. The red flag on our mailbox was always up that autumn, those letters traveling across the ocean, for Nanny or Vanessa or Aunty Janet to open them, at home where the coils of the little electric fire were glowing and the kettle was just burbling up to a whistle and there was always a knock on the door in the afternoon, always someone dropping by to say hello and have a cup of tea. And now all of that—it would just be script on the blue pages of RoyalAir letters. Already Vanessa and Colleen, her friends, were trailing away in their correspondence.

The balance steadily grew in her savings book. A few hundred dollars: enough for a single one-way fare. Her mother, father, and sister, all her aunties and uncles, waiting at home for her . . . the echoing clamor of O'Hare, feeling cramped and short of breath on the flight over, too panicked to sleep and yet strangely peaceful, weightless, unmoored, touching down in the early morning mist, the coach to Southampton, a quick taxi to Belmont Road, couldn't she just . . . couldn't she—she snatched up an envelope, went to the kitchen, put the kettle on high, and stood staring, barely feeling the heat of the steam as the stamp began to curl away from the paper.

SHE'D MADE an English friend, Hillary, through the gardening club. Hillary and her husband, Martin, were from Devon. Martin owned a farm implement business and sailed. They were members of the yacht club, a place we'd been invited a couple times. It was an odd mix of people: big-money hobbyists from Chicago, a few world-renowned competitive sailors, and a bunch of local eccentrics in commodore's caps. Dad seemed to enjoy himself immensely there and even took the trouble of changing out of his work clothes. At the club he got a gleam in his eye, and when we came home he always had to go off on one of his constitutionals along the lakeshore path and ogle the big houses.

Hillary and Martin had been in Wisconsin twenty years now. They'd become U.S. citizens. Mom often took Rory and me with her to Hillary's, where the two of them would have tea together while we swam in the big, contentedly humming pool. It was heated. You could swim even in the middle of winter.

One day we were standing in the drive saying our good-byes when we heard a mewling sound coming from the garage. The door was rolled up just a crack. Rory and I got down on hands and knees and peered into the darkness. A kitten—gray and white, pink and gray nose, a chewed-up ear—pushed out from under the door and came squinting into the light. "He's in rough shape," Hillary said. She was used to strays on her property.

Mom and Hillary discussed taking him to the animal shelter, but it was already at capacity; they'd no doubt put him to sleep. Mom picked up the kitten and stood there, cupping it in one hand, stroking the top of his head, pulling his eyes back to slits.

"Mom," I said, "it probably has fleas."

"Oh, never mind about that. Don't you worry so much. You'll give yourself an ulcer worrying like that."

"I'll help look after it," Rory said. He reached up and delicately touched the kitten's ear.

"Looking after an animal is a big responsibility," Hillary said, kneeling down to speak to Rory and me. "You have to make sure to look after it and feed it every day."

Mom looked on, nodding as Hillary spoke but not saying anything herself.

Dad was not pleased. He couldn't stand cats, always underfoot, always getting in the way. "Tough luck," Mom said. She wasn't going to take this poor animal to the shelter just to have him killed.

The cat crept around the house for a week or two, only appearing when Mom put down a bowl of Whiskas. He grew quickly, already more a young tomcat than a kitten. Rory wanted to call him Puffball. I wanted to call him Spitfire or Biggles, something aviational. But she told us those names were no good. We had to honor the way we'd found him. Something had put us there that day, she told us. It was a one-in-a-thousand chance.

The name she finally settled on was Kismet. Fate.

6

DISCRETION

Did they look like my dad? I felt somehow they didn't, or that if they did, they must be imposters, bogus versions of Rory and me (when, in fact, they were the originals; we were the second-generation product). If I couldn't picture Arthur and Harry, they didn't exist. And if they didn't exist, I didn't have to write to them.

I knew practically nothing about my half brothers. I'd hoped Nanny, Aunty Jan, and, especially, Aunty Sarah could fill me in. But over thirty years there'd been almost zero contact with that part of the family. My dad had separated from Sara, without an *h*, when Arthur was nine and Harry only seven. From that point on, Aunty Sarah told me, he'd been cut off completely. He wanted to see his boys, but his phone calls went unanswered and his letters were returned unopened. He sent presents at Christmas; they were sent right back. Sara ran with what Aunty Sarah called a "bohemian crowd." She was older and more "worldly wise" than my dad. When they married, he was just a pup.

After he and Sara split up, my dad never saw Harry again, but he did run into Arthur once—both Nanny and Aunty Sarah recalled the meeting—years later, in a pub in Southampton. Dad was having a drink with Glenn, his best friend in England. They were several pints in when Glenn pointed to the other side of the bar and said, Listen, Andy, that's Arthur over there. Arthur, your eldest. Go over and say hello, why don't you? Arthur had been maybe twenty or twenty-one then. He had his hair combed into a towering pompadour and wore some equally preposterous getup. Dad downed another beer to work up his courage, crossed the barroom, shook Arthur's hand, and offered to buy him a pint. According to Nanny and Aunty Sarah, who had the story from my dad (the whole thing appeared to have upset him greatly, but true to form he said next to nothing about how he actually felt about it), the first thing Arthur did was ask him for a hundred quid.

And that was it. Was there anything more to the conversation? Did Glenn know Arthur would be there that night? Did Glenn perhaps set the meeting up? Did Dad loan Arthur the hundred pounds? Nanny and Aunty Sarah couldn't give me answers. It was a half-remembered, secondhand, murky story—strangely, the money was never mentioned again—and neither my aunt or grandmother had seemed eager to tell it. Whatever happened to my dad's first two sons after that last little episode, I understood, was a mystery to them, and they weren't fussed if it stayed that way.

The last scrap of information came from an old friend of Mom's. Barb seemed a decent person to me, but Dad had often railed against her—"always putting her nose in." She came to the house just before my nanny and aunties left for England. "*Will,*"

Barb said, her voice low, confidential, excited, "your aunt tells me the secret is out." I sat there, smile frozen on my face. Mom and Dad had kept the secret of his other family from Rory and me for twenty-four years. Apparently, Mom hadn't kept it from her friends.

"There's something I should tell you," Barb went on. Several years ago, she'd been over having tea with my mom. Rory and I were upstairs playing. A knock came on the door. It was Arthur. He'd flown into Chicago, driven up to Wisconsin, found his way to our address in Fontana. He'd come all that distance, he said as he stood there on the front steps, to see his father. My mom wouldn't let him in, Barb said, not with Rory and me in the house. Finally, she sent Arthur away, saying she'd call the police if he turned up again.

Quite a dramatic story. Nanny and Aunty Sarah said nothing to confirm or deny it. "Better not to go into it," I was told at the time. Maybe Barb got her facts mixed up, Nanny suggested when I finally got around to asking about it again, or she heard something about Arthur from Mom and got carried away. Very little goes on in small towns, Nanny implied, and some people have outsize imaginations.

Or maybe it's just that these sorts of stories—so tangled up with fears and allegiances—just keep multiplying in implications and permutations. It's a lesson told to us often enough, but somehow it's always so hard to credit: There is no definitive version.

Whichever way—incomplete or half- or wholly imagined— the things I'd been told had impressed upon me one very clear notion: My half brothers might not be people I wanted to know. So I was wary of them, and even a little annoyed by their sudden intrusion into my life. But, in the end, it was curiosity that got me to write the letters. Curiosity and a sense of duty: Whoever

Arthur and Harry were, they ought to know a little about my dad and what kind of a man he'd been.

I started roughing the letter out, keeping the tone polite but cheery, making sure to substitute British for American English wherever possible. The hardest challenge, stylistically, was deciding how exactly to refer to my dad. I ended up alternating between calling him "our father" and, clumsily, "Andrew": "I knew Andrew as a very private person who enjoyed working around the house and in the garden." The less pleasant stuff I left for last: "Toward the end he was not in good health. He had trouble with his weight and lived in some discomfort. He also had a drinking problem. I believe, however, that his passing was fairly painless." (Here I was, already repeating the coroner's lie.) As a portrait of my father, this was terse to say the least. I offered up even less about myself, telling them only that I lived in a small city in the Midwest where I took courses in English at university. "It must be strange receiving this letter out of the blue," I wrote in closing, "but I hope it finds you well. I do look forward to hearing from you."

How careful—how bland! I'd managed only the barest reference to Rory and Mom and hadn't mentioned the divorce between my dad and their mother even once. Everything I hoped to conceal—my despair, confusion, rage—was only made more conspicuous by its absence.

It took me weeks to write those letters, but as soon as they dropped through the mail slot, they swung right out of my thoughts. I had other things to worry about, not least the bills and other paperwork having to do with my dad's death piling up, all of which was urgent, whereas the idea that two men out there somewhere shared half my blood remained tenuous and unreal. (On top of this, they both went by their mother's maiden name, Cartwright, which made them seem even more distant to me.)

So I forgot about Arthur and Harry and got back to work. I'd set myself the task of narrating an entire story through the thoughts of a fly, but the fly was proving too dumb to cooperate.

WITH SUMMER approaching, I booked a flight to England. It would be a relief to be home—a good, long span of dull, uneventful calm. But in the weeks before the trip, things started getting bad. As I sat down in a restaurant with friends, the floor started to slide away, the walls leaned in, collapsing. I muttered some apology and got out of there quick. Lying in bed, I swam in and out of sleep, sinking slowly through the darkness, my body clammy and numb, then prickling and stinging. These things I'd learned had hit me like a muffled blow, the kind you shake off at first, don't even know you're hurt. Death had taken my father's body and the gruff voice on the phone I hadn't realized I'd relied on so much. Now these dredged-up secrets were polluting even my memory of him.

I could see why Dad and Mom might have kept his secret from Rory and me when we were young. But why not tell us later, when Mom was sick, when I was already away at college and Rory finishing high school? By that time plenty of my friends' parents had gotten divorced or were only slogging it out a few more years "for the kids' sake." Rory and I could've accepted that it hadn't always been Mom and Dad, together forever and ever. With Mom dying, it might not have even been so terrible a revelation. If there was ever a time to get things out in the open . . .

Maybe he was just too embarrassed. I tried to picture Sara. Beautiful? Probably. Beautiful women make nineteen-year-old boys do idiot things. Dad had always prided himself on self-possession. Maybe he'd known from the start to stay away from difficult, bohemian women. Maybe he was ashamed to admit how easily he'd been snookered.

Still, when it was just the two of us left, he might finally have come out with it. *When I'm gone, guy, you'll be taken care of.* But if he had all his other paperwork meticulously organized and ready for me to find, he'd left the most important business jammed in the back of a drawer. Jesus, why didn't he just *tell* me? That morning on the phone, our last conversation before he died, I wonder if it crossed his mind, or if he'd pushed those memories down so deep, it wouldn't even have occurred to him to unearth them before it was too late. For fuck's sake, how much more English could you get?

And then, even after he was gone, my nanny and aunties wanted to wait a "few months" to tell me. Just as likely they never would've said a thing. *Better not to go into it.* Strangely, I was angry at my dad, but not at them. It was his secret to tell, not theirs. I respected their silence, admired their discretion, so effortless, so absolute.

I WENT on a walk. I don't remember where I was going. A glare knifed off every window and parked car. The sweet rotting of gingko leaves crushed yellow on the sidewalk filled me with thick, sluggish hate. At that point I was near catatonic. I didn't care, I truly didn't care, if I was alive or dead. Whatever bright future I had once imagined for myself was going dark at the edges, narrowing to just one choice. I turned onto a busy street crossing the southern edge of town, walked head down, kicking gravel. An eighteen-wheeler rumbled up behind me, suddenly so close the sound seemed to disappear.

A slab of hot air hit me as the truck shook past, and then

its acrid exhaust and the soft ripping sound of tires on melt-
ing asphalt. I heard a horn blast and startled. "Fucking idiot!"
I screamed. "Watch where you're fucking going!" Then I found
that I'd stepped off the sidewalk and was walking in the middle
of the right lane.

7

NEAR MISSES

Mom's first bout with cancer, ovarian, going into remission. This was when I was eleven and Rory nine, and neither of us really understood what was happening. She spent a few days, a week maybe, at a dingy cinder-block hospital in Elkhorn, and then she was home and nothing seemed different, only that she had to take pills, hormone replacements that played hell, she said, with her emotions.

Rory skidding the Lumina across three lawns and into that parked Cadillac and coming away without a scratch, without even a ding on his driving record.

Mom in her Renault Fuego, a semi hitting a patch of ice on a highway on-ramp, sliding sideways, and missing her by inches.

The four of us getting T-boned in our Taurus station wagon by a two-ton pickup hauling a horse trailer, and everyone walking away. Dad never quite forgave or trusted himself afterward. He was supposed to be our protector, the expert on everything, the one who had it all in hand, and then he pulled out into the middle of the road and got us creamed. But we were fine. Mom had to wear a neck brace to the hospital—that was all any of us suffered.

THE STRANGE THING was that earlier that day, we'd been at a soccer tournament up in Stoughton. Halfway through the second game, the air went still and heavy, the noon light turned yellow-green, and the wind started stirring in the tops of the trees. We had to spend all afternoon in a shelter, eating peanut butter and cheese crackers and listening to the warning sirens. The tornado hit a county away, and they let us go, back into the green evening and that lazy, luxurious feeling of relief—disaster had visited some other place.

Then Dad pulled out from the stop sign, at what was not a four-way stop, and from nowhere there was a truck, a huge black truck hauling a huge black trailer—how could he have missed it? From then on, he always did five below the limit and kept to the back roads whenever he could, the state and county roads, those long, straight, wide open stretches where you could see the horizon slowly unscroll before you, where you could see everything coming from miles away.

THE NIGHT Rory came into my room, fumbling at the buttons on his shirt.

I was reading, something weighty, naturally. He stood in the doorway, head down, trying to button his shirt, his checked Tommy Hilfiger shirt that he treasured and had gone to such lengths to weasel out of Dad. This was after Mom was gone, when he could get pretty much anything out of Dad. He kept trying to do it up; the buttons kept slipping out of his fingers.

"Will," he muttered, "shirt, I . . . my shirt, I can't," and then a bunch of stuff, all garbled, that I couldn't make out.

"What are you doing, retard? It's eleven thirty, go to bed."

He looked up at me, his face bunched in confusion.

"My shirt . . . No, my neck, hurts—the buttons . . ." He went back to his fumbling, twisting and turning the buttons and doing everything but putting them in the buttonholes. "Just really tired—Will, look . . ."

"Yeah, it's late. I'm trying to finish this." I waved the book at him. "You love that shirt so much you want to wear it in bed or something?"

"No, it's just—" He leaned on the door frame, blinking, looking at his fingers, watching them miss the buttons again and again.

"So you're tired." I figured he was probably high. "Go to bed already."

The next morning I woke up five minutes after Dad always got us up for school. I went downstairs. It was quiet. I went into Dad's room. He wasn't there. I went up to Rory's room. Gone. Then I sat down to a bowl of Weetabix and found the note on the kitchen table, just a few scribbled words: *Went to hospital. Will call later.*

They had to give Rory a spinal tap. They never actually said "meningitis," or at least Dad never said it to me. He and Rory were back that afternoon, and Rory spent the next couple of days in bed. He was fine. Another near miss, disaster hit somewhere else.

But for a few minutes, before I found the note, before I understood what I'd missed, what I should have seen the night before when my brother needed my help, I wandered the house in the glassy morning light, going room-to-room in the eerie quiet, exploring this new world, mapping out what it was to be alone.

8

ENGLAND, WHY ENGLAND?

I t was raining, of course. Outside, everything was a bluer green, the green of raw broccoli, the color I've always associated with the damp, sunlight-bereft land of my birth. Maybe it's jet lag beating all the nerves and tension out of me, but I breathe easier in England, and the air leaves me feeling melancholy and pleasantly leaden, as if I could sleep through the passing of another empire or two. I leaned against the car window, let my eyes close.

"Try to stay awake, dear," Nanny said. "Otherwise, you'll never be able to adjust."

I was seven when Mom, Dad, Rory, and I moved to Wisconsin. Still, growing up, I thought of myself as English. We went back once a year or every couple of years, as often as Mom and Dad could afford it. By thirteen I was a snob. I loathed everything American, fetishized everything English: the BBC, Thomas Hardy, Cumberland sausages, Twiglets, Jaffa Cakes, nationalized health care, the constitutional monarchy, Blur, Oasis, Supergrass, Pulp, Radiohead. (I worshipped Brit rock, even when the bands were ripping off American ones.) Though I'd lost my accent—an Irish accent, not an English one—when I was just a kid and spoke now with a nasal midwestern honk, I still insisted on keeping up a few little quirks, pronouncing, for example, each of the fussy syllables in *a-luh-min-e-um* or the long round *o* in *pro*-gress and *pro*-cess. When we went "across the pond," things got even more muddled. The diction came shoving its way back in; suddenly it was "holiday," not "vacation," and I even started thinking in the queen's English again, or tried to anyway. (Rory and I got in fights over this. He hated the clumsy, gummy sounds of those peculiarly English words in my mouth.)

The England I knew and loved was a shopkeeper's England, and in Wisconsin I scoffed at my classmates' quaint notions about taking high tea and rambling along the misty moors. At the same time, I let those illusions stand, hoping they'd let me claim a special distinction, an air of sophistication and genteel disdain for all things low, crass, and Yank. At Big Foot High, I didn't fit in with the farm kids, whom I made fun of, or with the rich kids who lived on the lake, whom I despised and secretly envied, so I became the most zealous of anglophiles, a true native who'd somehow gotten stranded in "the States." As soon as I finished college, I vowed, I'd be going back for good. Three years had already passed since then, and somehow my return kept getting postponed.

"Almost there now," Nanny said, as she always did when we came into the shambling outskirts of Southampton. "Recognize where you are?"

Redbrick terraced houses stretched out on either side of the motorway, the cement monoliths of council tower blocks looming among them. Rust-spotted container ships bulked dirtily on

Southampton Water. I cracked the window to get a breath of air; the thick smell of diesel exhaust atomized on wet asphalt left a film on my tongue. The bus stops were scrawled over with graffiti—bad graffiti. Every road seemed to have a strip of vacant shop fronts, with only the bingo parlors, betting shops, and discos thriving. Men stood on corners trying to flog stolen and cut-rate goods: jewelry, power tools, knock-off England jerseys. Clusters of teenaged boys with shaved heads hunched along the sidewalks in tracksuits, getting soaked and seeming not to care.

The last seventy years had not been kind to Southampton: German bombs, dockers' strikes and brutal unionbusting, dumb city planning mistakes, several grandiose new shopping centers gone bust, the opulent Southwestern Hotel closed down, the Royal Pier destroyed, twice, by fire. Southampton continues as the berth of the *Queen Mary 2*, the *Queen Elizabeth*, and the *Queen Victoria*, but the world remembers only its great maritime disaster: The *Titanic* sailed from here. Look Southampton up in a guidebook; there's no mention of its original Roman walls and mosaics, the ancient Bargate, or the Tudor buildings that miraculously survived the Blitz. Just a few pithy remarks about the "unsinkable" ship and a note that reads "little else of interest here." My hometown. I felt the need to defend it against the general indifference of the world, but it seemed to get drabber every time I came back.

NANNY FED ME enormous meals: fish and chips; chicken curry and chips; bangers and mash with gravy, freezer peas, and chips. In the evenings, we played Rummikub and Scrabble or put together jigsaws. We went out to see Nanny's brothers and sisters, my great-aunties and -uncles. In dim, underheated living rooms crowded with overstuffed settees draped with lace doilies, I sat listening to my great-aunties (the uncles hardly spoke) talk about their gardens, swap news of the vast extended family, and rehash stories of bad service received in restaurants. Over the years, I like to think, I've become a keen observer, a student even, of families, but my nanny's family is like few others. At the time I'm writing about now, eleven of the thirteen brothers and sisters were still alive, all but one of them living in Hampshire. They all grew up together in a big, mold-infested house with an open well at its center, with an eccentric father who roamed the county poaching game and a mother who, well, birthed thirteen children. During the war, the older siblings worked in government offices and munitions factories, drove supply vans, riveted the wings onto Spitfires (I can't help but laugh every time I picture frail, skin-and-bones Great-aunty Cis, her body vibrating to each jolt of the pneumatic riveter), and looked after the younger children. Now the younger looked after the eldest, who had finally started to succumb to heart trouble, aching joints, dementia, and a lifetime of surviving off English cuisine circa 1945.

I took a lot of pleasure in my grandmother's family. And I envied them. When they all got together, the jokes passed so fast between them, the store of shared memories was so great, I struggled to keep up. The siblings who had passed away lived on in that endless conversation, spoken of as if they were only momentarily indisposed, sent upstairs, perhaps, for bad behavior, and sure to come back down to join the fun soon.

Everyone was very gentle about my dad. A good man, they said. Good but quiet. Great-uncle Bob remembered him as being rather "deep." (Which is not to say unusually thoughtful or sensitive, as meant in America, but introverted and a little dour.) When I told my great-aunties and -uncles how I'd learned about my dad's first marriage and his two other children, they quickly changed the subject, as if to say, *Well, never mind about all of that.* They were worried about me living "over there" all by myself. "And how is Claire?" they wanted to know. "Lovely girl, isn't she?"

". . . lovely, but we . . ."

"What?" gruff old Uncle Spadge said. "Enunciate, William. E-nun-ci-ate."

"Very lovely," I said. "We haven't been talking much."

"What? Sorry? Honestly, I can't understand a word the boy says."

All through my teens I was a mumbler. Over here I was also painfully self-conscious about what my relations called my "awful American accent." Anyway, my great-aunties and -uncles were most of them so deaf I could get through an entire visit saying barely a word. Finally, the conversation swung back to the usual: the family, the garden, and wasn't the service so much better in American restaurants? And the portions so large! Now and then, someone would tell a story about life during the war or dust off some antique turn of phrase—"those mucky little pups," "we were at sixes and sevens," "she had a face like thunder," "I didn't come up on the down train, you know"—and I'd file it away in memory or sneak off to scribble it down in my notebook. Research for the great Anglo-American novel.

In private I asked Uncle Bob, whom I'd always gotten along with, if he'd known about my dad's other family. "Well, old chap," Bob said, "I did hear about it all, yes. Through the grapevine, you understand."

I TOOK the train to Salisbury to see Aunty Sarah, her husband, Roger, and my cousins. I can only describe Aunty Sarah, somewhat at my peril, as matronly. Uncle Rog comes home to a cooked lunch every day of the week and has only recently been seen to wash a dish, but Aunty Sarah is the unquestioned head of the household. She exerts a gravitational pull over her three sons. Greg lives just across the road, and Iain less than a half mile away. Martin, her eldest, jokes about his inevitable return with fatalistic dread, but he has only strayed a half hour away. My dad never got along with his older brother, John. (The only boyhood story I remember him telling about Uncle John had something to do with his brother tormenting him at the dinner table and Dad giving him a smack upside the head with a smoked kipper.) But Dad and Aunty Sarah were fiercely loyal to one another. I'd always liked visiting Salisbury, going to see the famed cathedral, the medieval town market, and, of course, Stonehenge. In my teens, my cousins would hustle Rory and me into the discos—the Chapel, the Spire, American Rock—and get us stonking drunk. Aunty Sarah scolded, fed, and teased me like one of her own. I could almost imagine her adopting me. I could almost see the glimmers of a new life there in the village.

What a fantasy! I was way too old to be an orphan, and now that Iain and Greg were both married with children, the discos had begun to resemble seedy church dances, everyone too young and too horny. I'd seen the tourist sights many times over, and even Stonehenge underwhelmed, never mind the lesser-known Woodhenge, where all you could see was the concrete markings indicating where the barrows, long since rotted away, *used* to be.

I arrived midafternoon. We had tea and watched quizzes on the telly. We had supper. I took Aunty Sarah's terrier, Sandy, for a long walk. We watched another quiz, a rerun of *Flog It!*, in which modest people have modest reactions when their family heirlooms go for modest prices at auction, then an episode of *Rosemary and Thyme*, about two gardeners who get embroiled in murder mysteries. At ten, I yawned conspicuously and excused myself off to bed.

"Will," Aunty Sarah said—her eyes danced for a moment, some decision playing back and forth behind them—"a letter came for you."

"A letter?" Why would anyone write me at Sarah and Roger's?

"It came last week. I was going to give it to you in the morning, after you'd had a rest. I wasn't going to forget about it." She went into the hallway and came back with the letter. It was addressed "William Boast, c/o Sarah Smith." The name in the top left corner—Arthur Cartwright.

"Of course," I mumbled. "Thank you."

My aunt leveled a steady, questioning look on me. "You don't have to read it now. You can save it till tomorrow. We can read over it together."

I said I'd be fine and that I'd see her in the morning. I brushed my teeth, washed my face, being very deliberate about it, as if sprucing myself up for a date, then took the letter upstairs to the attic room my three cousins once shared. Uncle Rog used it now to store his fishing tackle and tie his trout flies, and it smelled, not so subtly, of the lacquer he used to waterproof the flies. The letter was typed, single spaced, and went on for several pages. Mine had barely edged over a single, ruthlessly revised page.

Arthur thanked me for my letter and apologized for not having responded sooner. He realized it must have been very difficult for me to write to him, especially as I had only recently learned of his and Harry's existence. And, of course, for the awful losses that I had suffered, he extended his warmest sympathies. "Andrew's death has upset me terribly," he wrote. "The very sad thing is there was no reconciliation between us before he died."

He said that he'd also found it very difficult to write me. He'd known he had two half brothers since he was twenty-one, the last time he'd seen his father. Since then, he'd always felt he'd one day find a way to reconnect with my part of the family. About ten years ago, he'd done some traveling in America, and the idea had been very much in his thoughts: "I contemplated contacting Andrew. But doing so might have caused incalculable damage, and I decided against it."

I stopped and read this first part again. The style was formal, but the tone friendly, heartfelt even, as if someone were reaching out to touch me lightly on the shoulder and share a few reassuring words. But I was suspicious. The letter seemed to confirm what my nanny and aunties had told me about Dad meeting Arthur in the pub. (I could only assume Arthur was referring to that accidental, or ill-conceived, meeting.) But it also contradicted what Barb said about Arthur traveling to Fontana only to be turned away by my mom. And "incalculable damage"—what did *that* mean exactly?

"Well, then, what would you like to know about me?" Arthur went on. He was writing me on a Sunday morning, he said, while having a long breakfast on the balcony and listening to *The Archers* on Radio 4. He lived on the seafront and had a lovely view of the ocean. The Georgian architecture in Brighton was gorgeous, and the city itself a mad place—"the San Francisco of the UK." He liked strolling along the promenade in the evenings, meeting friends for dinner, watching the sunset on the beach with a bottle of nice dry white wine. He enjoyed reading, John Irving novels especially, and music—"mostly obscure, classical pieces." He'd lived in London and France but preferred Brighton. For the last five years, he'd run a gallery near the city center, dealing in mostly contemporary painting.

Arthur remembered his father as a fit, athletic man, and how excited he'd been about his work. Dad used to bring home prototypes for the switches he was designing and spend whole evenings explaining how they worked to Harry and him. When his parents split up after nine years of marriage, things got messy. "It was an age where children were put in the middle of the battle-field," Arthur said, but didn't elaborate further.

Very recently, he said, he'd met up with our cousin Adrian (Uncle John's eldest son, whom I hardly knew) for the first time in twenty-eight years. He was almost certain that Adrian secretly harbored a plan for him to meet our father again. Then, just when it seemed he was getting close to that reunion, when he'd finally grown comfortable with the idea of finding his way back to his father and his father's side of the family, when the whole wild notion was threatening to become a reality, Adrian had rung up to tell him my dad was dead. My letter arrived several weeks later. "It's sad," Arthur wrote in closing, "that only now, in this way, you and I can get to know a little about each other."

I tucked the letter back in its envelope and hid it between the pages of my notebook. This faceless person writing me—a complete stranger, really—somehow knew intimate details about my family. In his words, I felt a gentle insistence, a sense of initiation, as if I were being taken by the hand and led to some unfamiliar place. But reading about Arthur's desire to reunite with my dad got my back up. It even seemed wrong for him to say "our father." And that bit about my dad showing him and Harry his prototypes from work—that was *my* memory.

I turned off the light, tried to sleep. Not a chance. I paced the small attic bedroom. In the corner, Uncle Roger kept the little desk where he tied his flies. I paged through one of his manuals, studied the fly he had up on the vise. The smell of his fly-tying lacquer was making me light-headed. The only booze in the house was a bottle of homemade parsnip wine, and it was locked away in the shed. I took up the lacquer and breathed deep till my head swam.

✳   ✳   ✳

WHEN I WENT DOWN in the morning—which, for me, came well past noon—Aunty Sarah made me sausages, bacon, black pudding, and eggs.

"What did Arthur have to say for himself, then?"

I didn't know why, but I suddenly felt reticent around her. "He's in the art world, apparently."

"Yes, I'd heard something like that."

So why hadn't she told me earlier?

"Did you talk to him recently?"

"He rang a few weeks ago. He'd heard, through Adrian I'd imagine, you might be over. I expect he still had our address and number. Hasn't changed in thirty-odd years."

It was strange that someone I didn't even know should concern himself with my whereabouts.

"Did he sound nice?"

"He sounded very posh."

Aunty Sarah and Uncle Rog—a secretary and a plumber—are proud to have worked their entire lives. For them, a meal out is fish and chips or a curry in town. A holiday is a caravan trip to Dorset. London is loud, dirty, and much too dear, and "posh" is another world—them, not us.

Aunty Sarah sat down to her own breakfast, a bowl of oat bran. When she spoke again, there was a wary note in her voice, like the one I'd heard when she'd given me the letter to read, when she'd said to me, a day after the funeral, "There is one other thing."

"Well," she said now, "while you were having a lie-in this morning, I was taking messages for you. Arthur rang again. He says he'd like to meet you, if you have the time."

9

STRANGER

The next weekend I was back in Salisbury. Aunty Sarah and I had just finished lunch. Sandy was asleep under the patio table, his eyelids flickering over the scenes of a dog's dream. I felt sick to my stomach, a hard little knot of dread. For the last few hours, I'd been drinking tea compulsively, and my brain was shimmering like dandelion fluff on a stalk several feet above my shoulders.

Sandy perked up his ears. A moment later I heard a car pull up in front; I prayed it was just the postman or someone arriving home next door. I went to the front gate. A man was getting out of his car. He wore tortoiseshell Ray-Bans, dark blue jeans, and a pair of lavender slip-on loafers. In his left hand, he held a bouquet of mixed tulips. I thought for a moment that they were for me. I opened the gate and went out, extending my hand. "Hi, I'm Will."

"Of course," the man said, smiling behind his sunglasses. "Lovely to meet you."

Aunty Sarah came down the walk, also smiling, but at the same time looking suddenly very tired.

"Hello, there!" the man said, giving her the tulips.

"Oh, you needn't have." She sounded tired as well.

The man leaned over and quickly kissed her on the cheek, that prim little English greeting. "It's been, what, almost thirty years?"

"Thirty-two," Aunty Sarah said.

We went around to the back patio. Sandy came running up, yipping and jumping at the man's legs. Aunty Sarah called him inside—"Sandy! Leave off!"—where she was already putting on the kettle. Sandy turned and toddled over to her with that busy walk little dogs have, his tail up like an aerial. I don't know why I was noticing so much about the dog. I was clenching my jaw and had to tell myself to stop.

"Well, this is strange, isn't it?" the man said to me, his smile now conspiratorial. "Are you nervous?"

"A bit."

"Don't worry. I'm just happy to see your face."

Aunty Sarah brought out a fresh pot of tea. I knew she'd spoken with him again over the last week and could guess that the two of them hadn't much to say to one another. I might have called myself, but Aunty Sarah and I agreed it would be better if she arranged for him to come to Salisbury. I understood that I was being insulated from him. This meeting would take place on home turf or not at all.

"Milk and sugar, Arthur?" Aunty Sarah said, the first time since his arrival that either of us had spoken his name.

"Just milk," he said. "Thank you. Lovely."

He took off his sunglasses. His face took shape now: high forehead; prominent, wide-winged nose; blunt shovel of a chin; glinting, walnut eyes. His complexion was olive dark, almost Mediterranean, except he looked so thoroughly English. I only had to call to memory some old photos of my dad at forty. Arthur still had his hair—straight and glossy black—and my dad had been bald; still, at that moment it all suddenly became real, undeniably real, to me. There he was, my half brother, sitting right in front of me, looking more like his father's son than I ever have, and by a long chalk.

"How's Uncle Roger?" Arthur said. It only occurred to me then that Roger was his uncle, too. "Is he still doing plumbing jobs, or has he retired by now?"

"Still hard at work," Aunty Sarah said.

"I remember when he got his first van," Arthur said. "That tiny, bubble-shaped van. We used to call it 'the Bubble,' anyway. Dead proud of that van, wasn't he?" He smiled at the memory, laughed. He had a surprisingly deep, hearty laugh. His accent was more or less uninflected—what the Brits call "received pronunciation"—with no trace of the low, slangy Hampshire dialect he would've heard growing up. Each word he spoke had a pleasing roundness and came welling up from deep in the chest. An easy, persuasive, oddly familiar voice—it resonated in me. I was nodding along before I even knew what he was saying.

"How are your boys?" Arthur pressed on. "Are they all established in the world?"

"All doing fine," Aunty Sarah said. "Greg's a nurse. He's married now. Iain's an electrician. Martin works for Southampton City Council. Expect you'll only remember Martin."

"The last Harry and I saw of him, he didn't have hair." Martin had leukemia when he was young. The doctors had given up all hope, but then, just in time, a new treatment had been introduced. "Harry and I worried ourselves sick over him. We cried whenever his name came up. We never found out what happened, not till years later."

"Right as rain now," Sarah said. "Keeps active. Keen on windsurfing."

Was I being oversensitive, or was she being a little short with him? I thought of all those long distance calls Dad made to his sister, every fortnight, ten o'clock on Sunday morning; they were loyal to one another, no mistaking it. Aunty Sarah would be hospitable—Arthur might be there to rob the place and she'd still sit him down and serve him tea—but thirty-two years didn't evaporate in an afternoon.

"So you work at a gallery, Arthur?" I said, speaking for what seemed the first time, coming out with that most American of questions: What do you do for a living?

He told us about the various roles he played: looking after the artists they represented, watching the secondary market, balancing the serious work with a sideline in prints, something to keep the tourists coming through the doors. And new talent—he was always hunting for new talent. He loved what he did. And the gallery was in a beautiful spot, just beautiful.

"Sounds awesome," I said, nodding along.

"Your mother well?" Aunty Sarah asked Arthur. "And Harry?" Two polite questions to clear all the other family business out of the way.

"Mum's had some health trouble," Arthur said, "though she's all right at the moment, I'm happy to say. Harry keeps busy with work and the kids. They're lovely kids. Mum's remarried. I don't know if that news ever reached you?"

Yes, Aunty Sarah said—not sounding eager to discuss Sara without an *h*—she'd heard something to that effect.

She took the teapot in and brought out a plate of shortbread.

Sandy came toddling out beside her and stood at Arthur's feet, whining to be let up into his lap. "Sandy!" Aunty Sarah said in the stern voice she reserved for the dog and her husband. "Leave it!" Just as she sat back down, Sandy jumped up into her lap. "Oh, you little terror," she said.

"He's gorgeous," Arthur said.

"He's a right nuisance."

"Jack Russell?"

"Border terrier."

We ate the shortbread in silence.

"Will," Arthur said, turning to me, "I thought you and I might take a walk."

He might as well have been asking me to join him in a quick round of Russian roulette—the thought of the two of us talking alone . . . Still, that voice. I found myself nodding in agreement.

"Should we go up to Old Sarum?"

"Sure," I said, then felt the need to anglicize. "Lovely."

"Dinner's at six, Will," Aunty Sarah said at the front gate, putting a curfew on our expedition. Arthur drove a red Toyota. Not so posh. As we pulled away, Aunty Sarah stood cradling Sandy in her arms, the breeze blowing her gray hair about. Arthur made a right turn, and she vanished—and at that moment my stomach turned over and I felt I'd made a very big mistake.

SARUM IS an ancient place, settled by the Romans, Saxons, and Normans in their turn. The barren, wind-beaten hilltop gives a vantage across the entire Salisbury Plain, which meant that for a couple of thousand years people thought it worth dying to defend. Now it's where old-aged pensioners go to walk their dogs.

"I really am nervous now it's just the two of us," Arthur said as we came past what had once been the moat and the gatehouse and dropped our 50p in the National Trust box. "Harry and I have been wondering about you for ages."

"Shit, I didn't even know you existed until a couple of months ago."

I laughed, trying to make a joke of it. Arthur smiled shyly. I was noticing more about him now: the boyish ruddiness of his cheeks, his thoughtful, penetrating gaze—he was scrutinizing me as well. Which pieces of his father, or his memory of his father, was he seeing in me?

"We did hear a few things about you over the years," he said. "That you'd all gone off to Ireland, and then to America. I really was very sad when I heard about your mum and brother. It must have been very hard for you." Thanks, I mumbled. "Your brother's name was Rory, wasn't it?" I nodded. "How old was he when the accident happened?" Seventeen. "That's terribly young. I am sorry, Will. And your mum had cancer?" She did. "Rotten disease. Rotten. I get checked every couple of years. You should, too, come to think of it." Yes, I said, probably should.

We wandered through the ruins of the castle, the cathedral, the bishop's palace. There was so much to talk about, and yet I seemed to have nothing to say. Friends have since wondered, if I knew so little about what had happened in the past, why didn't I just *ask* Arthur? A fine question. To which I've always been tempted to reply, Jesus Christ! Pick a reason! Shyness, modesty, grief—which gathers up its own silence—a hyperdeveloped respect for the privacy of others. Back in Wisconsin, working as a bag boy at the SuperSaver, I'd eavesdrop on the conversation between the cashiers and customers—a running ticker of small-town gossip spooled out from that checkout line—and couldn't help but be appalled at the kinds of things Americans revealed about themselves and others. The English are more forthcoming and less polite these days, but I took my lessons from my parents and grandparents, and their generations exalted privacy above all.

And, of course, I was afraid. I could admit that I was excited to be here with Arthur—the very *idea* of the two of us having this conversation—but in that excitement I also felt danger. *Better not to go into it. Incalculable damage.* If there'd been almost no contact between the families for thirty-two years, maybe it was for good reason. Aunty Sarah's wariness around Arthur had caught in me like the flu. It had occurred to me that he might want things: money, someone to complain to, to cry with, to blame, to hate. But most of all I feared what seemed his greatest desire—which, of course, was also my own: to have his father back. Arthur was a stranger to me. Yet in our desires, I was closer to him, in the early part of that afternoon, than anyone else on the planet.

"So, how long have you done, you know, art stuff?"

He'd taken studio courses at university, he said, but it was always the behind-the-scenes work that interested him. Some of the art history got a bit stultifying, but what he'd learned study-ing the Renaissance and even medieval murals, well, he ended up using it. He really did end up using all of it. The gallery was beautiful, he said again. Lovely old building. I'd have to come see it.

An invitation? I made some noncommittal reply, said I'd look it up on the Internet. "Who's your favorite painter?" I said, trying to keep up the evasive questions. But this one set me off on a run of talk. I told him that I'd been to the Tate Modern on my last trip over and that when I saw the Rothko room, I was almost paralyzed. The huge canvases were so overwhelming, so intense, like stepping through a fiery doorway between this life and the afterlife. "I mean, that kind of power with a paintbrush . . . Rory was always the more artistic one. I wish that—" Despite myself, I was getting carried away. "Do you like Rothko? As a painter? Because, I mean, he was really great, right?"

Arthur smiled at me curiously. Of course, Rothko was brilliant—one of his absolute favorites. "Well, then, William," he went on, and I knew it was coming, the conversation was swinging over to me, "you said you were on a university course. What is it you hope to do? What are your ambitions?"

"It's hard to explain." Back then, I always tried to play my dreams down. My people were working people: secretaries, plumbers, house cleaners, merchant seamen. In a sense, my dad had been our big success story—project manager at an international plastics company. Go back two generations, he liked to remind Rory and me, and the Boasts were down a Welsh coal mine. "I want to be a writer," I muttered and felt embarrassed about it.

"You seem like you'd make a good one."

"Thanks." I stared at the ground, Arthur's lavender loafers against the gray-green grass of Sarum.

Arthur wanted to know where I'd lived in America, and I told him about the endless cornfields of southern Wisconsin, the scrappy liberal arts college I'd attended in downstate Illinois, the two years I'd spent in Chicago, and how I was already getting bored in Indiana. Generally, I tried to make my life seem so dull it was hardly worth talking about—yet again concealing and flaunting my pain. But this time it was different. Here, after all, was someone who had his own stake in my loss.

"Do you think you'll come back to England?"

"I mean, I love it here. And my nanny's getting older; I'd like to be around. She has trouble with her hip—I feel like I *should* be around . . ." I hesitated. This was getting too intimate.

Because now I was betraying the central fact of my life, the thing I was laboring the hardest to conceal: I was in utter despair. There were days, many of them, when I didn't want to be around, period. I hadn't realized exactly how much I relied on my dad—for wisdom, for company, for reassurance that life wasn't spinning out of control. If it hadn't made much sense for him to hang on in America after Mom and Rory died, it made even less for me to stay now. Besides my friends, I didn't have any real attachments. I still had my British citizenship. I could look into jobs (what I was qualified for I didn't know), stay with Nanny till I got on my feet. When everything went to hell, you went home. And England was still my real home, wasn't it?

Arthur let out a sympathetic sigh. "It's hard seeing your loved ones get old."

"I could be a better grandson. I don't call as often as I should."

"I'm sure she understands. You're a young lad. And, really, you should do whatever it is *you* feel like doing. I'm sure your gran isn't going away tomorrow."

Maybe it was the obvious thing for Arthur to have said; he didn't know me well enough to lend any real advice. But that voice—roughen up the accent a little, and I could almost hear my dad. With all that tea I'd drunk earlier, my shimmering mind was dancing wildly from thought to thought. My father's face, my father's *voice* . . . I was clenching my jaw again, this time to keep from bursting into tears.

"You really should come to Brighton," the voice said. "There's loads going on."

Another invitation. I nodded, mumbled a vague "uh-huh," and left it at that. "Harry lives in Southampton, doesn't he?" I managed to get out.

"Yes, he never did leave. I think he's quite happy there." The voice grew quieter now. It was telling me that Harry had also gotten my letter to him, and that I shouldn't be upset if he took his time getting in touch. "Harry took our mum and dad splitting up very hard—our dad just walking out on us."

It was at this point that the fluff blew away, and my head thunked back down on my shoulders. *Walked out on them?* My dad's first wife had all but *forced* him out. She'd sent back his letters unopened, told him to stop calling, returned the Christmas presents he sent. I was furious now. *Walked out?* I looked hard at Arthur. He didn't seem to think he'd said anything out of order. But then, he'd only been a boy when his parents separated. Aunty Sarah said his mum was difficult—who knew what nonsense she'd told her sons about the divorce?

"Is Harry married?" I said tightly. "You mentioned a partner in your letter."

"He's quite unconventional in that way. I don't think he ever thought marriage was for him. He and Rose have been together, what, twenty-odd years now? He's settled down tremendously— used to get into all sorts of trouble. Do you like sport?"

"I like soccer. Football, I mean."

"Harry's mad for it. He's a Saints fanatic. Do you know them?"

Saints were Southampton's beloved, and usually beleaguered, football club. Before I'd had no mental image of Harry at all; now I couldn't help picturing the sorts of men I'd seen, as a kid, swamping the Dell on match day: thick necks, big bellies, shaved heads, broken, crookedly healed noses. Men clad in trainers and tracksuit bottoms, sucking out of tall cans of Carling, roaring out football songs. Hooligans. Yobs.

"Well, if you're interested in football," Arthur said when I didn't reply, "I'm sure you two will get on brilliantly." He let out a clipped, sardonic *ha* of a laugh. We came to where the footpath led down the hill. Over the ragged, pagan expanse of Salisbury Plain, the sky was scurfed with the dishwater wraiths of high rain clouds. "We should get you back in time for your tea."

"No rush." All I wanted was to get away from there.

Arthur smiled at me, the same fond, conspiratorial smile I'd seen before. "I was dreading this in a way. You could've been a horror, actually. But you're lovely." He reached over and touched me gently on the arm. I recoiled. Male, midwestern, English— you couldn't touch me, tell me you loved me, or ask me to talk about myself without things getting awkward.

"Good to meet you, too," I said brusquely.

Arthur gave my arm a quick squeeze and let go.

"You mustn't blame him, you know," Arthur said quietly. He was talking about my father again. "They were both very young. There was a lot of pressure raising a family back then. There wasn't anyone you could go to and talk things out."

Blame him? Except for not telling me his secret, I didn't think I needed to blame my dad for anything.

"I think they'd only been dating a few months before I was conceived," Arthur went on. "And once I was on the scene— well, really, I don't think they ever should've gotten married. But Granddad Boast wasn't having that. He wasn't having that sort of shame brought on his family. 'Shotgun wedding'—that's what they say in America, isn't it?"

Who'd told Arthur these things? I was suspicious again of his mother's influence, though, given my own ideas about what Granddad Boast had been like, I had to admit there might be some truth to what Arthur said. If my dad had put his first wife in the family club, Granddad Boast wouldn't have given him any choice but one.

A worried look came over Arthur's face.

"It's all right," I said before he could ask. "It doesn't bother me."

"Should we make tracks, then?"

"Yeah, let's make tracks."

We drove back to Sarah and Roger's. Arthur came up to say a quick good-bye to Aunty Sarah. "See you again soon," he said to her. "Hopefully it won't take another thirty years." She thanked him for the flowers. They haven't seen each other since, and I don't know that they ever will.

Arthur and I went down to the gate. We stood there, studying one another, staring into the imperfect mirrors that each held one of our father's faces.

"Here," Arthur said, drawing an envelope out of his pocket. "I thought you might like to have these. A few snaps from the family album."

I went to shake his hand. He pulled me into a hug. "Thank you," he said. "I needed this." Then he was getting in the Toyota and driving off down Laverstock Road, and in another moment he was gone.

10

RELICS

bought a pair of running shoes and started panting my way up and down the narrow park that begins at Cobden Bridge and follows the Itchen River for a mile and a half. The rough hillocks of the common, the manicured cricket pitch, the ducks weaving among the cattails after the river passes through the Old Mill and goes from salt to fresh water, a solitary blue heron gliding silently over the water—for good long stretches in that park, you can almost be fooled into thinking you're in some idyllic country village. My family history began at the other end of Southampton Water, the industrial end, where my parents met on the job—Dad the foreman on the line, Mom in payroll—flirted with one another on their breaks, and, after six months, began dating. As I ran the length of that park, to the White Horse pub, then back to Cobden Bridge, where the view opened up on the muddy expanse of the salt side at low tide, the boats tipped over on their rudders and stranded in the mud, the grim factory estates in the distance, the gulls squabbling overhead, bright spots of rubbish stuck to the river walls, it was as if I were passing back and forth between those two Englands: the green and pleasant land of the imagination and the gray desperation that's held on since the 1970s, the lean, troubled era when my parents came of age, and from which the country never seems to have recovered. Up the path from me, two dogs strained at their leads, lunging at each other's throats while their owners cursed each other. "Mate, you'd better get your fucking animal under control!" I kept at it, going back and forth, slapping the wall of the pub, slapping the bridge. The smell of grease from a kebab shop hung slickly in the air. On a nearby corner, a man in a dirty raincoat was selling hammers out of a suitcase.

It kept gnawing at me: I'd done the wrong thing. Aunty Sarah and Nanny would let me make my own decisions, but I could feel that they silently disapproved of me meeting Arthur; they hoped this would be the first and last I'd see of him. What was worse—I'd betrayed my dad: He'd never wanted me to know my half brothers. Not only had I met Arthur, I'd blithely discussed the family with him. Dad would've been mortified if he knew what was happening. But I hadn't meant for it to happen. I'd just been curious, and when Arthur said he wanted to meet me, I'd been too polite to say no.

Oh, but now I'm being coy. Part of me *wanted* to throw myself into this drama, the same part that had been secretly fascinated by all the gossip that passed through the SuperSaver checkout lane. I was at war with myself already: the Yank and the Brit; the discreet, loyal son and the aggrieved, angry, bewildered young man. I couldn't eat, couldn't sit still. Heaving my way across the common—out of shape from cheap beer and cheaper food—I slapped the bridge, turned back for another lap.

"You're worldly people," Dad used to tell Rory and me. "You've been all over the world." Life in a series of provincial towns isn't exactly globetrotting. It was just what he told us to stave off the homesickness. We left England, I understood, because we were broke. Yes, Adventure, Opportunity, a Better Life—and then all Mom and Dad did was fight about money.

The fog was sliding over the Itchen. Empty cans of Carling rattled across the path in the half-dark. My head was pounding, my breath ragged—the pub, the bridge, the pub, the bridge. Voices kept shouting at each other in my head, scattering with each footfall, then roaring back.

The junior partner had called about the will. I'd given him Nanny's phone number, in case anything important came up. He called under pretense, something that needed my signature. Really it was to give me another prod. The court was getting impatient. Did I want to go to trial and have the county judge make the final interpretation of the will? The safer route, he said, would be to settle out of court with Arthur and Harry.

"Arthur and I met."

"Well, that's great. That must have been some experience. I mean, that must have been *weird*." Somewhere along the way he'd gotten wrapped up in this case.

"We had tea and went for a walk."

"And did you talk about the . . . ?" He hesitated, unsure how sensitive he needed to be. In general, he made a big show of being sensitive with me, sensitive and friendly. No doubt he meant well. "So, what did you talk about?"

"Mark Rothko, modern art."

"Good, good. It's good for you to have a personal connection with them. And did you meet the other brother?" I heard him shuffling some papers, looking for the name.

"Harry. No, I didn't meet him. I'm not sure if he wants to meet."

"Remember, we're going to have to move on this soon."

"How soon?"

He made various speculations—within the month, by the end of the year—before admitting he didn't know: "I've never done one like this before."

The settlement over Rory's accident, all that money I knew nothing about, I hadn't rejoiced when I found out about it. Dad might have spent some of it, *any* of it, on himself. He'd always talked of opening a restaurant—Chez Andy, he only half-jokingly called it—or retiring to San Remo, on the Italian Riviera, where he and Mom had taken a belated honeymoon, paid for by Nanny and Granddad Snook. Like all misers, my father dreamed of the day he'd blow all his cash on the thing that would finally make him happy, then forever postponed that day. *When I'm gone, guy, you'll be taken care of.* He waited until the very end, so he could blow it all on me.

I slapped the bridge, the wall of the pub, the bridge, the pub, the bridge, one day after the next, pounding out the rest of my summer, and then I took off my new running shoes, dropped my wallet and keys in the little bin, and shuffled forward in the security line at Heathrow, Nanny waving good-bye to me—"Ring when you get back!"—until I disappeared past the metal detector.

Back to bachelor life, back to my books and LPs, back to my 1964 Rogers Holiday drum kit with matching Powertone snare set up in my bedroom, back to my fruit flies. Back to pitchers of High Life at night, pot of black coffee in the morning. Back to Gender and Globalization, Politics of the Detective Novel, and pretending to be a grad student. Back to . . . what exactly? After a month and a half, it seemed I'd embarked on a sensible, grounded life in England. I was finally *home*, and now I was leaving again.

I felt sick the whole way over, couldn't concentrate to read or to watch *Cold Mountain* or *Shrek*. But as I drove down I-65, the road shimmering in the late August heat, the corn seven feet high, a vague excitement started creeping back in. The next morning I woke wrapped in sweat-soaked sheets, planted myself at my desk, scratched out a few paragraphs—and found myself blank. I wailed away on my drums, sweating and grinding my teeth. I wrapped a T-shirt over my mouth, Lysoled fruit flies in the bathroom. I flipped channels on the TV, finally settling for the news. The presidential campaign was already full-tilt, and one of Bush's flunkies was rattling on about "defending the family." I was back under the sheets again before eleven.

EARLY THAT SUNDAY the phone rang. I crawled out of bed, made sure I wasn't imagining things. On the line there was the faint, oceanic static of long distance.

"Morning, squire."

That voice again, right at the time my dad always used to call.

"Oh, hey," I said, recovering, "good morning. Hey."

We made some talk about our weekends. Arthur had gone for cocktails at the Grand. I'd done shots and chugged PBRs at the Video Saloon, then driven home with Walnut Street swaying and blurring in front of me.

Arthur asked if I'd send him a photo of where I lived. "I'd like to picture you somewhere, even if you are just sitting there in your knickers."

"I think you'd call it 'student accommodation.'"

"Is it covered in fag ends and girls' pants?"

I laughed. "Not just at the moment."

He asked if I'd enjoyed the photos he'd given me. They were still packed away in my suitcase, where I'd hidden them from myself and tried to forget they were there.

"Oh, right. Haven't had a chance to look at them yet."

"Not to worry." But he sounded hurt. It couldn't have been easy for him to part with those photos.

"Well, this is probably costing a fortune," I said, the way Dad always ended his long distance calls to Aunty Sarah. Then I added, in a high-pitched voice, "Hope to hear from you soon!" Suddenly I didn't want to get off the phone, didn't want this to just be another budget conversation where no one really got around to saying anything—didn't want to let that voice go.

"Everything okay?"

Fine, I told him. Everything's fine.

THERE WERE four photos. The first two were of a group of children standing on a patch of grass in front of a small stucco cottage. It looked like a sunny day—they were all squinting against the light—but the boys were dressed in long-sleeved shirts and corduroys. There was one girl. She wore a brown skirt and a blue sweater. The children stood facing in slightly different directions, none of them really smiling, as if the photographer hadn't been able to corral them into a pose and had to settle for this somewhat forlorn tableau. The prints were overexposed, or maybe faded by time. On the back of one, Arthur had written, *Summers in West Gomeldon! Harry and I on the left!* West Gomeldon: the Wiltshire hamlet where Granddad Boast built Greenfields, the family cottage, after he came back from the war.

As a boy, maybe seven or eight, Arthur had the same dark hair. Harry was much fairer, with sandy hair, almost blond, like mine. In both pictures, Arthur had his hand up to shade his eyes, a peculiarly adult pose. Harry looked down. The other children were Uncle John's three eldest: Adrian, Tim, and Paula. I'd only known them as adults (the little I did know of them), and it was odd seeing these miniature versions.

The next photo was a black-and-white of a young man, in his early twenties maybe, standing at the steps of a large stone building. He leaned casually against a stone pillar, one hand in his trouser pocket, a foot up on the first step. He held his head cocked to one side and looked coolly into the camera with either calm self-possession or a certain reticence. His hair was swept to one side, and he wore knit trousers and a wool sweater over a collared shirt, fashionable clothes and expensive-looking.

It was my father. The long hair had thrown me. (The hair, period.) And that he was so skinny. In school photos and pictures of his rugby team, when he was sixteen or seventeen, he'd been wiry but broad-shouldered, suntanned and rugged, like his father. Here, he was lanky and elegant, with a foppish, Continental air about him. I realized that I'd never seen a photo of him at this age, though I could recall any number of photos of him in his thirties, from the time just after I was born, when he was already going bald and starting to put on the weight he'd carry through the rest of his life. He was still handsome, even then, but here he was confident, debonair, and, well, beautiful.

In the last picture, the same young man stood in a flower garden with a woman in a caramel-colored sundress on his arm. The day was bright, the garden in full bloom. He wore a three-piece suit. It was a party of some kind, but he stood so stiffly he looked more like he had a court date. The woman had an olive, dusky complexion, and her hair was whipped up like cotton candy into a towering beehive. The young man, my father, seemed caught out by the camera, but the woman stared demurely, patiently into the lens. Her smile was restrained, cryptic, knowing. She was several years older than my father, a woman, not a girl. Here, then, was Sara.

Nothing was written on the backs of the last two photos. I looked at them all again, then tucked them away in my desk drawer and pretended to go about my day. The realization came slowly, but when it arrived, I had to stop and sit down on the bed.

In a corner of my apartment, several boxes were stacked, the contents of a chest of drawers in our house in Wisconsin that had been filled with photos. I'd nearly left them in storage, but Claire had convinced me to keep them here. The big bottom drawer of the chest always stuck on its rails. Rory and I used to wrench it open and dig through the old black-and-whites of our great-aunties and -uncles, the round-cornered snapshots from when we were toddlers, pictures of the two of us in school uniform, baby photos of me pulling up grass from the garden and shoving it in my mouth, Granny and Grandad Snook visiting Ireland, Mom and Dad in San Remo. Most of these snaps were loose and had been shuffled, out of order, back into the paper envelopes from the developers. One envelope might cut a swath across forty years and three or four countries.

Rory and I would handle the oldest photos like relics: Grand-dad Boast and his brother Will (my namesake) in the Welsh countryside, looking like old-world peasants, dressed in baggy trousers and flat caps and leading a shaggy-maned pony along a dirt road. Great-gran Rawlings dressed for her job as a cigarette girl at the famed Southwestern Hotel. And plenty of posed wedding pictures: the men in their military uniforms, the women trussed up in billowy dresses, the children in wool jackets, short trousers, long socks, and polished dress shoes. All the aunties and uncles and second and third cousins—we could never remember all the faces, let alone the names. To us, these were images from a foreign country, a world Rory and I were unmoored from. They belonged more to *Masterpiece Theatre* than our own history.

Often, Mom would kneel beside us as we spread the photos across the carpet. She loved going through them as well; they were her way of keeping England alive in memory. *Who's that?*

Rory or I would say. *Is it Nanny?* No, she'd say, that's Aunty Cis.
Where was that one taken? That's the river by Bunratty Castle.
We went on the paddleboats afterward. Remember? When we
had to fish you and your silly brother out of the water . . . Another
photo. Another. *Who's that, Mummy?* Question after question.
We were fascinated by the contents of that bottom drawer, so
hard to open and nearly impossible to close again.

I got up from my bed, took down a box, and started digging,
fanning the envelopes of photos out around me as I searched.
Until you know what's missing, you don't know what to look
for. Maybe they were in there somewhere, unnamed and unre-
marked on, lost in the sprawl of the extended family. I took down
the next box, and the next, and it wasn't until late that evening
that I finished and I knew for sure.

MAYBE HE DID IT before he met my mom, or later, in the weeks
before we left England, as we were packing up the house on
Clarendon Road—he put all those old pictures in the rubbish, or
in the fire. Maybe the memories were just too painful to haul all
the way to America. But to cut out and discard a whole chunk of
his life . . . I could hardly bring myself to throw away Rory's old
clothes.

No, not the fire. Too melodramatic. In a story, I could never
bring myself to write that scene. And not the dump. I couldn't
imagine him leaving images of his family to molder among old
newspapers and food scraps.

The river. I picture my father in black and white, a young
man with long hair and fine clothes, walking along the Itchen, a
cardboard box under his arm. It's evening, just as the people of
Southampton are sitting down at home for their tea. Yes, the sun
has already set—a clear, cold evening, the fog not yet curling in

over the valley. He follows the riverside walk, passing the football fields, the playground, the cricket pitch, his steps hurried but tentative as he moves toward the point where the river runs through the mill and goes from salt to fresh water, the point where he can get close to the top of the millrace. He crouches there, dropping the photos into the current, watching them accelerate toward the sluice. Maybe he pauses over a few of the photos before letting them go—his boys—but the job doesn't take long. Sliding away on the quick current, another print of him and his first wife at the garden party—or, God, their wedding . . . The glossy paper begins to wrinkle. Through the millrace and past the sluice, the image flutters and wobbles but doesn't tear. And then the wide channel of the Itchen at high tide, the leisurely flow of the green water, the oil and scum on the surface, the gulls and terns flapping along the bank. The photos make dark spots against the dark water. In the dim light, no one out walking sees the little flotilla of baby pictures and birthday parties and family portraits, and besides, who would worry themselves, on that mucky river, about more rubbish making its way out to sea?

11

LECTURES

We're riding bikes, whipping through the back forty, dodging branches and briars and puddles. We're pulling on our long blue socks for T-ball—going to swimming lessons, soccer practice, Cub Scouts, coloring in pictures of Jesus at Bible study (it's cheap day care, Mom says, believe whatever you want). We're breaking branches off trees, sharpening their tips with my Swiss Army knife, jousting each other on our bikes, until Mom comes running down the lawn— "Oh, streuth, stop! Stop!" We're playing war and dodge ball and TV tag with Cal and Bree. We're playing Nintendo at Jeff Cates's (he's technically Rory's friend, but I always go along). Hole eight of the golf course, we're searching in the long grass for Titleists and Bridgestones to sell at the clubhouse, taking off our flip-flops to wade into the pond, mud sucking our toes. "Look, this one's personalized—'Doug Davis.'" "It should say, 'Doug Davis sucks at golf.'" We're chasing around the lawn, giggling, while Dad sprays us with the hose. The old couple in the big house at the end of the block comes past in their big Coupe de Ville. They tap the horn, and we tear up the street to carry their groceries inside. We're mowing their lawn, fighting over who gets to weedwhack, watering their flowers, taking their garbage out, picking their garbage off the gravel drive when the raccoons get into it. We're down by the lake, helping Mom clean someone's summerhouse, on our backs making angels on the thick, cream-colored carpet. We're riding bikes to the Card Coin Comics shop attached to the bowling alley, pockets full of dollar bills and quarters, fighting over *X-Force* or *Amazing Spider-Man* or *Youngblood*, pulling the almost translucent wrappers tight on packs of baseball cards, looking for rookies and All-Stars. We're hiding out in our fort in the living room, chomping on stiff, dusty-tasting sticks of Topps gum, counting down the days with dread. We're at Wal-Mart with Mom, buying notebooks and folders and protractors, at Geneva Sports gulping the bright, rubbery smell of new Nike Airs, Rory giggling while Mom asks the guy about jock straps for me. We're on the bus while Mrs. Laugen screams, "I told you to sit down and shut up!"—the first day back, and now I'm in middle school, Rory's in fourth grade, and when I don't see him in the halls anymore, I feel tight in the chest, like swallowing something down the wrong pipe, and at recess I stand on the edge of the blacktop watching the other kids play tetherball, alone but terrified to talk to anyone, the trucks rolling out of the gravel quarry next to the school thundering in my ears, and the rest of the day I'm only waiting to have him beside me again on the bus ride home.

AT NIGHT I couldn't sleep. I'd lie in bed, my mind churning. Finally, I'd go into Rory's room, sit down on his bed, and lecture him. I railed against the popular kids at school: They were popular because they were rich, because they had designer clothes and designer jeans and Trapper Keepers. The teachers treated them better because their parents were on the school board and town council. They got good grades by cheating and copying. Cheating was stupid, because . . . well, you were just cheating yourself. Wearing designer clothes was stupid because they were no different than what Mom bought us at the church sale, they just had a name stitched on them. "School isn't a fashion show," I told my brother. Kids at our school cut the leather tags off the backs of their jeans if they couldn't afford Jordache or Guess—I couldn't even *begin* to describe how stupid that was. Rory sat up in bed, *Return of the Jedi* comforter pulled up to his chin, nodding sleepily.

"But you have to be nice to girls," I instructed him, "even the popular ones."

"They're always prettiest."

"But don't be nice to them *because* they're pretty." This didn't quite make sense, so I changed topics. "You know what the worst thing is?"

"What?"

"Being gay."

"You're gay."

"Shut up," I said, a little too vehemently. I hadn't actually figured out what was so great about girls yet, and this had me worried. "If you're gay, you're just . . . No one talks to you anymore. It's just, you know, gross. If you're in the locker room and some guy looks at your dick, that's gross."

"How's your new jock?"

"I'm not wearing that thing. It sucks."

"You suck."

"Yeah, wait till you have to wear one. It's like getting your balls in a choke hold."

"Balls," Rory said, a blink away from sleep.

IT SEEMED he'd always be shorter than me, he'd always be husky and chubby-cheeked. He had Dad's broad nose and strong, blunt chin, Mom's blue eyes and hale complexion. He blushed a lot. His classmates all liked him, though he kept to himself in school, doodled in his notebook or just stared out the window. I always got good remarks on my report cards, but Rory needed to *apply himself, try harder,* and *develop better work habits.* Art was the one subject he took to—in fifth grade, a painting of his won an award sponsored by the governor—but, really, the art room was just a place where he could goof off a little, where the teacher wasn't always telling him he was falling behind.

In middle school, I felt constantly judged. My clothes, my hair, the suck-up things I said in class, the frantic way I played basketball and kickball—I went around sighing and rubbing my eyes with the heels of my hands, like Dad after he got home from work.

One day, Nick Law came to school wearing a new pair of LA Gear Lights. These shoes were special: Red LEDs in the heels flashed every time you took a step or landed from a jump. You could even make them flash different patterns by doing a double tap on the heel. Nick, who was already considered pretty cool, had cemented his status in one brilliant move. I went home in an aspirational frenzy—better principles gone out the window— and told Mom how awesome Nick's shoes were, how everyone said they were getting a pair, too. She listened carefully. Behind her eyes I could see a plan forming. She had coffee with Nick's mom every couple of weeks. She could find out where Nick had gotten those shoes! "Well," Mom said, smiling, "we'll just have to see."

A few days later, she came home carrying something bulky in a shopping bag. I could already see the red lights twinkling under my feet. "Here you are, then," Mom said as she brought out a battered blue and gray shoe box. She opened it, and there sat . . . Nick's old shoes, a scuffed pair of Keds that were still perfectly wearable. "Look, you and Nick are the same size!"

BIG FOOT HIGH drew from Fontana and several other neighboring towns. Most of the other kids knew your name, but they didn't know every detail of the social suicide you'd been committing since age seven ("Cheerio, everyone!"). Grunge arrived in Wisconsin, five years late, and suddenly it was cool to wear ratty thrift store clothes. I signed up for school band and started working evenings at the SuperSaver. I made friends with a few of the guys who hung out in the music room, bagged groceries at the store, and made dry, cryptic quips within earshot of the jocks—"Hey, Reece, I sacked your mom the other night." Before I knew it I'd betrayed my most cherished principle: I'd joined a clique.

In seventh and eighth grade, Rory made some new friends, too. Like him, they were the kids who stared off into space in class, who were considered lazy or troublesome. They lived way out in the country, where they worked on their dads' cars and raced four-wheelers and snowmobiles through the woods. They took a week of excused absence every year for hunting season and, the rest of winter, wore camo and blaze orange coats to school. Rory and I still spent a lot of time together, riding bikes or roaming the back forty, pocketing lost golf balls out of habit.

When my buddies came over, I'd let Rory play video games or watch dumb movies with us. I was proud, in a proprietary way, that he got on so well with the older guys. When Rory's friends slept over, I stayed upstairs reading. It wasn't that I disliked his friends; I just considered them a little beneath him. Or beneath me, which amounted to the same thing.

A year later Rory started at Big Foot. (The Swiss-Germans who first settled the area marched the local Potawatomi chief and his tribe off to the Dakotas; a hundred years later the town named the high school after him.) Rory's locker was down in an obscure corner of the school where the Ag Science room, the wood shop, and the boiler room were secreted away and the kids in 4-H and Future Farmers of America hung out. Mom and Dad hoped high school would be a new start for Rory, but in most of his classes he struggled to get even C's. The teachers at Big Foot were used to kids dropping out to go work on the family farm, at the resort hotels on the lake, or in the mink barns over in Delevan. Big Foot never won at football or basketball, so the school funneled its resources toward its honors students, who'd go on to the UW or Marquette or Lawrence. A few of the lake-front kids even went out east to the Ivies. These were the kids I truly despised. They were on student council and honor board, yet they drank and did drugs and even cut school. They partied on the weekends, usually at the house of whoever's parents happened to be away, though sometimes, like most other midwestern kids, they just got drunk out in the middle of a cornfield.

My junior year I started shaving. Little else, it seemed, had changed. Rory was still himself, bashful, a little husky, clumsy on the soccer field and basketball court. Like me, he dutifully wore the clothes we got from our aunties and nanny on birthdays and Christmas, though he'd started to style the bowl cut Mom always made him get with some goop called L.A. Looks. He was still easily distracted and quiet. He laughed and smiled a lot. Even when someone was telling him he'd failed a test or was going to sit on the bench for most, if not all, of the game, he would smile—a restrained, embarrassed smile that seemed almost an apology.

I started to see him in the hall. The popular underclassmen shared lockers with juniors and seniors. Rory didn't have one of these lockers (it never occurred to me to share mine with him), but I saw him tagging along with a few of the sophomores who'd attained such lofty heights. I wasn't worried. Rory's current friends, farm kids and grease monkeys, didn't help his cause. He was always on the periphery with the cool kids, and after a time, he disappeared back to the obscurity of freshman hall. I figured he hadn't really had much of a shot anyway.

That summer Rory took a month-and-a-half-long trip to England. He stayed with Nanny in Southampton and spent a fortnight in Wales with our great-aunt and -uncle Angela and Lawrie in their bungalow in Caerwedros, a place so remote that two weeks, at his age, could feel as vast and empty as two years. But he enjoyed himself, helping Aunty Angela in her garden, going with Uncle Lawrie to dig for Victorian-era pots in the local dumps, or just wandering the hilly, windswept countryside. Unlike me, Rory was never much of an anglophile. The four of us had just gone over for Christmas. Why he wanted to go back again five months later, I didn't know, but he'd gone to Mom and Dad and practically begged them for his ticket. He said it could be his birthday present *and* his Christmas present that year—that year and the next and the one after that. After he left, the house felt weird, abandoned almost. I asked for more hours at the store and got put on the night shift. I read H. G. Wells, Jules Verne, and a shelf of Star Wars novels. Four friends and I started a band that we called, for some reason, the Honky Sandwich. I wondered if I should've gone home to England as well. It only occurred to me afterward: Rory hadn't even asked me to go with him.

When he came back, everyone suddenly seemed to be commenting on how tall he was becoming, how handsome. He'd let his hair grow out of the bowl cut. He'd caught some sun and slimmed down. He'd even bought himself some new clothes with the pocket money Nanny had given him: rugby shirts, khaki shorts, a couple of knock-off Ralph Lauren polos from a car-boot sale. Overnight, he turned into a clotheshorse. Dad had his wool Yves Saint Laurent shirts hanging in his closet. They were hand-stitched, and Dad claimed they cost him, in 1965, a hundred quid apiece. As if the tailor had cut those shirts for the son as well as the father, they fit Rory perfectly.

In photographs from that time, Rory was already starting to pose. He casually slouched against a wall or looked steadily, coolly into the camera. When he was younger, he clowned for photos. He'd pull faces, beam winningly, or look away at the last moment as if someone were calling his name. Now he was all restraint and—if he hadn't been my little brother, I could say it more easily—elegance. When I asked about his trip, he said it was cool but boring. It was just good to get away for a while. "Away from what?" I said, but he didn't answer.

For Christmas that year, the memory of his pleas for the plane ticket already faded, Rory asked for a pair of designer jeans.

WHEN SCHOOL started again, he was sharing a locker with Alex Lindbeck, the younger brother of one of the popular girls in my class. The kids in the circle Rory had been aspiring to join took him in readily now. The sons of lawyers, businessmen, and ortho-dontists, they dressed in ball caps and khakis but wore their hair in dreadlocks and listened to stoner music. They were like hippies who'd wandered into a J.Crew catalog.

At the end of fifth-period Concert Band, I'd see Rory coming down the hall with his new friends. They were going off-campus for lunch, like all the smokers and the kids with cars did. My friends and I made a point of eating in the cafeteria, because it was so uncool. When Rory came past, I'd stop and shake his hand. My friends and I were into shaking hands.

"What'd Mom pack you?" I'd say. "Liverwurst and cucumber again?"

To stretch the weekly check Dad gave her, Mom bought the lunchmeat for our sandwiches from the very bottom of the deli case: liverwurst, spicy headcheese, old-fashioned loaf. I mentioned the liverwurst because I thought it might embarrass Rory in front of his new buddies.

"Yeah. I got Chips Ahoy, though." He swept his hair out of his eyes. "You want my sandwich?"

"Sure, liverwurst's fine with me. You want my apple or something?"

"Nah, I'm cool. Peace."

"All right, peace. But, you know, eat something."

We shook hands again. He went off to cruise around town for forty minutes with Alex and their other pals, and I went to my cafeteria table to make fun of the cool kids.

HALFWAY THROUGH my senior year, I started to have vague thoughts about college. Mom and Dad seemed to think I should go, but where and how and, more importantly, how much it would cost was beyond them. I was so glum (or realistic, as I thought then) about my prospects that Big Foot's guidance counselor didn't know what to do with me. He suggested I look at vo-tech schools, but I was offended by the idea of going down-market. I sat down one night with a stack of brochures, chose four almost at random, and wrote an application essay on the life of John Philip Sousa (having played sousaphone in marching band, I was a fan). Dad reassured me that if I didn't get in anywhere, he could get me a job on the shop floor at Filtertek.

Another dull, dark winter passed. I got A's in all my AP classes and took second place at the conference math meet. Rory was failing everything but Painting II. One afternoon he passed out in study hall and had to be driven by the vice principal to our family GP. Dr. Almgren only needed one look at Rory to see what was wrong, but he let him off the hook, saying he felt faint because he'd skipped lunch. Later that night Rory told me that he and Alex had hotboxed in Tyler Nystrom's Jeep Cherokee. He'd felt as if he were falling through a crack in the earth, he said, his eyes still red, a crooked grin on his face. A month later Dad found a crumpled pack of Camel Lights in the pocket of Rory's coat; he tried to ground him for a week but relented after just a couple of days. I chipped in one night by expounding on what a filthy, expensive habit it was, how all the chemicals they put in cigarettes were what made them addictive, so that you were basically paying to get hooked on tar and arsenic—what a waste of money.

"Jesus, chill out," Rory said. "It's not like I've been smoking for forty years." There he had a point. Both Mom and Dad had smoked as long as I could remember and had only recently quit, Mom on Nicorette gum and Dad, fired by his thrift, cold turkey.

LATE THAT MAY, Mom and I took a last-minute trip to western Illinois and Iowa. I'd gotten into the four colleges I'd applied to but had yet to choose one. Mom thought we should go see these liberal arts schools that looked so well burnished and perpetually autumnal in the brochures. We went to Knox College, a tiny school in Galesburg, Illinois, that prided itself on its English Department and its jazz ensemble. We planned to visit Grinnell, in Iowa, and check out the University of Iowa on the way. Unfortunately, I'd left my decision so late that when we got on Iowa's campus, the university wasn't even in session. We wandered Iowa City for an afternoon, had burgers at a bar and grill, and started thinking about heading home. Mom had a pounding headache. She'd taken four or five aspirin, but it hadn't gone away. We'd have to see Grinnell some other time, she told me. She hadn't touched her burger, so I wolfed that as well.

"So, are you excited to go away to uni?" Her voice was thin and weak. She kept wincing. "Won't it be nice to get away from boring old Fontana?"

I didn't know how I felt about college. I still didn't think we could afford it, though I'd gotten good scholarships to Knox and Grinnell. Both schools were a half day's drive from home, about as far away as I wanted to venture. Most of my buddies were going to UW–Madison, but I'd heard it was a party school.

"It's going to be lonely. I'm going to miss the guys. I suck at making new friends."

I went on, working myself up with all the reasons why I shouldn't leave home, feeling a little sorry for myself, because I actually longed for an education and definitely wanted to get the hell out of Fontana. Still, I told Mom I didn't really see the point of college, especially when it was so expensive.

"Oh, don't be silly. That's for your father and me to worry about. And of course you'll make friends. Loads of them."

Her voice—I wish I could remember her voice. I used to have a recording of her doing story time for the tots at the library, but somewhere along the way I lost it in a move. I'd give a lot to have that tape back.

Our waitress brought the bill. She was pretty, in that all-American pep squad way. I knew Mom could see me staring.

"Are you a student at the university?" Mom said.

"I sure am," the waitress said brightly.

Mom nodded at me. "Will's trying to make up his mind."

"Oh, it's really great here." The waitress blushed, seemed suddenly self-conscious. "I love your accent," she said to Mom. "Are you guys from England?"

Mom looked at me.

"Well, originally," I said.

"That's so cool. I've always wanted to go."

"You should!" I said, slipping back into—some kind of accent. "It's brilliant."

When the waitress went to get our change, Mom gave me a big wink. "Loads of new friends," she said. Then she winced again.

We hadn't been on the road more than half an hour when she pulled over and said I had to drive. I didn't have my license yet, I told her. (I'd failed my driver's test, twice.) Yes, she knew *that*— she spoke sharply, pressing her knuckles against her temples— but there wasn't any other way we were going to get home. I got behind the wheel. Mom lay down on the backseat. I thought maybe she was preparing me for my third test, an impromptu trial by fire to get me over my nerves, but she hardly spoke. When we got home late that night, she went straight to bed. The next morning she called me into her room as we were getting ready to catch the bus. Dad was already at work. Rory and I didn't have to go to school, she told me. She was lying in bed still dressed in the same clothes she'd worn the day before. She said I'd better take her to the doctor.

We went to Dr. Almgren, who sent us to the county clinic, who in turn sent us, late that afternoon, to a clinic at St. Mary's in Madison.

Rory and I spent that day in waiting rooms. We ate candy bars from the vending machines. We thumbed through *Time* and *National Geographic* and even *Highlights* when we got bored with all the adult articles. We made a game of hopping around on the different-color squares on the carpet. We sat slumped in the bench seats, punching each other in the arm. We had thumb wars. We arm-wrestled. Maybe we knew what was coming. Maybe we wanted to feel like kids again, if only for a couple more hours.

Finally, Mom came out. We asked how she was feeling. She sat there, very quiet. Fine, she said. Fine. It was evening, and there was no one in the clinic except the receptionists and a janitor who kept passing by whistling the theme to *The A-Team*. The doctor came out. He sat down next to my mom and rested a hand gently on her knee. He asked if she wanted to hear the diagnosis. Yes, she said. He asked if she wanted Rory and me there to hear it. "Yes," she said, "I want them here." She nodded once as if to affirm it, her lips pursed, her chin held firm, and then she burst into tears.

12

STRANGERS

Dad came to get me from school. We drove through winter-barren western Illinois, listening to the Modern Jazz Quartet. Dad kept rewinding the tape. We must have listened to the MJQ's "God Bless Ye, Merry Gentlemen" seven or eight times before we crossed the state line.

When we got home Mom was asleep. I said I'd look in on her, but Dad said better let her rest, he'd get her up just before dinner. It was the day before Thanksgiving. The last time I'd seen Mom was at parents' weekend back in October. She'd stayed in the hotel nearly the entire visit, and the one time we got her to venture out, she had a forgetful spell in front of the parents of a guy in my hall. She thought they were two of my professors and told them what a good boy I was, what a clever student. Physically, she'd seemed a little sturdier than before I left for school, or at least the steroids had helped her put on weight after her final round of radiation. Her face had gotten puffy, her cheeks fat and mottled red. The rest of her body had puffed up, too, uneven and lumpy. It looked as if she were hiding a sack of potatoes under her clothes.

Dad had prepared an egg curry the night before, and now he slid it into the oven, fixed himself a 7&7, and dropped, with a weary grunt, into his easy chair to rest his back after the drive.

Upstairs, Rory was watching TV in his room.

"Hey, what's up?"

"Nothing. Got wasted last night."

I'd just started drinking and, despite disapproving of him doing the same, wanted to impress my younger brother. When I think of that time, it's like I'm continuously falling backward, a stunned grin slowly spreading across my face.

"Heard the new Outkast album?"

"Alex got it. Good shit."

Rory and his new friends listened to hip-hop and stoner jam bands almost exclusively. Before, every band I loved, Rory loved, too.

"I dig their last album better," I said, trying out my hep cat slang on him. "You know, the more austere approach."

I unpacked my overnight bag and took a long shower. When I came downstairs, Mom was sitting by herself in her place at the dining table. I started with surprise. She was wearing her new wig.

Julia and Barb had taken Mom up to Madison a couple of weeks back to pick it out. Over parents' weekend, Mom had worn the old mousy brown wig Dad had helped her choose. Her friends had decided it was time for something more glamorous. The new wig was strawberry red, shot through with orange and crimson highlights. It shone with a silky aura. If it were real hair, you'd have thought a stylist had labored over it, chopping, spritzing, and teasing. The top was spiky. In back it ran flat against her neck, curling up just at her shoulders. Overall, the effect was reminiscent of a look that, a few years back, had been small-town chic for both men and women. "Hockey hair," we called it up in Wisconsin.

As I came into the room, Mom tracked me with her gaze. Her face had puffed up even more, which made it seem like she was furrowing her brow and pursing her lips, and there was a strange, feral look in her eyes. She had on her favorite housedress, though it fit her pretty snugly now. I went around the table and hugged her. She clung to me tightly.

"Hello," she said softly, "hello."

AT FIRST we were hopeful. From the things everyone was saying going into the surgery, you got the idea that cutting a chunk out of somebody's brain was a tricky but routine procedure. "Procedure," that's what they called it—the doctors, Mom and Dad, pretty much any grown-up. It was my job, I thought, to take their optimism and drill it into Rory. "These guys are experts," I told him. "They're professionals. Plenty of reasons to stay positive."

I should remember the days leading up to the surgery, but searching back in memory they're mostly blank. Did we speak just before they put her under? Did she take my hand, squeeze it, tell me everything was going to be all right? If anything should happen, I was to look after my little brother—did she say that? I don't know. It's all gone, and now I only have the things I'm sure, absolutely sure, she *didn't* tell us.

I would eventually learn from her friends, both Julia and Barb, that there was a time when Mom wanted to tell Rory and me Dad's secret. She and Dad argued over it. She gave in to him— he'd make her life misery if she started dredging up his past. But did she reconsider? Before the anesthesiologist and the surgeon's knife, did she think that perhaps now she had nothing to lose?

Well, but in that moment other thoughts must have been roaring through her head—her death, her own death. She blamed herself for the cancer coming back. Too much fatty food, too little exercise. All those packs of B&Hs she'd sucked down on the back step. Too much stress, all the volunteering and little jobs she'd taken on. Her diets, she could never stick to them. And then there was her theory about the digital alarm clock she kept on her bedside table, right next to her head, all the radiation leaching off its big red display. She threw it away after the diagnosis.

I have my own theory: all those years of homesickness and fretting over money, the fights over credit card bills, the worry and frustration slowly tightening into a little knot, a dark snarl down in the folds of her brain, growing, pulsing, beating like a heart. And Dad's secret, having to carry it so long, wanting to tell us, having to push it down every time, until it began creeping into everything, the way secrets do, corrupting, tangling everything up, a little snarl growing down in the darkness, pulsing, beating, pushing out and out, until that day the headaches began . . .

HER FIRST WEEK back home, she did little but sleep. When we came into her room, bringing her a cup of tea or something to eat, she'd push herself up in bed and do her best to indulge us; it was difficult for her to hold anything down. We asked how she was feeling. She'd try to tell us, but her sentences wandered off. Before the heat of the day, she was bright-eyed, a little confused, happy. We were all smiles and easy laughter. In the hospital she'd seemed like some other person, a half-corpse. Now she was home. But from midmorning on, she had us keep the curtains closed and did nothing but doze. While we were talking to her she'd fall asleep without warning, and when she woke she was groggy and irritable. Rory, Dad, and I looked in on her in shifts. When I saw her eyelids begin to flutter, I stepped quietly from the room, thinking I'd leave her to rest. Rory stayed, perched on the chair we kept beside her bed, not saying anything, just watching her.

The hair that had been shaved off for the surgery was already growing back around the stitches. She was embarrassed by them and kept her head turned so we couldn't see, though sometimes she'd reach back and finger them wincingly. Only when she fell asleep and her head lolled on the pillow did we see the skin around the stitches going blister red. It turned my stomach, and I looked away.

For another week she stayed close to bed. After that she seemed to launch back into her old routine. Despite our protests, she insisted on doing housework, and if anything she was more fastidious than before. Her friends came to visit and sat drinking tea, catching her up on the village gossip. I drove her to a few meetings of the garden club, and we stopped in at the library to say hello to the other librarians. When she had to be in bed— exhaustion caught up with her quickly—she sat up, buoyed by several pillows, anxiously thumbing through one of her garden-ing books or a paperback novel.

On a follow-up, the surgeon told us how neural pathways sometimes reconnect. It took time, he said, but it was possible. At home, we could almost see it happening, the way she would struggle to find a word, her eyes searching as if it were written in the dust dancing in the light streaming through her window, then her tiny, girlish grin as she pronounced it—"handbag," "toothbrush," "cookbook"—even when she'd forgotten what she wanted the thing for in the first place.

*   *   *

THAT JUNE I graduated from Big Foot. Mom was ready for the ceremony. Two weeks ahead of time, she'd already chosen the dress she was going to wear and insisted on picking out my shirt and tie as well. But at the last minute, just as we were about to leave, she had a forgetful spell and then, in the middle of all the confusion, wet herself. After we got her cleaned up, she was exhausted and had to go back to bed. She kept apologizing for having to miss my "special day." I told her not to worry, she wouldn't be missing much, just a few corny speeches and some rednecks blowing air horns. When I said this, she started to tear up. I decided not to press the point.

After the ceremony, we picked her up on the way to the party the Meyers were throwing for Cal and me. Our families mingled on the back porch, eating brats and corn on the cob. When it came time for toasts, Rory brought out a bottle of champagne he'd been hiding in the car. "Where'd you get that from?" Dad said, but Rory only flashed a sly, darting smile. Looking back at the photos now, I see what could almost be a normal family. Me, wiry and bespectacled. Rory, cool and handsome. Dad with a forbearing but proud expression. But in each picture, there's a woman that looks like my mother. She's wearing my mother's favorite dress (a checkered pink and red housedress not terribly appropriate for the occasion). She has her hands crossed demurely in front of her, and she's grinning giddily, almost maniacally. It isn't her smile at all—it belongs to a woman none of us had ever known. I don't think even Mom knew who that woman was.

Early that July, Rory and I drove her to the first chemo appointment. In the parking lot, she told us to wait in the car. No need to hang around a stuffy clinic. Besides, she said, she didn't want us catching anything in there. Rory and I sat on the curb outside and pitched stones at a fire hydrant. An attendant appeared and told us to cut it out. "Fuck that guy," Rory kept saying after he went away. "Stupid motherfucker." An hour later, Mom came out on the arm of a nurse, looking dazed. She sat up very straight in the car and said almost nothing. At home, apologizing to us, she went straight to bed. When I went to check on her, her eyes, squeezed shut in sleep, were rimmed red from crying. I stepped out, as careful and quiet as always, and eased the door shut behind me.

Between the chemo and then the radiation treatments, she was cheerful and self-deprecating. But when the next was approaching, she'd snap at us for hovering over her constantly, for whispering outside her door. She started mixing up our names, calling me Rory or Rory Andrew. When we tried to get her out of bed to use the toilet or to help her undress for her baths, a process that was as embarrassing to us as it was to her, she'd shout—"What is this? What do you think you're doing?!"—and kick and squirm and flail until we stopped. She'd sit crying on her bed, her housedress half unzipped, the beige straps of her bra fallen from her shoulders, pantyhose rolled down to her ankles, the varicose veins showing darkly on her pale legs.

Sometimes she didn't know where she was. She thought we were in Southampton or Ireland or in a villa in the hills of San Remo. Sometimes she seemed to believe she was back in the classroom and would sit, legs crossed at the ankles, one hand on top of the other, and answer our questions as if she were being called on. It was like she was anthologizing her life. Sometimes she slipped back into her radio role as the queen.

"Everything okay, Mom? You comfortable?"

"Yes, fine, thank you." She considered for a moment, regal in her detachment, then dismissed us. "Yes, quite fine."

Finally, Dad gave in. I remember little about the hospice

nurse who came to the house four or five times a week, only that she was very firm with my mother. No more talk of going back to work, no more housecleaning, no more garden club meetings. She was to stay in bed and rest for her next appointment at the clinic. A small, pink-covered Bible appeared on Mom's bedside table. Whether it came from the nurse or one of Mom's friends, I didn't know. It was stamped with the name of Pastor Dan's congregation. I was livid at the sight of it but didn't say anything.

It usually fell to me to drive Mom to the clinic. Rory kept track of her pills, brought her tea in the mornings, and sat by her bed when she couldn't bring herself to get up, talking about his day and what all of his friends had been up to. A couple of times a week, he went off into the night and came back late, red-eyed and reeking of smoke, and went straight up to his room. He was hardly eating, his jaw and cheekbones chiseling out, the dark circles under his eyes making him look wary and hunted. By the time I started to wonder whether I should leave for college or stick around and help look after Mom, Rory had passed his driving test (the first time). He drove her to the last of her appointments, taking on the responsibility willingly, and even with a hint of pride.

Late that summer I woke to a loud thump. I crept out of my room and met Rory on the landing. "What the fuck?" I said. We went downstairs and found Mom lying on the kitchen floor, not asleep but in a stupor, her eyelids fluttering. Rory knelt and shook her gently. She didn't respond. He looked up at me, his eyes wide, questioning, a look that stripped me of all my authoritative, instructive words.

"Should we wake Dad?" Rory said.

I just stood there looking down at her, horrified. Her underwear was around her ankles—maybe she thought she was using the toilet (she hadn't, thank God)—and a thin trail of drool ran out of the corner of her mouth. Where was she then? Was she conscious? Did she know she was lying on the kitchen tile? Or was she in some other state of being, caught in some strange, miasmic place between sleeping and waking?

"Maybe we should wake up Dad," Rory said again, his voice shaking.

I eased open the door to Dad's room, stepped into the salty, close smell of his sweat, and called softly, "Dad?" I thought he hadn't heard, but he sat up suddenly and rolled out of bed with a heavy grunt. In the kitchen, none of us spoke. Dad got a dish towel and wiped her face. "I'll call 911," I said tentatively, but Dad held up a hand to stay me. The fluttering of her eyelids slowed to a steady blink.

"Come on, Nancy. That's a good girl."

"Don't worry, Mom," Rory said. "It's okay."

Together, the three of us got her up off the floor, back into her room, and into bed. We stood in the dark watching her. Dad whispered for Rory and me to go to bed, but Rory wouldn't leave. He said he was going to stay until she was better. But Dad insisted—just as later he would insist, at the beginning of the school quarter, that I go back to college. I was the scholar in the family; no way would he let me miss out on my education. Both times I was happy to do as I was told.

"GRUB'S UP!" Dad called from the kitchen.

Rory came down and laid out the knives and forks. I found the place mats stacked on the chair I usually sat in. Dad brought in the egg curry, the popadums, the rice, the lime pickle. I watched as he took up Mom's napkin and tucked it into the front of her dress—a bib. I tried to act natural, talked about college, my courses, my new friends (I'd made a few after all). I was auditioning for the jazz ensemble again, I said, but everyone was better than me, and I never had time to practice, or maybe I was just too lazy or it was too boring to work on scales and études. Or maybe I just sucked. Rory and Dad half-followed what I said. Mom didn't seem to be paying attention at all. She fought with her bib—it kept getting in the way as she tried to fork up her food—and finally she yanked it off and crumpled it on the table.

I tried to look her in the eyes, those strange, small, animal eyes, but my gaze kept drifting up. The wig sat a little cockeyed, strands of her own sparse hair wisping out underneath. Couldn't her friends have helped her choose something more *subtle?* Christ, after all the indignities she'd suffered—the weeks of bed rest, the endless treatments and consultations, the sponge baths, having to be helped every time she needed to piss—now my mother had to be saddled with this ridiculous hairpiece. I knew the wig had nothing to do with me, and that Julia and Barb had only gone along to support her—she'd chosen the thing herself. But my anger was almost choking me. And still I kept on talking, detailing my minor triumphs and failures at school, terrified to let any silence at all enter the room.

Halfway through the meal, she started drooling. Her mouth gaped. The food went in, then came sliding back out. Rice, curry, and flecks of mashed-up popadum slowly ran down her chin and neck. "Come on now, Nancy," Dad said, scolding her gently. She felt around with her hand to wipe off the mess but just spread it around, leaving her face ringed yellow with curry. The third time it happened, she made no attempt to clean herself up but sat perfectly still, her mouth hanging open. I sat there, frozen by revulsion.

"The curry is good," Rory said. "Right, Mom?"

She looked around at us.

Dad reached for the napkin crumpled on the table and tried

to wipe off the curry that had dribbled down her chin. Just as he touched her, she pushed herself back with a trembling screech of chair legs.

"No!"

"It's all right, Nancy. Come on now."

"It's okay, Mom," Rory said. "Everything's okay."

When I heard the caution in my brother's voice, I knew that while all of this might be new to me, it wasn't the first time since I'd been gone that they'd been in this sort of situation. Rory and Dad didn't have my luxury, the luxury of distance. They lived with her illness every day. For me, it had become abstract, unreal. *She* had become unreal. When I looked at my mother now, I saw only that other woman, the one grinning maniacally out of those graduation party photos, the one who would choose this new wig. Dad went for her again with the napkin.

"Leave me alone!" She stood up suddenly, flinging out her arms, then just as suddenly letting them flop to her sides. She sank back down to the chair. "Stop him!" she said, staring at me. I thought she was talking about Dad, but she shot her startled gaze over at Rory. "Who is he?" She began to cry. "Who *is* he?"

"Mom . . ." I began.

"Who is this person in my house?" she cried out.

"Mom, it's me."

"It's Rory," I said. "It's him."

"Don't tell *me* what to do! Leave me alone. I don't know you." She tried to stand but could only drop back into the chair again. "What are you doing?! Get out of my house!" Her gaze darted from me to Rory to Dad. Panic made blanks of her eyes; she didn't recognize any of us now. "You heard me, get out!"

The three of us—three strangers at her dinner table—sat in silence, looking at each other, unable to look at her. Her face was screwed up in horror and indignation. "*Get out!*" she screamed—

one last try. For all the force of her words, she couldn't even raise her arms to strike us. She shut her eyes tight. She opened them. We were still there. Her shoulders slumped; her chin dropped to her chest. The wig had come half-unclasped. Part of it was folded underneath itself, showing a patchy chunk of her scalp. When Dad reached over to straighten it, she didn't stop him.

We put her to bed. She slept all through the night and most of the next day, though it wasn't true sleep but that stunned, floating state she had lofted into that night on the kitchen floor. Dad, Rory, and I wandered the house. We kept getting in each other's way, meeting in doorways and crowding each other at the sink and fridge. I'd brought Neil Young's *Live Rust* home for Dad, but he made me turn the stereo down so low I could barely hear it.

The next few days I looked in on her every couple of hours, sneaking into her room and staring down at her as she drifted through her uncertain sleep, sneaking out again as quietly as I came. I was seized by nausea, the ice hardening in my stomach, pushing through my veins. The terror I felt that night at the dinner table, and the night I stared down at her on the kitchen floor, comes back even now, quick and paralyzing—the mind enfeebled and erased—total helplessness.

Just before Dad and I left to take me back to school, the hospital bed arrived. I balked at leaving when I saw it, but Dad said going back to my studies was the best thing for me to do. And I wanted to believe him.

When I came home for winter break four weeks later, she had lost nearly thirty pounds. Her skin no longer had the weird pink hue it had taken on after the radiation but had turned a papery gray. She slept with her hands curled into loose fists. Her nails were turning yellow. She chewed them when she was awake, her fingertips red and raw. Her own hair had begun to grow back, though it was sparse and thin and fell out as quickly as it came in. As for the new wig, I never saw it again. I think Dad threw it away.

A week and a half before Christmas, Nanny and Aunty Janet arrived. Mom seemed to sense they were there and would sometimes call softly for her mum. When you squeezed her hand, she squeezed back, a pressure so faint it was hard to tell if you were imagining it or not.

Four days before Christmas, the hospice nurse came out of Mom's room and spoke to Dad. He sat Rory and me down in the living room. If there was anything we wanted to say to her, he told us, or if we just wanted to say good-bye . . . I told him I'd already said my good-byes. Rory just sat staring at the carpet. A little later, he went into her room and didn't come out for over an hour.

The rest of that day, she hardly moved. She kept making small puckering sounds with her mouth. We couldn't pick out any words. Before, there had been a constant smell of urine and sour bedclothes in the room. Now there was almost no smell at all. We kept opening the door a crack to peer in at her sleeping in the half-dark. Finally, Nanny had to tell us to stop: "Your mum needs her rest now more than ever."

The next day, Dad sent Rory and me down to the SuperSaver to buy groceries for Christmas dinner. He gave us a long list, but I knew those grocery aisles too well; it didn't take us more than a half hour. When we got home, she was gone. I went in to take one last look. Nothing seemed to have changed. Her skin was the same pallid newspaper gray. She had only stopped breathing.

A pair of men came that afternoon and took her away. The people who'd delivered the bed arrived an hour later and took that away, too. All that was left was the chair that had sat next to the bed and the dust balls in the corners. The briskness of the removal, which was Dad's doing, upset Nanny and Aunty

Jan, but they agreed that he was in the right. Better not to linger over things. I put myself to work cleaning up around the house, though there wasn't much that needed doing. Rory barely left his room the rest of that day and all the next. He only came out late on Christmas morning when Dad called him downstairs. It was time to open presents.

The whole village seemed to turn out for the funeral. We'd expected a crowd. I hardly remember the service itself, or what I said when I got up to speak. As the guests filed in and then out, there was one thing we were told again and again. I heard it at the funeral and in letters and cards, on the street, in line at the store, the post office, the bank. Her illness had been tragic, people kept saying, but at least it would bring the three of us, the three men in the family, closer together.

13

HOSTAGE

Christmas in England: presents at ten in the morning, tea and cakes at midday, then into the kitchen to start on dinner. Roast goose, roast potatoes, roast parsnips, sausages wrapped in bacon, brussels sprouts, bread sauce, mince pies, Christmas cake, Christmas pudding. I eat too much, drink too much of the sloe gin Aunty Jan and her husband, John, bring down to Southampton. I pull my cracker, pretend to be amused by the little prize inside, read the joke printed on the curl of paper that never fails to fall out onto my dinner, unroll the paper crown and sit smiling with it on my head. At seven: cheese and biscuits, a glass of sweet sherry, then a few games of Scrabble before we settle down to the inevitable *Doctor Who* special on telly. It's not a bad day. I know it's not meant to make me, personally, feel miserable. Everyone, they say, gets depressed around Christmas.

But that Christmas, 2004, I could hardly stand to hear some-one whistling "Jingle Bells" without rage and spite welling up in me. The last few months, I'd spent a lot of time driving around in my dad's Impala, having panic attacks in which I saw myself spinning and cartwheeling into cinematic accidents. Runaway eighteen-wheelers, swan dives through guardrails, pileups, head-ons, wrong turns into oncoming Escalades, the sickening thump of caving body panels, the heavenly shower of shattering glass. Since things had ended with Claire, I'd thrown myself into a series of drunken flings—making out in dive bars, waking up on futons and floors in strange apartments, not knowing where I was, sneaking out, then back in again to get directions home. For six or seven weeks, I actually dated someone, until her fiancé came back from his research trip in India. Late at night she'd get calls from her "friend." "No, it's okay, I'm awake," she'd say to him on the phone while I lay naked under the covers. "What am I doing? Oh, not much." Then, mid-November, Kerry lost to Bush in the election, and Bloomington sank into gloom. I'd made up my mind I was leaving; I wanted to start my degree over at the University of Virginia. But the thought of saying good-bye to all my friends in the Midwest panicked me more than chang-ing lanes in rush-hour Chicago traffic.

In Southampton, we opened presents, and I feigned excite-ment over socks, ornaments, and a giant Cadbury's Fruit and Nut. When we gave Aunty Jan's border collie, Kree, his present, instead of watching him tearing the wrapping off his new chew toy, his eyes gone white with delirious pleasure, I had to get up, leave the room, and spend the next hour fuming upstairs. That evening, instead of taking Chris and Bob, my great-aunt and -uncle, up on their invitation to go carol singing in Otterbourne, I went out alone for a long, dreary walk along the Itchen, despis-ing everything in sight.

* * *

EAST WORTHING, SHOREHAM-BY-SEA. The dead-sounding, pre-recorded voice announced the last stops before Brighton. The train began to empty, the passengers getting off at local stations— *Southwick, Portslade*—going home to their families. I sat grinding my teeth, willing myself not to get off early and catch the next train back to Southampton.

Arthur and I had been e-mailing since the summer. I wrote him brief messages about the weather or records I thought he should hear, and he sent me funny little images: Bush Photoshopped to look like a monkey or Prince Charles mounting a horse with Camilla Parker Bowles's face, the caption reading, "His royal steed." Now and then, Arthur also strayed into more personal matters. He told me that when he was seventeen, away at university, he would sometimes turn and look up from his spot in the lecture hall and see a figure sitting in the balcony, looking down on him with obvious interest. Somehow he knew it was his father, though when the lesson was over and he raced up to the balcony to meet him, he was always gone—just an empty row of seats.

I'd spent the last week coming up with reasons not to go to Brighton for New Year's. If I wasn't feeling up to it, Nanny told me, I should just ring Arthur and say I wasn't feeling well. No one would think less of me. I shouldn't feel obligated. But somehow this *was* necessary. Out of some stubborn desire, if only just to play the drama out to its end, I had to go. When Nanny saw I'd made up my mind, she laid out an overnight bag for me: several changes of clothes, a bath towel and face towel, a packet of Polo mints for the journey. "Now, mind you don't come back gay," she said at Southampton Central. She meant it as a joke, I think.

Arthur was waiting on the platform. When I saw him again,

my breath caught. My dad, back from the grave. As soon as he spotted me, a grin spread across his face. "Welcome to Brighton!" he said in that uncanny voice. I went to shake hands; he drew me into a hug and gave me a kiss on the cheek. I shrank back. "We're very Continental here," he said. "You'll just have to get used to it!" We went out to the car. "Wrong side!" Arthur called out when I went round to the driver's door. "My little Yankee brother!"

We drove into the city center along a street lined with cafés and tattoo parlors. We crossed the high street, the pavements thronging with shoppers, and drove along the seafront past a row of hotels—the Old Ship, the Royal Albion, the Grand—with ornate, glass-fronted entries and valets in long red coats, clapping their white-gloved hands together to keep warm. Palm trees—stunted and wind-beaten but palm trees nonetheless—poked up between the buildings. A pebble beach sloped down to the water, and there the ocean swayed back and forth, hugely black, shot through with silver. We passed several enormous buildings with elegant, scalloped facades, painted all white and then, farther down the seashore, all butter yellow. The Regency crescents, Arthur explained, where the Georgian nobility once summered. We turned up a narrow road and parked. "Here we are," Arthur said. "Welcome to Treetops." In most of England, you only named your house if you had a thatch cottage in the country or were to the manor born. On Arthur's road every house had a nameplate.

A man with sandy blond hair stood in the doorway saying, "Come in, come in. Oh my, cold out there, isn't it?" He looked about forty and wore tan slacks, a rumpled Oxford, and rimless glasses.

"William, Phillip," Arthur said. "Phillip, William."

This, finally, was Arthur's partner. He'd mentioned Phillip

any number of times over e-mail, but somehow I hadn't believed there was really a man behind the name. We shook hands, and I brought my duffel inside.

"Your first visit to Brighton!" Arthur said, putting a glass of white wine in my hand. "Shall I give you the tour?"

I was used to English homes crammed with knickknacks and overstuffed furniture, homes that smelled of ancient dust, oven grease, and the damp bags of potting soil kept in the conservatory. Here everything was sleek and minimalist—black leather couch, glass-top dining table, a rack of high-end stereo equipment, real art on the walls—tasteful, expensive, and spotlessly clean.

WE WENT to a restaurant on the seafront. Arthur ordered up a feast. The last time I'd had such an extravagant meal was when Dad and I took a trip to Chicago, and in an expansive mood, he'd decided we should dine at the Drake. "My treat, guy," he said. "My treat." Toward the end, he was always treating me. When the bill came, I swallowed hard and tried to slip my credit card in, but Arthur insisted on paying.

We walked along the promenade and turned up a winding lane of salons and restaurants with one-word names. Girls in short skirts and boys with gelled-up hair queued to get into clubs. Two rugged, beautiful men in evening coats were kissing in a doorway. We stopped at a bar called Vanilla and ordered martinis. Phillip sat in silence, listening to Arthur and me talk, and trying not to listen, trying to give us our space.

"He would have found this quite strange, wouldn't he?" Arthur was talking about our dad. "The two of us getting to know each other."

"I don't think he could ever have imagined it." And if he had, it would've been as a nightmare.

"Did you and he get on? Were you mates?"

What could I say? When I was young, I feared my dad's anger—it always seemed coiled inside him waiting to strike. Later it was his detachment, his analytic mind so obsessed with work and money, that gave him his awful power. Yet this was also what I admired in him, his inventiveness, his curiosity, the way his eyes lit up when he had an idea—an *idea*—and reached for graphing paper and mechanical pencil and started deftly sketching it out. He passed those same habits on to me, and blamed himself for not inspiring them in Rory. Rory and I were the products, the print and the photonegative, of his manias. But was I friends with my father?

"Toward the end," I said. "When it was just the two of us."

Did Dad ever open up to me? Arthur wanted to know. Were we ever able to really talk?

Maybe it was just two sides of the same coin, I said. He was closed off because I was closed off. Most of the time, when he tried to talk about Mom or Rory, I just felt embarrassed.

"You mustn't blame yourself," Arthur said. "I spent most of my adolescence and my twenties wondering, why didn't I have a dad? What did *I* do wrong?"

"I could've bugged him to go to the doctor. I could've said something about his drinking." On business trips, he'd pack a handle of Seagram's in his overnight bag. Not a fifth or a liter but a *jug* of whisky. Toward the end, his guts were so rotten he had to take a roll of toilet paper and a change of underwear in the car with him, even on the twenty-minute drive to and from work. "Sometimes I *wanted* him to die." I'd had more to drink than I realized. "I wanted to be, I don't know, unburdened of him."

"You weren't his keeper," Arthur said. "You were his son." He reached over and gave my shoulder a squeeze. This time I didn't recoil. "Come on, let's make tracks. Big day tomorrow."

* * *

ON THE PALACE PIER, its fun-fair games and rides shuttered and forlorn in the gray December afternoon, Arthur and I leaned on the railing, squinting at the ocean. Arthur had been excited to show me the city, but I was hungover and quiet. In the city center, making our way through the crowds, I felt remote from the holiday bustle, sunk in the stifled rage that'd been hanging with me for months. Arthur ran into a few people he knew and introduced me. I could barely mumble out a hello.

We stopped at a record shop, flipped through the albums, gave each other recommendations. We bought a couple of records each and went back out into the early evening. The winding lanes and the tidy little squares that opened off them were all hung with lights. They started to come on now, casting the curving lines of all the redbrick buildings into soft relief. The barest snowfall was coming down—it so rarely snowed in England—and stylish, red-cheeked shoppers streamed all around us. Some of the passageways were so narrow that whenever someone rushed by carrying bags stuffed with wine and food for that night ("All right, Arthur?" several people called out. "Happy New Year!") we had to squeeze against the wall to let them pass. Despite everything, the excitement was rubbing off on me. An elegant middle-aged woman stopped to give Arthur a hug and a kiss. She seemed thrilled to see him and apologized for having to rush off.

"Carry on, my dear, carry on!" Arthur said. "Just giving a little tour. This is my brother William! From America!"

It was the first time I noticed it: not "half brother" but "brother."

"Nice to meet you!" I said. "Love your city!"

"Oh, marvelous!" She seemed confused why I should be complimenting *her* on it.

Arthur and I stopped to say Happy New Year to a few more people; then suddenly we were back on the promenade, on our way home. "Bit chaotic today for the full tour."

I must have looked disappointed.

"You'll be back, won't you?"

"Sure," I said vaguely. "Of course."

THE PARTY was at the flat of an artist friend of Arthur's, an open loft with her stacked paintings spilling over into the living area. Arthur introduced me around. I shook hands, kissed a few cheeks. Here in Brighton most people kissed on both cheeks. I was unaccustomed to this and ended up headbutting one woman.

My champagne glass was never empty. Lips gone numb, I felt light and talkative—except when I opened my mouth all my conversation evaporated. The artist buttonholed me in the corner with questions about America. At some point, I told her that I was English, actually, and saw myself as a bit of an outsider back in the States.

"What on earth happened to your accent, then?"

"Kids are cruel. I wanted to fit in."

"I adore American accents," she said, touching my arm. "I find them sexy."

Her husband came over, a thick-necked guy who made documentaries. He nearly pulped my hand shaking it.

"Tell me," the artist said, "what do you think of this Bush fellow? Bit of an imbecile, isn't he?"

I put out both hands, shoving away any association with the dubiously reelected president. "No love lost here."

"He's a fucking travesty, your Bush," the filmmaker cut in. The artist gave him a sour look and drifted away, leaving me alone with him. "Who'd you vote for, then?"

"I didn't vote. I'm still a Brit."

"Don't bother yourself much with politics?"

"No, I mean, I get involved in my own way. I . . ." This was going to sound lame. "I try to talk to people."

"You lot don't like to get your hands dirty, do you? I've been to America. Everyone complains, and then they just let the fucking pols do as they please."

I couldn't tell if he was joking or if he really wanted to give me a hard time. That year being a Yank in Britain, or pretty much anywhere abroad, wasn't going to get you draped with grateful, liberator-embracing hugs. Still, hearing someone slag off the U.S., I couldn't help feeling personally insulted. I tried asking the guy about his films. I mentioned a documentary I'd seen recently.

"An American film? All gushy, sentimental stuff they like over there."

Listen, I wanted to say, I'm not here representing all of America. I'm here because my dad died. Because he had a family I never knew about, and I found a folder of papers in his desk, and usually I'd love a good argument, but it's been a really fucking crazy year, so please, whoever you are, please just leave me the *fuck* alone.

"It's September 11," the filmmaker went on. "You Americans think everyone can be a hero—firemen, soldiers, any ordinary bloke—and that's what you want on screen: One man against the whole world. It's all a fantasy. Fucking dangerous fantasy at that."

Arthur came over with a bottle of champagne. "You look like you need a top-up," he said, filling the filmmaker's glass. "I think our lovely hostess was looking for you." The guy went off to track down his wife.

"Thanks," I said.

"They're going through a rotten divorce," Arthur explained. "You okay?"

"Fine," I said, but I was obviously shaken.

The night was now in full swing. Arthur hung by when I had trouble making conversation, slipped off now and then to work the room. I watched him charming everyone, wishing I could, too. Suddenly everyone was putting on coats and hats. We pushed outside and headed for the beach, gliding along on a silvery trail of booze. I heard my feet crunching on the pebbles, the waves rushing and fizzling. There was already a crowd down there, silhouettes moving in the dark, voices laughing and calling out. Then the commotion died—everyone checking their watches—and the countdown started. There was a loud cheer, then happy confusion as everyone started hugging and kissing. The glasses came around, and the pop of several champagne corks cannonaded at once. The beach was lit by the flares of rockets spiraling off into the night, Roman candles sputtering brightly to life, flash bombs blinking against the dark sky, then exploding with a heavy *boom*. In all the disorder, the group next to us fell into our circle, and I was embracing complete strangers, drinking to their health and happiness, toasting to the New Year. Arthur gave me a big, wet kiss on the cheek. I gave him one back.

"Lovely to have you here," he said, pulling me in tight. "I'll always remember this weekend—when my little brother first came to visit."

For a moment, I couldn't speak. Then someone handed me a bottle of champagne, and I was shouting out into the darkness, "Happy New Year!"

Arthur looked at me, held me with that steady gaze of his. "Let's hope it's better than the last one."

"I'll drink to that," I said, tipping back the bottle.

AS SOON as we got into the taxi to go home, the alcohol hit me. The shops on the high street passed in a smear of light. I hung on to the sound of Arthur's voice. He had the driver go past the Royal Pavilion, so I could see it lit up at night. A sprawling building with a massive, onion-shaped dome surrounded by minarets and saw-toothed spires went by in a long streak.

"Beautiful," I said weakly.

Back at Treetops, I was about to declare that I was going to bed when Phillip brought out a bottle of scotch and three tumblers. "A little nightcap?"

"Yes, please, and thank you very much," Arthur said, answering for both of us.

I tossed back my head and drank it down in one shot. I winced at the burn, wiped my lips, exhaled a sharp *ha*. Arthur and Phillip stood looking at me.

"You're supposed to sip that, you know," Arthur said.

"That's how me and the boys back home do it."

"Bloody Yanks!" Arthur said, and both he and Phillip broke out laughing. "Can't do anything properly!"

"Listen"—I stood there, swaying—"one thing I know how to do is drink."

Arthur reached over and gave me a little slap on the cheek. "Only teasing, little bruv," he said. "Only teasing."

We said good night. I went unsteadily down to the guest room, lay on top of the sheets, and observed the ceiling tilting back and forth. I closed my eyes, tried to sleep, and kept bobbing back up. I tried to hold it back, but the torrent roared through my skull, all those voices shouting at once. I kept turning over the things I'd first been told about Arthur: the meeting in the pub in Southampton, when he'd asked my dad for a hundred quid. Barb's story about his failed visit to Fontana. *Stay away*, the voices told me. When I first met Arthur I'd felt such a strong connection between us. But I was still nervous around him. *Better not to go into it. Incalculable damage.* My imagination—my overactive, small-town imagination—churned with drink and suspicion. Maybe Arthur was angry, jealous and angry that I'd had a father and he hadn't. He'd brought me here just to tell me terrible shit about my dad. He'd brought me here to . . .

I slipped into woozy sleep—then woke with a start to the sound of voices and footsteps coming down the stairs. The idea flashed into my head (an idea, I'm ashamed to admit, that had been lurking since I got on the train in Southampton): *They were going to hold me hostage.* They wanted the money in the estate, and now they'd succeeded in getting me fall-down drunk and were going to hold me hostage until I gave it to them. One moment it seemed absurd; the next, I really believed that I could *feel* them waiting just outside the door. It was all going to turn out to be a cruel trick. All the e-mails and phone calls, all the kind, sympathetic things Arthur had said—what reason would he have other than to scam me? How could he love a brother he'd only just met?

Five minutes, or an hour, swam by like this. Finally, I got out of bed, dragged the chair over from the desk in the corner, and propped it under the door handle. *There,* I told myself, *either way I'm safe.*

14

A BALANCING ACT

Nanny and I were watching *University Challenge.* She'd answered more of the sadistically obscure questions than any of the cabbage-pale Oxbridge contestants. All the teachers in Southampton were evacuated during the war, and my grandmother never had a day of school past age eleven, her education coming instead from TV quizzes, the *Daily Mail*, and doing the books at the newsagents she and Granddad Snook had run together for forty years. Usually, I could only sit there marveling at her. My grandmother in her sea green recliner, adjusting her bifocals, primping the curls of her perm, making little gestures of delight every time she got a question right—seeing her was always a comfort to me. But now my toes were wriggling in my shoes. I kept getting up to check the time. And when the doorbell went just before eight, I nearly leapt out of my seat I was so startled.

"You'll have to ring him," Arthur had told me. "He's quite shy. But he'd love to take you out for a pint."

I went to the door, opened it, held out my hand. He was tall, a couple of inches taller than me, with dark brown eyes and thick brown hair, curly and neatly kept. We stood there, me staring at him, him staring at me. He wore khakis and a crisply pressed short-sleeve shirt; I had on one of my threadbare western wear snap-ups. But it didn't matter how we were dressed, there was no mistaking it: Arthur was the son of my father, but here before me was my brother. Harry had my dad's eyes, and I had my mother's blues. Still, we looked more alike than even Rory and I had. Just that summer, my hair had started to go curly. I didn't know where it came from—everyone else in my family had straight hair. Recessive genes. Here were two examples, gawking at each other on the threshold.

"Welcome! Come in!" I said in a strange, booming voice. "Don't worry about your shoes!" We went into the living room. "Go ahead, have a seat!"

Harry perched on the edge of the high-backed leather armchair, Granddad Snook's chair. Hardly anyone sat in it, even with my grandfather ten years dead. I sat on the settee, elbows on my knees, chin cupped in my right hand, tapping my foot furiously, the same ulcer-courting pose I used to take before my tuba solos in school band contests. "Well!" I said, thinking I would kick off the conversation, then suddenly not knowing a single thing to say. "Well!" But that tug didn't get the engine going either.

"Will tells me you're in the motor trade," Nanny said, stepping in to fill the void.

I sat there smiling and nodding as if the meeting were between the two of them.

"I'm at the BMW garage in town." Everything he said came after a long, embarrassed pause. He shifted restlessly in the high-backed chair. "I'm the service manager."

"And have you always lived in Southampton?" Nanny said.

"All my life. Moved around a fair bit when I was a lad. In Shoaling now."

Christ, twenty-four years and at least as many visits home to England, and all that time the second of my half brothers was living just the other side of the river.

"Hasn't the weather been rotten these last weeks?"

"Absolutely dire, this weather."

"Rotten," I put in. "Absolutely rotten."

Harry shifted positions again. He was ready to be on his way.

HE'S LYING on his back, knees pulled up to his stomach, arms held straight up in the air. The carpet is strewn with Christmas wrapping paper, all the new toys pushed under the tree to clear a space. Rose looks down at him, already laughing. She's blond, blue-eyed, petite. In school she did gymnastics and dance. In America, no doubt, she'd have been a cheerleader. She closes her eyes, doubles over, holding her stomach.

"Come on, then!" Harry says, trying to keep from laughing himself.

"Pull yourself together!" Rose admonishes, herself or Harry or both. She leans forward, so that her stomach presses into the bottoms of Harry's socked feet. He takes her weight, then slowly starts to press up, lifting her with his legs. She makes her body stiff, reaches out for his hands, holding on until she gets her balance. Then she spreads her arms wide, straightens her legs, closes her eyes again.

"Mummy, don't fall! Mummy!"

Charlie and Violet are dancing around, giggling and calling out and tumbling over on the carpet in their excitement. Charlie's five, blue-eyed and fair, with smooth, pale cheeks and dusky wisps of eyebrows. Violet, three, has her father's dark, serious eyes—that *is to say,* my *father's eyes. Just twenty minutes ago, they were both hiding behind their mother, clinging to her legs, too bashful to even speak, not knowing what to make of the unshaven stranger with the funny accent and cowboy clothes.*

"Right, Charlie," Harry says, a quiver in his voice from keeping Rose aloft. "Come on, your go."

ACTUALLY, the weather wasn't rotten that night. Harry and I rolled down the windows. We crossed the Itchen and drove along Southampton Water, hardly speaking.

"How long you worked for BMW?"

"Oh, years."

"Great cars."

"Good company, too."

"Great, great. Good to know."

Harry turned onto a dark, narrow lane and parked under a copse of willows. A path led to a wooden gate and stone steps going down. I could hear waves lapping against pilings, a sound that took me back to Fontana and the lake and touched something wide and lonesome inside me. A marina opened up below us, a flock of white sailboats, masts ticking back and forth against the inky water. A sudden panic trilled through me. What were we doing here—at night in this out-of-the-way place? My antic mind frenzied through every scenario. I was picturing robbery, murder, my body floating facedown. Then I saw the pub at the bottom of the steps.

No big-screen TVs, no video gambling, no fruit machines. No one was falling down drunk. The copper beer taps shone invitingly. "What's yours?" Harry said.

"Pint of bitter," I told him. "Courage Directors."

"Good brew, that one."

Harry's accent was thicker in person than in the halting, awkward phone call we'd had to set this meeting up. It was a Hampshire accent, all dropped pronouns and inverted syntax, a mellow singsong that sounded nothing like the rather proper locutions Arthur had acquired at university.

We took a table in the corner. The windows were open, letting in the salt air and the warm, insistent breeze. Harry sipped his pint and stared across the water, a vigilant look on his face, as if he were trying to spot something out there in the dark.

"Used to bring Rose here when we first started dating. Liked to come for lunch, watch the boats going out."

"It's great. I didn't even know there were pubs like this in Southampton."

We sat drinking our beer. It felt like the end of a conversation, not the beginning.

"Arthur tells me you're a Saints fanatic."

"Told you about the turnstile, did he?"

"Sorry?"

"Rose let me have it on condition I put it in the garden." He explained that he'd bought at auction one of the entrance turnstiles from the Dell (the Saints' former grounds, torn down a few years before). He'd put in eight bids before he won the lot.

"How much was it in the end?"

"Three thousand quid."

At the time that was nearly six thousand dollars. Despite myself I was making calculations: Who needed Dad's money, who didn't. Who deserved it—who'd *earned* it.

Harry went on, telling me that when Saints played their last match at the Dell, he and a few other season ticket holders had unbolted their seats and lugged them home. He'd also bought a square of turf from the pitch and planted it in the back garden, next to the turnstile.

"How do you tell the Dell grass from the grass grass?"

"Turf died two weeks later."

I told him I'd seen Saints play a couple of times—an exhibition against a Dutch club where Matt Le Tissier put in a rocket from the edge of the penalty box, and then, in season play, I'd watched Tottenham Hotspur trounce Southampton, with goals from both Gary Lineker and Paul Gascoigne. I tried to sound very expert, but my knowledge didn't go further than what I'd learned playing JV soccer at Big Foot. I said I loved "the footie" but that they never broadcast the English leagues in America. I asked how Saints were doing this year, not even knowing if the season had actually started.

"They're a young team," he said. "Loads of promise. Haven't played together much. Find their pace eventually."

We sipped our beers again. I felt swept up by Arthur—his energy, his charm, that voice. With Harry, it was like having a pleasant chat with a distant acquaintance. We just had to have a couple of drinks, say a polite good-bye, and carry on with our separate lives.

Except that every time I looked at him I saw my chin, my nose, my jaw . . .

CHARLIE STRADDLES *his dad's head, getting into position. He reaches for his mum's outstretched hands, picks up one foot, then the other, and puts them in his dad's palms. He bites down on his lip, not just playing, not just having fun, but solemn, determined.*

After we'd said our hellos, Harry, Rose, and I had sat down in the living room. The kids kept their distance, studiously investigating their new toys, a Scalextric race car set for Charlie, a Bratz doll for Violet. We opened a bottle of wine. It was good to see that Rose and Harry were fairly casual about drinking around the children. I remembered the secretive way Dad had about his whisky, how he hid it away on the top shelf or in his bedroom.

Charlie came over, clutching Violet's doll. "Look, Daddy, she has blue hair."

"Yes, son, very strange indeed."

Violet got up and tried to pull the doll from Charlie's hand.

"Violet, don't! Don't be rude! I'm showing it to Daddy."

"I was playing with it. Give it back. Give it back!"

Violet's lips started trembling. I steeled myself for tantrums and sobbing.

"Calm down, please, Violet," Harry said. Now Violet was indeed crying. "Oh, I know, it's tragic."

"Violet, stop whinging," Charlie scolded.

"Would you like to give your sister her doll back?" Harry said, patient and unruffled. "She was playing with it, wasn't she?"

"But Daddy, I—"

"That's enough, Charlie."

"But—"

Charlie gets both feet in his dad's hands, wiggles a little to find his equilibrium. Harry pushes up, cantilevering Charlie between him and Rose, raising his son slowly into the air. Harry's legs tremble at the new weight—it looks dicey for a moment—then go rigid again. Violet looks on thoughtfully, toying with a pink barrette in her hair, inspecting the work like an architect on a job site. Then she risks a glance at me, and her face pops into a wide-eyed, gap-toothed look of disbelief.

"YOU'RE A STUDENT, then," Harry said. Outside, the riggings of the sailboats were clanking and moaning. "What do you study?"

I launched into a jumble of an answer, something about

taking literature courses, doing odd jobs, living cheap—ramen, hot dogs, Miller High Life, the ninety-nine-cent Dunkin' Donuts breakfast special I once ate for a month straight. I figured that anyone who worked for a living either wouldn't be interested in or wouldn't understand my antinarrative, Frenchified, prose-poetic pursuits.

"Arthur's always been the intellectual one," Harry said. "He had a rough time of it in the Southampton schools. Got sent some nasty places. A few years in there I had to look after him on the playground. Done well for himself, though. I was always more into clowning around, taking the mick. You regret it in the end, you do. No one knew about dyslexia back then. Didn't have a proper diagnosis till years later."

I nodded, made a sympathetic sound. I could see the pattern emerging: the elder son clever and driven, the younger fun-loving, a little wild. Just like it'd been with Rory and me.

"You live alone? Have your own flat? Apartment," Harry corrected himself.

"A real bachelor pad."

"Anyone special in your life?"

I came close to unloading on him then: my breakup with Claire, my moronic pursuit of the Smithie, that shameful night I'd tried to use my grief to get Claire into bed. I could've gone on, about feeling constantly menaced, threatened, hunted—thinking that God or Death or whatever was after me. About my sudden impulses to throw myself in front of traffic, the dark, despairing stories I'd been cultivating in my notebook. About Rory. About Mom. I *wanted* to tell Harry all of this—but it would wreck the whole evening. You couldn't talk about these things with someone you hardly knew.

"No one special at the moment," I said, repeating what I'd told Dad on the phone on his last morning on earth.

❊　❊　❊

VIOLET TAKES OUT *her barrette, drops it on the carpet without look-ing where it lands, intent on the task at hand. She gets herself into place, grabs onto her mom's thighs—"Violet! Steady on!"—puts her bare feet on Harry's butt, and leans back, poised and elegant, countering Charlie's pull in the other direction. For three, maybe four seconds, they balance together, making the shape of a letter from some inscrutable alphabet. Then Charlie starts giggling.*

I'd been gulping down the wine and rambling on—about the Midwest, grad school, bands I'd played in, all of it sounding completely frivolous as soon as it passed my lips. Violet had for-gotten about her doll and started stomping around, blowing big fat raspberries for no particular reason. Then she got down on all fours and neighed like a horse. Charlie asked if he could bring out his cornet and play a song, but Harry gently said no. Charlie and Violet were performing for me, that much was clear. But I never knew how to act or what to say around kids. I enjoyed adult conversation, *intellectual* conversation, and found it irritating to have children forever interrupting.

Charlie came over again. He looked up at me under his deli-cate lashes with his bright blue eyes, and I felt a quiver of fear, of something foreign and unnamable, go through me.

"Uncle Will," Charlie said, "why do you talk that way?"

Uncle Will! Until that moment it hadn't occurred to me that, properly speaking, this little boy and girl were my niece and nephew. I didn't know if Harry and Rose had prompted them to call me "uncle" or if Charlie had said it spontaneously. Either way the words were out there, hanging balloonlike in the air.

"Uncle Will! Uncle Will!" Violet burst out. She started danc-ing around, twisting her hips, windmilling her arms, and gig-gling. Harry smiled down at her indulgently.

"Why do I speak like this?" I said, looking at Rose. She nodded toward Charlie. "Well, I live in America," I said to him in a high-pitched voice, the kind you'd use to tell a dog to fetch.

"Is that very, very far away?"

"All the way across the ocean. I used to live here, in South-ampton. A long time ago." There was a lot to say about what came in between, but how the hell could I explain it all to a five-year-old? "I come back to visit."

"Can you come to my birthday party? It's in . . ." He counted on his fingers. "Three weeks!"

"I don't think I can. I'll be in America."

"But we're going to have a bouncy castle. All my friends from school are going to come. And all my friends from swimming class. And we're going to play football—"

"Charlie," Rose said, "I think it's getting close to bedtime."

"But Mummy—" When Charlie laughs he blushes and turns his face away.

"Yes, speak up, Charlie."

"Can we do our family trick for Uncle Will?"

"Our what?" Rose said, smiling, pretending not to understand.

"Oh, Mummy, you know, our trick!"

"Yeah!" Violet said. "Yeah, yeah, yeah! *Oh, Charlie, don't!*"

Now Violet's scolding her older brother for giggling, for upset-ting everyone's balance. Harry's legs tremble again—Rose's grace-ful flight shudders. Everyone's trying to correct, shifting in different directions at the same time, the wobble flexing through each of their separate bodies. I make some encouraging sounds but have no idea what to say. What am I ever supposed to say?

"DO YOU LIKE to cook?" I asked Harry. "Andrew loved to cook."

I was reluctant to bring up my dad (his dad, *our* dad?—I didn't even know what to call him anymore). Yet hadn't we both come here, to this cozy pub, to get drunk enough to talk about him?

"He was really good at Indian. I remember his lime pickle." I laughed. "Shit, it was so hot only he ever wanted to eat it. But he always made us sit down, have a proper family meal together."

Harry watched as a boat, probably the last to come in that day, glided into the marina. Some memory seemed to glide past his eyes as well. For a moment, I recognized Rory in him.

"Arthur and I are both good cooks," he said quietly. "Men in the kitchen. Maybe it's inherited." He made a motion with his empty glass, asking if I wanted another.

When he came back from the bar I made another attempt.

"Do you like music? He and I both liked jazz. We sort of bonded over it."

More than that, in Dad's last years, it was our way of communicating; those little grunts and moans of surprise, approval, and exquisite pain we made listening to Bill Evans or Cannonball Adderley or Milt Jackson were our way of telling each other that there could still be beauty and grace in the world. For just an instant, concentrating so intensely, so desperately, on just one single passing note, the perfect note, the one you would never have expected, Dad and I weren't resigned to picking through the wreckage of the past but could live again in the bright, lazy comfort of the present.

"Trouble is," Harry said, "once you have kids, you find yourself listening to whatever they want to hear. 'Old McDonald,' that kind of thing. You just go along with it, you want to make them happy."

We sat smiling at each other. Arthur had *wanted* to talk about my dad. With Harry, it seemed like every word I spoke about him was a wound.

"I've always wanted to do something with boats," Harry said.

"Rose thinks I should chuck it in at the garage, start training for the Coast Guard."

"Sounds cool. You should do it."

"Can't just quit everything when you're raising two young children."

We sat there inspecting our drinks very closely.

ROSE LOOKS DOWN *at Harry, her eyes bright, their gazes locked together. Harry makes small adjustments with his hips, juggling Charlie's feet as Charlie's little body shakes, not taking his eyes from Rose's, judging every correction through the silent instructions passing between the two of them.*

After the kids were in bed, we sat down with another bottle of wine. Now the words came more easily. "So, when you guys got married," I began, "did you—"

Rose corrected me. They weren't married, actually.

"Right, sorry. When you got together, did you think you'd have kids?"

Harry had been listening to us, a distant expression on his face. "You start to thinking maybe it wouldn't be so terrible after all—you know, giving up your freedom and all of that." He faltered, searching for the words. "Right up till Charlie was born, I still wasn't sure. But when they finally arrive, you just . . . you just say, yeah, this feels right."

"Do you think you'll settle down, have a family?" Rose asked me.

Here I launched into a stoic-sounding bout of self-pity: about my dire romantic prospects, about saddling a child with my poisoned bloodline. There was just too much cancer in my family for me to pass on my crappy genes, I said, trying to sound pragmatic about it.

Harry shook his head. "You can't think about that. We decided right from the start we wouldn't worry over Charlie and Violet every waking moment. Of course, you want them to be safe. But you can't plan for the worst."

No, I wanted to say, you always had to plan for the worst.

"Do you think you'd have another?"

"Two is enough for us." Then Harry understood the other half of my question. "When Arthur and I heard about your brother's accident . . . and your mum before that . . . we wanted to get in touch, to send our sympathies. But we didn't even have an address."

I nodded. "Thanks."

We all fell quiet. Harry got up and put on some music, the Pet Shop Boys. From his DJing days, he explained. "That's how we met," Rose said. "I used to go out dancing with my girlfriends, and there was this lovely boy in the DJ booth."

Harry blushed. I thought I saw how the story went: As a teenager, Harry was flunking school, getting drunk, running with the yobs. He'd lived in the shadow of his overachieving older brother—that old story—and wreaking havoc was the only way he knew to distinguish himself. Then he met Rose. Now here we were, sitting in this modest, comfortable home—a happy home, that was clear, too—and it was all because she'd loved him and brought into his life the stability he'd never known growing up. Sometimes the right one just comes along. Maybe it could've happened to Rory, too—if only he'd had the chance to meet her.

"Do you think you will get married eventually?" I said. "I mean, I think it's really cool. Love without marriage, family without marriage."

The distant look came over Harry's face again. He stared down at the carpet. Rose took his hand in hers. She tucked her legs underneath her and snuggled closer to him. "And your parents never told you?" she asked me. "They never told you that you had half brothers?"

I'd racked my brains trying to remember, I said—if there was ever a hint dropped and I just didn't understand. I'd looked for photos; there wasn't a single one. It was like that part of my dad's life just stopped existing for him.

Rose turned to Harry. "It must have felt . . . well, like you'd just been discarded."

That word rang out—discarded. Whether my dad had walked out on his first family or Sara had forced him out, the effect had been the same: Arthur and Harry's dad disappeared from their lives completely. Eventually, he took up with another woman, started another family, then moved out of the country, first to Ireland, then all the way to America. To Arthur and Harry, growing up, it would've felt as if he wanted to get as far from them as possible. And now here I was, telling Harry his dad hadn't kept even a single photo of him. I saw him struggling to speak. But the words wouldn't come. Two bottles of wine between the three of us weren't enough to get them out.

Charlie's giggling quieted. Harry went on correcting as Charlie's legs pistoned up and down. He pulled in a breath and pushed Rose back up, straight and level. Violet went on riding comfortably, her head tipped back, her hair hanging down, aloof as an acrobat. But it was coming apart. Now Rose was laughing, setting Charlie off again. For a few last seconds, Harry brought it all together once more, held them all in place. He kept staring up at Rose, biting his lip, grinning—and concentrating hard.

15

OVERDUE

Saturday morning, seven thirty, Mom and I arrived at the library. It was the basement of the village hall, all acoustic tile, wood paneling, and worn-down teal carpet, made more inviting by a few mismatched lamps and the comfy leather chairs in the atrium. The sour stink of the vinegar Mrs. Janssen, the fastidious, bookishly glamorous head librarian, used to clean the coffee urn hung in the air. As it faded the smell of the books rose, dry and earthy. I was twelve, almost thirteen, and they smelled to me like fall leaves, like jumping into a big pile of them and coming up giggling and spluttering leaves. Mom and I stood in the half-dark, letting the library wake up with us, before we flipped on the lights, got the copy machine and the free coffee going. To one side of the circulation desk stood my task: eight or nine carts of returns, often more, waiting to be reshelved.

031.02 *Trivia*

They were a chaos of call numbers, as varied and random as the tastes and obsessions of the patrons of a little Wisconsin public library could be. Mrs. Janssen, who came in at eight with a swooping of her long dark hair and silk paisley scarf, didn't tolerate sloppiness in her stacks. But to keep numbers like 914.56SL1968 and 914.565S1968 in order you had to squint hard. I stood over the first cart, head swimming. I was too young to be on the payroll; Mrs. Janssen paid me my thirty-five bucks a week out of petty cash. Mom had gotten me the job. Her title was "assistant librarian," meaning she had no degree, and I was assistant to the assistant, meaning Mrs. Janssen was doing us a favor.

Mom looked up from her morning's work jacketing the new arrivals and saw me blinking like a mole. She came over—"Here, look, group them together"—and shuffled the books around on the cart. "The fat ones first." I pushed a couple of thick car repair manuals together. She tousled my hair; I shied away. "Come on, you great lump," she said. "No sense moping about."

I'd start in trivia, a couple of shelves of hefty paperbacks that went in and out of the library quickly: *The World Almanac*, *Ripley's Believe It or Not!*, *Guinness Book of World Records*, *The Book of Lists*, *The New Book of Lists*, *Best Book of Lists Ever!* They were a pain in the butt, always spilling over and flopping off the shelf. When I picked them up, they'd fall open, their spines too weak, their insides too sprawling to keep them closed. Sitting on my rolling footstool, I couldn't help a quick look—World's Fattest Twins: the McGuire brothers, North Carolina, 1,300 pounds combined. On his famous flight Charles Lindbergh took with him four sandwiches. The common housefly always hums in the key of F . . . I kept glancing up nervously, in case Mrs. Janssen caught me loafing. I didn't mean to. It was like those books, so stuffed with facts and curiosities, kept squirming off the shelf by themselves.

At eight thirty, the library opened, and if there weren't a few patrons already waiting in their cars, they started arriving soon after: the retirees who'd been up since five, coming in to sit in the atrium in the sunlight and read the *Trib* or the local *Shopper-Advertiser*; the harried mothers hustling through to check out videos for their kids before soccer practice; the pulp novel junkies darting in to ravage the shelves of Mysteries New. You could hardly keep people away. All of the books, books-on-tape, VHS tapes, dusty old LPs, maps, atlases, boxes of slides and microfilms and microfiches . . . The library was straining at its stacks. It and the village hall had been shoehorned into the old firehouse in the mid-1920s, the last years of a national spree of public library building floated on ideals of Classical learning and Andrew Carnegie's money, back when people called librarians things like "apostles of culture."

My mother could hardly stay away either. Halfway through the summer after she got sick, in the wake of the chemo and radiation, when we were all just hoping for a few more good months, she actually went back to work. She spent a few afternoons shuffling around returns and straightening the magazines and newspapers. She was hardly strong or coherent enough to leave the house, but she wanted badly to be back at the library. The call came after only an hour or two, her voice weak at the end of the line: "Bring me home."

358.4 *Air Warfare*

From the end of General Nonfiction aisle two, I listened to Mrs. Janssen making her calls, informing a patron that *Bridges of Madison County, I is for Innocent, Popular Mechanics Complete Band Saw Fundamentals,* and *The Bodyguard* were now overdue, and the fine was twenty-five cents a day, seventy-five cents for the video. (The other librarians, Mom especially, were always fudging the overdues, waiving fines or discounting them.) I listened to the burbling of the coffee urn, the old men rustling newspapers or snoring in the atrium, the clacking of the bulky blue-gray IBM Selectric Mom used to type out catalog cards. I raised and lowered my weight, squeaking the pistoned wheels of my stool. Two books were in my lap: *Aces over Malta* and *SR-71 Blackbird: Revealed!* I was pretending to check whether their title cards were slipped into the pouches glued to their back covers, stalling until I heard Mrs. Janssen go into the kitchen for her morning cup of chamomile tea.

I'd already been through my dinosaur phase (560 Paleontology) and my spaceship phase (387.8 Space Transportation), months-long imaginative pitches into the distant past, distant space, and obsessive detail. Still, these were, relatively speaking, passing fancies. After Trivia and the tall, easy-to-sort Time-Life serials (The Emergence of Man, The Old West, True Crime: Crimes of Passion), I'd roll a cart to the end of aisle two and the clutter of diagram-stuffed books I found there. I'd slip one or two off the shelf, make it look like they were returns . . . B-52 Flying Fortress, max payload 70,000 pounds, max range 8,000 miles; Hawker Siddeley Harrier V/STOL assault striker, capable of short/vertical takeoff, in service USMC, Indian Navy . . . But, more than any other plane, I loved—*Spitfires.* Their cunning, low-slung airframe and elliptical wings, all kitted out in desert or naval or fighter-bomber configurations, their mythic role in the Battle of Britain, dogfights over Dieppe and Malta, bloody carnage over the Mediterranean, Spitfires threading between German convoys, their 20 mm Hispano machine guns making lace of the Messerschmitts and Junkers, balls of fire blooming like roses—yes! Direct hit! Biggles bags another Jerry, Biggles, greatest ace of them all, scourge of the—

"William, how are you coming on these?"

I snapped the book closed and pretended to be shelving it—383 Postal Communication.

"How's your system working?" Mom said, inspecting my cart, which held returns for every section but the one I was actually in.

"I'll get it done," I said grimly, with a face like I was staring down the entire Luftwaffe.

"You need to get a move on. Can't just moon around all day."

She looked down at the other book in my lap. She'd seen the multicolored drawings of fighter jets I spent hours on at the kitchen table, labeling everything with made-up specifications, wearing out whole boxes of pencils. And she knew how I could lose myself in Dad's photography books and cookbooks and even the JCPenney catalog, anything appropriately dense with lists and tables and instructions.

"Well," she said, "keep at it." She opened her eyes wide and gave me a backward tilt of her head, back toward Mrs. Janssen, who'd just come out of the kitchen. "Can't expect to get them all done every week," she all but whispered, "but keep at it."

Teen

In seventh grade, I threw myself into Book It!—literacy promotion brought to you by Pizza Hut and your participating teacher. You bought books at the monthly school book fair, read them, wrote a brief report, and in return received Pizza Hut coupons. Encyclopedia Brown or the Hardy Boys went down easy, and helped you rack up the Personal Pan Pizzas, but Dad wasn't going to shell out for more than a couple of paperbacks a month. My appetite was larger than that.

The library's Teen section was not what you'd call up-to-date. Most of the titles had been acquired in the late fifties, when the Hardy Boys still wore sensible sweaters and did a lot of flashlight-related investigating. There was an entire shelf of The Adventures of Tom Swift, an even more antique series about a boy inventor, and fifteen or so volumes of The Dragonriders of Pern, with its quasi-mythic stories of lonely heroines with weirdly punctuated names, all of them trembling on the brink of self-discovery. Nancy Drew, Sweet Valley High, the Boxcar Children—it didn't matter whether it was targeted to younger kids or preppies or girls or whoever, it all added up to more trips to the Pizza Hut two towns over. Still, I was inefficient. After racing through to the last page and the last sugary hit of formula, I started wolfing down the same book again, just to be back at the bottom of the ocean with Tom Swift and His Electronic Hydrolung or to soar again, dragon-borne, with F'nor and T'ron.

"Don't get greedy now," Mom said when I brought a small tower of books up to the circulation desk at the end of one Saturday. If I finished shelving all the carts, she'd cut me loose to "tidy" Teen until the library closed. By now I had my own library card. She'd typed it up for me herself, and I kept it in a protective plastic sleeve, tucked away in my Velcro wallet. There was a limit of ten books per patron, but I'd gotten carried away. I started agonizing over which to put back.

"Oh, go on then," Mom said, slipping the first title card into the punch machine—*chunk*—and inking on the due date.

"Mom, it's more than ten."

"Don't worry about that. That's for the videos. That's just so people don't take out every video in the place."

But when she'd gone over ten, I saw, she checked the rest out on her own card.

020 *Library Sciences*

The clunking of books sliding into the book drop, the chatter across the circulation desk or at the urn of free coffee, the clacking of typewriters, the footsteps of the village hall clerks overhead, the low, hoovering sound of the copy machine, which, being five cents cheaper than the one at the gas station, had its own thriving community. The voices of our regulars: Craig, the young, floppy-haired architect, whom all the librarians gossiped about whenever he came in. Sam Franklin, the harmless old guy who made a joke of always asking for *Sex*—Madonna's book (Mrs. Janssen thought it unsuitable for the collection). The heavy novel readers who rambled through plot synopses by way of recommendations. The friends Mom made among the gardeners in the village, the *Masterpiece Theatre* fans, the patrons who came in just to chat with her and sometimes left without checking out a thing . . . Most days, all that actually kept quiet in the library was the chunky, green-screened Tandy PC that sat dustily in the corner of Reference. *For patron use*, a little handwritten sign taped to it read. The patrons passed by the computer all the time, on their way to the encyclopedias. We had five different sets, each bound in leatherette with titles stamped in gilt letters.

As Mom grew comfortable handling the circulation desk, Mrs. Janssen started working half days on Saturdays and on occasion took the day off—leaving me free to indulge my contraband reading. Sometimes Mom would catch me and tell me to get back to work with a soft clucking of her tongue. There was never any real hurry. In Fontana, people hung around the gas station or the bait store or the SuperSaver gossiping or just shooting the bull—but you couldn't stay all day without buying something. The library was the only place where you could really linger, thumbing a few magazines or poking around in the stacks before you wandered back up to Circulation to continue the conversation.

Still, we sometimes got a little midday rush.

"William"—Mom appeared at the end of an aisle, framed by the light slicing through the atrium windows—"leave those for a moment and come help up here."

I sat frozen to my rolling stool. "But I don't . . ."

"Oh, come on, it's easy. Easy peasy."

She showed me how to file the title cards for the books she was checking out. I felt ungainly and exposed up there where the grown-ups talked so casually with one another. I'd stand next to Mom, slotting the cards into order, concentrating hard, but also listening to her chatting with the patrons. Librarians are supposed to always be shushing people. Mom, thanks to her accent, tended to launch conversations.

"Oh, wow, where you from, hon?"

"We're from Southampton"—she'd nod toward me; I'd look down at my feet—"where the *Titanic* sailed from. Isn't that right, William?"

". . . Spitfires . . ."

"Huh?" the patron said.

"They built . . . Spitfires there too."

"Okay, sure. Right, those planes."

"Oh, yes," Mom said, "he could tell you all about it."

"They built the first production models at the Supermarine factory, at Woolston. The K9787, with the Merlin engine. Then they opened a big factory at Castle Bromwich. But they kept making Spitfires in Southampton, mostly the Mark IA, with the Merlin III engines and the de Havilland three-blade, two-speed propellers . . ."

The patron stood there, nodding and smiling stiffly while the detail piled up.

Discards

Every three months, Mrs. Janssen made a list of books for me to pull from the shelves. I'd box them up, move the boxes to the back hallway, then haul them up to the garage of the village hall, which we called "remote storage." Most of these were outdated reference or titles that hadn't been checked out in decades or were simply falling apart. But none of us liked to see them disappear upstairs, where they sat behind a couple of broken-down lawn mowers and some rusty file cabinets. We liked to pretend they stayed there indefinitely. After a few months the discards disappeared, carted off to the dump.

When the men came to remove my mother's body and then the reclining bed, it left a blank in her room, an absence framed by the dust balls and snarls of hair that had gathered over her decline. The discards I pulled left gaps, notches in the permanent dust that, even when the shelves had been cleared, cleaned, and refilled, still wouldn't disappear.

799.1 *Fishing*

Our patrons' tastes did not run to the literary. We're talking here about a small library in a small, midwestern town where people like 799.2 Hunting, 796.94 Snowmobiling, and sitting around in ice-fishing cabins all day waiting on fish (see 362.2 Insanity). By eighth grade, I'd spent enough time reshelving in Outdoor Sports to make me a vicarious enthusiast on all these subjects. I was working the circulation desk on a regular basis now, sometimes helping to check out books.

"How the crappie feeding?" I mumbled to the guy who took out the guides to local fishing holes and back issues of *Outdoor Wisconsin*. Huh? he said. I repeated myself, adding, "There's a good spot over by Black Point."

"Yeah? What you been catching over there?"

"A few perch, couple good walleye. Real nice smallmouth. Good fighter."

For upwards of three or four minutes, we traded stories. Mine were invented off the pages of those same guidebooks, with some secondhand expertise from Time-Life how-to serials mixed in. His were real, probably. As I went on about spinning reels, muskie baits, and jigging for crappies, Mom sat typing up new catalog cards, listening, smiling to herself, the keys chattering under her fingers.

Romance/Fantasy

It was worse than Trivia. Next to the newspapers hung on their wooden poles stood a wall of thumb-worn paperbacks. With their slick covers and gaudy embossed titles, they were always slipping around and falling off the shelf, and the coarse, pulpy stock they were printed on smelled worse to me than cleaning vinegar. Still, I couldn't help staring at the cover illustrations: barbarians poised on rocky outcroppings, swords aloft to the heavens, where two suns blazed maliciously. Innocent maidens in ragged, revealing clothes being encircled by pythons or menaced by robots. And, farther down the shelf: women in low-cut ball gowns and pearls the size of golf balls, men with unbuttoned shirts and virtuosic hair, their eyes intent yet strangely distant, as if they were gazing not at one another but at the reader.

"Don't worry too much over those," Mom said, catching me lingering over a particularly suggestive cover, a woman in a lacy bodice, kneeling on a four-poster bed and reaching out imploringly to a man in a business suit. It was summer, and girls from my school had been coming into the library. Hiding in the stacks, I caught glimpses through the shelves—a suntanned arm, a book-sized slice of thigh—while I played at doing my job, shuttling back and forth on my stool to get a better look. They'd check out *Adventures in Babysitting*, R. L. Stine, *Flowers in the Attic*, back issues of *Seventeen*. I could picture them lying on towels at the beach or the country club pool, books or magazines tented over suntan-oil-glistening bellies. They even smelled of the sun, those girls, sun and bubblegum-sweet perfume and all the bright world outside that I had previously been content to ignore.

"Well, they keep falling out," I said. "Nothing's in order."

I was supposed to keep the paperbacks alphabetical, more or less.

"You think anyone's paying that much attention?" Mom said. "Streuth, we should stock them by the pound."

People took these paperbacks out by the boxful, and new ones, donations, were always coming back in the same boxes or crammed into SuperSaver grocery sacks.

"Anyway"—Mom took the book from my hand and shelved it alongside a copy of *Thongor at the End of Time*—"don't spend all day over here. Loads to do."

Children

She wore a purple ball gown she'd found at the church sale, comically stuffed with pillows, with a gray, old lady's wig—a fairy godmother/Good Witch of the West/pantomime dame costume, depending on the story: *Cinderella, The Wizard of Oz, Puss in Boots, Jack and the Beanstalk* . . . The tots sat Indian-style on the teal carpet, staring wide-eyed while Mom hammed it up, doing characters, delivering the dialogue in a posh accent—"Oh, I *say*, hasn't this beanstalk grown tall?"

Children's I usually left till last. It was a playpen—battered toy cars and Lincoln Logs and a dog on wheels strewn across the carpet. The books themselves were dinged and torn and juice-stained and teeth-marked and generally loved to the last threads of their bindings. Reshelving was just trying to rein in the chaos, though sometimes I found myself on my hands and knees, zooming the cars around or taking the dog on wheels for a wobbly walk. And when I heard Mom doing story hour—"Fe, fi, fo, fum, I smell the blood of an Englishman!"—I heard her reading Paddington Bear or Narnia to Rory and me. She wasn't paid for story hour. She often went in and did it on her days off. The library was her refuge. It never changed. Always the smell of slightly toasted dust, the dark wood paneling, the worn-out carpet, the sedate voices and deliberate movements of the other librarians, the heavy footsteps overhead flexing the dropped ceiling, the hum and rattle of the water fountain, all of the hushed conversations, always rising in volume. The books and magazines and videos and patrons and children and friends came in and went out, but the library, it seemed, would never change.

Fiction/Literature

I have before me her old school reports. In grammar school she came first in English term after term—her successes ended there. "Her arithmetic is despicable" was the judgment of her headmaster. In her other classes, she was "too sociable" and didn't "even seem to *want* to try." She'd dreamed of being a writer one day and, over the years, bored at home while Rory and I were at school, penned a few sentimental, sweetly sad poems that were as complete and tidy as a winning composition paper. I don't think she had the temperament for anything more rigorous. She was not a shy, reclusive person lost in her own head. She was, as the headmaster put it, "more interested in other people than in her studies."

A family friend remembers Ursula Hegi and Annie Proulx as among Mom's favorites, the authors she always recommended to patrons and friends. I'm not so sure; those wintry voices seem unlike her. In her bedroom she kept a shelf of gardening books, James Herriot's *All Creatures Great and Small* novels, and a few of Wilbur Smith's outlandish South African romances. Diamond barons, high intrigue, treacherous safaris—I found my way into Smith as well. It was like following Tom Swift off on yet another adventure, racing off across the savannah toward the final page.

Reshelving in Fiction went quickly. It was strictly alphabetical and so unmired in the swamp of Dewey Decimal call numbers. Michael Crichton, P. D. James, and Terry McMillan bulked large and glossy alongside the books marked Fiction/Literature with their ugly, pea green covers or black and white photos of old men with frazzled, homeless-guy beards. In a few months I'd be fourteen and in high school. With a dutiful, cod-liver-oil sense of virtue, I started to peer into those yellowed, broken-spined books. On my bedside table, they usually sat underneath whatever *Dragonriders* novel was still enthralling me. James Fenimore Cooper's *Red Rover*, Melville's *The Confidence-Man*, Hardy's *Far from the Madding Crowd*—I read the ones with impressive-sounding titles or that came with a dark red ribbon attached to the spine, a kind of regal bookmark. It took weeks, sometimes months to finish them, not a good strategy for Personal Pan Pizzas. But especially over winter, when there wasn't much to do but homework, no other obligations, no distractions, they made the nights stretch out, they made thoughts unfurl, out from the small pool of light cast by my bedside lamp, into the night and out over the prairie, pushing forward like that slender red ribbon, slowly finding its way across the flat white landscape.

Mom's favorite job at the library was entering the new arrivals into the system, dressing them in their polyurethane dust jackets, giving them their catalog cards and call numbers. She did this with great care, fussing the jackets till they fit just right, the same way she fussed over Rory and me before sending us off to school. Maybe I find it hard to remember exactly what she read herself because I've come to think of her as looking after *all* books.

004 *Data Processing/Computer Science*

The barcode scanner, truth told, made life at the circulation desk a lot easier. One brief beep, and the work of punching, stamping, and filing cards was done. The cardpunch machine remained on the desk, for older books that hadn't yet been bar-coded, but we used it less and less. Still, it was hard to resist—

sometimes I slipped a blank card into the machine, just to hear that low, definitive *chunk*.

When the old green-screened Tandy finally went the way of "remote storage," it was replaced by a new PC with a bank of four CD-ROM drives. The card catalog, with its narrow, handsome, unwieldy drawers became obsolete almost overnight. (People kept using it anyway, unaccustomed as they were to the mute, cryptic blinking of an MS-DOS cursor.) The WisCat CD-ROMs held the entire catalog not only for the village library but for every library in the state, a fact that, at the time, seemed almost mystical to me.

"Oh, I can't be bothered with that thing," Mom would say, giving up in frustration whenever she made a halfhearted attempt at doing a search on the new computer. I got a new role at the library, research assistant, helping patrons with more obscure interests locate titles from other libraries. But, really, all the time I spent on that computer went toward locating books *I* wanted. The searching became an end in itself—searching and searching and never settling on anything, thoughts flitting back and forth like minnows, moving on to more lists, more holdings, more titles.

The new computer had an internal modem. Since the main library phone had to be unplugged to use it, I almost never had the chance to connect it, and, besides, it was too slow to load anything. But sometimes, as Mom and I were finishing up for the day, I'd plug it in anyway and listen to the hundreds of thousands of bits of information gurgling down the line, and then that distinctive digital hiss, like a snake about to strike.

A few weeks after she tried going back to work, Mom started getting so exhausted she could hardly do more than sit up in bed. Dad drove her down to the library, and she brought back a grocery sack of books: Sue Grafton mysteries, sci-fi, Harlequin romances. It seemed she'd just chosen at random. A pile of pillows behind her to keep her upright, she'd page through them, following the line with her finger, mouthing the words to herself. If she lost her place or caught herself reading the same paragraph again and again, she'd put down the book and with a look of exasperation murmur, "Silly me, silly me." There were other slips. She'd call for Rory or me, but when she tried to tell us what she wanted, her words got muddled. "The tup," she'd say when the tea was too hot, "the tup." Or when she had to use the bathroom: "I need to make some trouble." More and more we had to help her to the toilet. "William doesn't like it when I make trouble," she'd say. "He gets all cloudy. When I make trouble, he gets all cloudy." Sometimes we couldn't help but laugh at the things she said. She didn't seem to mind; she laughed right along with us. Then a puzzled expression came across her face, and she'd mutter crossly, "Never mind, never mind. Silly me."

It became difficult for her to hold a thought for more than a minute or two. She got distracted, forgot things, jumped from one subject to another when you tried to talk to her. Finally, in her morphine haze, all her words abandoned her. We could see her making shapes with her lips. No sounds came. Her eyes flicked back and forth, as if she were reading, but she was only searching, searching for the thing she was trying to say.

Overdues

I stopped working at the library when I was fifteen. I could get more hours bagging groceries at the SuperSaver, and, besides, all my friends worked there. But I still went into the library now and then to help haul the discards upstairs and to poach a few choice titles for myself. And I kept checking out books and magazines and videos, wearing out three library cards, in their little plastic sleeves, along the way.

After Mom died, I had some overdues. I didn't return them for months. (They never charged me for overdues.) One afternoon, I slid them into the book drop, waited for the familiar *clunk*, and then drove away before anyone saw me. I couldn't go in. I didn't want to see Mrs. Janssen or any of the other librarians. I didn't want to talk to the woman they'd hired to replace my mom.

Local Authors

There was a small shelf of them, half a shelf really. Just a few pamphlets on local history, an outdoors guide, and a couple of copies of *Black Point*, a romantic time-travel yarn set on the lake that had some regional success. Otherwise, books (and writers, it seemed) came from somewhere else: New York, London, Boston, Oxford. They were too elegant, too sophisticated, even the pulp paperbacks, to come from my village.

After reading in Madison on my first book tour, I stopped in Fontana to see the library. In the middle of a recession, when libraries all over the country were closing, having their budgets slashed, or being turned into glorified computer labs, I was expecting the worst.

Stepping inside, for the first time in twelve years, I hardly recognized the place. The carpet was new, and the copy machine, and even the circulation desk itself, now a big, shining swoop of lacquered maple with brass trim. Somehow, God knows, the village had found the money to expand the place. There was a big section for Employment—a job board, pamphlets. Where the magazine racks and newspaper poles had been, there were new comfy chairs and ottomans. The stacks had been completely rearranged. They were more open and inviting now. It was no longer possible to remain hidden down at the ends of aisles, but you wanted to linger over the titles, pull down one or two, find one of those deep leather chairs.

I introduced myself to the librarian on duty. I told her I used to work here, with my mom.

"Oh, Nancy Boast?"

She must have picked up a trace of my accent. It's so faint I rarely hear it myself.

"You knew her?"

"Honey, everyone knew your mom."

I asked after Mrs. Janssen and the two other full-time librarians Mom had worked with. They'd all retired. I told the librarian on duty that I'd written a book, my first. She seemed interested and promised to order it.

I wandered through the stacks, listening. The *chunk* of due date cards going into the punch machine was long gone, along with the burbling coffee urn and the soft thump of an encyclopedia being set down on the reference table. Even the precise beep of a scanner reading a barcode was missing, a passing vestige of a time when people still needed computers to beep and whir and clack to understand that they were working. All of the business at the circulation desk now transpired in sleek digital silence. It was unsettling, the quiet.

Then an elderly couple came in. And a mother and her little girl. A guy who needed to use the copier. Overhead, the heavy footsteps of the village clerks made the acoustic tile flex and tremble. The elderly couple went up to the desk to ask the librarian a question—or were they just saying hello? In the slow rhythm of village life, it was hard to distinguish the two.

I passed through the double doors back into the sharp winter air. She was still there—in the chat over the circulation desk that only starts in whispers, the grocery lists left in the middle of novels as bookmarks, the wide eyes of children at story time, the smell of dust and paper and morning light. She's there when the book falls open, almost by itself, and I can't help myself—without pausing to think about what I could be doing next, I start to read.

16

EMPTY THREATS

In little more than a week my father lost the two most important women in his life.

I knew Granny Boast only as a spindly old woman with thick National Health glasses and a right knee perpetually wrapped in an ACE bandage. Her bungalow on Laverstock Road—the narrow dark halls, her thimble collection arrayed on the mantel, the electric heater burning dust—glows brighter in memory than the woman herself. Like Nanny's house in Southampton, Granny Boast's bungalow was a family museum, crammed with photos of Granddad Boast, Uncle John, Aunty Sarah, Dad, Mom, Rory and me, our cousins and second cousins.

Whenever we visited, I came to learn, Dad called ahead and had his mother take down all the pictures of my half brothers. Even as teenagers, Rory and I got into everything. We explored every inch of that bungalow—and never noticed the empty spaces on the walls, the scattered patches of wallpaper unfaded by sun.

But what strikes me now, apart from the savage meticulousness of my father's secrecy, is that Granny Boast kept those photos of Arthur and Harry hanging, long after all hope of seeing them again had passed, restoring them to their rightful places in the family every time Dad had her take them down. It broke Granny Boast's heart, Aunty Sarah tells me, that she never saw her first two grandsons grow up.

Two funerals over the Christmas holidays. In England, Aunty Sarah buried Granny Boast. Then, a week later in America, Dad, Rory, Nanny, Aunty Janet, and I buried my mom. In any other circumstances, Dad never would've missed his mother's funeral. It speaks well of him, I like to think, that he stayed by my mom's side.

He lost the two most important women in his life . . . What I didn't know was that he'd already lost another. Who would he have called the love of his life—Sara, the older, bohemian woman he met when he was practically a boy? Or my mother, the chatty girl from payroll, with whom he decided to try it all over again ten years later? There's no way to know, yet I can't help thinking that first love was the greater love, the one that burned more fiercely, that left the deeper mark—that did the most damage.

AFTER MOM'S FUNERAL, Nanny and Aunty Janet stayed a few days past Christmas, then flew back to England. Suddenly, Rory, Dad, and I were very polite around each other, very considerate. We cooked meals together. We sat up watching *Fawlty Towers* and *Blackadder*, doing our best to laugh at all the gaffes and humiliations suffered by the characters. In the morning Rory and I helped each other make our beds. We went downstairs, put the coffee on, took a cup in to Dad, helped him make his bed. If

Mom was up there looking down on us, she might think we still looked like a family. We did our best to play one. It lasted right up till the Friday after the New Year, when Rory came home at four in the morning smelling of beer and cigarettes, and Dad, who'd waited up, got so furious he broke down in tears.

I hesitated to go back to college. Even keeping house, not such a simple business to begin with, was going to be hard with Rory at Big Foot and Dad working as devoutly as ever. The medical bills were streaming in. If I stayed, I could work, bring in a little extra cash, and act as a buffer between Rory and Dad. I believed I understood them both—why Rory wanted to get out of that house so badly, why Dad worried so desperately about him. If there was one thing I felt I'd learned in the first quarter of my liberal arts education, it was how to see both sides.

For the coming quarter, I was enrolled in another array of woefully unmarketable courses. I'd made the Jazz Ensemble and was also playing in Wind Ensemble, Jazz Combo, Afro-Cuban Conjunto, and a newly formed funk band, Sexual Chocolate. But most of all, it was the girls I wanted to get back to—girls who wanted to talk, late into the night, about Sylvia Plath, Egon Schiele, and Shipping News (the book and the band). "The nerd girls, Mom," I'd heard another freshman, even more bookish than me, say on the hall phone, "they *like* me."

I couldn't make a decision, so again I let Dad make it for me. On a certain level, I understood that he was living through me. Behind his rowdy tales of Bishop Wordsworth's, I heard the regret: What little schooling he'd had was only enough to prepare him for the factory line. He'd discovered too late that he was a brooder and a problem-solver, not the natural athlete and leader of men his father had been. Still, I can't shake the guilt. Three times I've been presented with a choice: my family or my education.

No, let's not dress it up: my family or myself. And every time I chose myself.

IT WAS a wet winter. On the phone, Dad fretted over slick, oily roads, black ice, hydroplaning, out-of-control snowplows. The roads were deadly at night, he claimed, and he forbade Rory going out, even when his friends were all at the movies or hanging out at Haney's, where they went to smoke Camels and Luckies and drink shitty diner coffee. In Dad's haunted imagination, every turn was a spinout, every stop sign a slide into cross-traffic. He and Rory spent too many long, dark winter nights penned up together. He tried to get Rory interested in cooking, taught him how to make coq au vin and chicken tandoori, how to make the best of a tough cut of beef, how to fry an omelet the way the French do, runny and oozing off the plate. But Rory was too quick a study and got bored easily. Dad tried to get him into jazz; all Rory wanted to hear was hip-hop, which Dad hated. "It isn't music, guy," he complained to me on the phone. "It's just shouting." Rory stayed up in his room playing Nintendo, beating the same games again and again, only coming down for dinner and going right back up when the dishes were done. It must have been torture for my brother being cooped up in that house. The smell of morphine, a sickly sweet smell like vanilla, had seeped into the walls.

Once the weather broke, Dad could do nothing to keep Rory at home. He started going out with his friends five, six nights a week. At first he was good about calling to check in, to say he'd be home an hour or two later than promised. Then his progress report—*sleeps in class, doesn't pay attention, quality of work very poor*—arrived from Big Foot, and Dad tightened the screws. Curfew was ten thirty on a school night, no exceptions.

Dad blamed Rory's buddies for distracting him from schoolwork. But Rory had fought hard to win his new friends and wouldn't abandon them. He started lying about where he was going, who he was with, how late he'd be out.

Dad threatened him with a month's grounding, no TV, no car privileges. He talked about packing Rory off to military academy. They were frustrated, toothless threats. A week's grounding never lasted longer than a day or two, and after a while, Rory started ignoring Dad's edicts altogether. He could get anything out of Dad: clothes, a new pair of Doc Martens, passes to the local ski hill, money for Phish concerts at Alpine Valley or weekends spent roaming the Chicago suburbs. When Dad refused the cash, Rory helped himself, skimming quarters out of the box of change in the wardrobe, slipping a buck or a fiver from the crumpled bills Dad left on his dresser. Rory was sly about it; Dad could never prove him guilty, or didn't want to. Sometimes I think he left those ones and fives on the dresser just so Rory would take them.

By the end of spring, they'd hit a dead end. The handful of times I came home from school, they were hardly speaking. They only saw each other at the dinner table, Dad already on his fifth or sixth whisky, Rory rushing to finish his meal so he could go out. When the truancy notices started coming in place of the progress reports, that's when Dad lost it. "You've blown it! Your one shot at school, and you've blown it!" He'd go on, telling Rory he didn't contribute to the household, didn't have a job, didn't help out. We weren't so well off he could just keep sponging his whole life. The way things were going Rory would have the cops to deal with soon enough, not just his father. Then Dad would sniff the air, as if only now catching a whiff of tobacco on Rory's clothes. Mom had died of cancer, and now he'd started *smoking*.

To meet my brother, you might never have known what he'd lived through that past year. He had an openness, a vulnerability, that made it hard to get really upset with him. Though he almost never did homework and ditched half his classes, his teachers liked him and tried pushing him to do better. That summer Rory ran Mom's Chevy Lumina off the road, skidding across two lawns and crashing into a Cadillac parked in a driveway. The retired couple who lived in the house, a big house across from hole two, must have seen that he was high out of his mind, and decided, by whatever miracle, they didn't want him to get into any trouble. They didn't call the cops and told Dad that Rory had swerved to avoid a chipmunk. Somehow, impossibly, the only damage to the Lumina was a tiny ding in the front bumper you had to catch in a rare light to even make out.

Rory never had a steady girlfriend, but I wasn't surprised when, later, packing up the house in Fontana, I found an empty box of condoms in his dresser. One weekend, he drove down by himself to visit me at college. We got drunk with my buddies at the Jazz House. After he left, all I heard from my friends—the nerd girls, no less—was how handsome Rory was, how cool, how confident. That year he took Ann Palmer, the prettiest girl in his senior class, to prom. (I'd refused to go to my prom; I didn't participate in American class rituals and popularity contests.)

He graduated, barely. There'd been talk of summer school and not letting him walk with his class, but at the last minute his photography teacher, who thought he had a good eye, changed his grade from a C– to a C+. After graduation he caddied at Grand Geneva and helped with the art classes for kids his friend Tyler's mom taught. I lived with buddies in Madison for the summer, drank beer, played drums. When I went down to Fontana, Rory was almost never home. His friends were all partying hard before they went off to college. Now and then, Rory talked about going to a community college in Madison or Milwaukee. He wasn't in any rush to be back in a classroom. I would've tried to give him a pep talk or two, but I only ever saw him on his way out the door.

WHEN THE DORMS closed for winter break, I looked for a way to stay on campus but couldn't get a room. With no great excitement, I went back to Wisconsin for the month-long break. Just after I arrived, there was a heavy snowfall. The temperature plummeted, the snow crusting over with ice. Through our frost-starred windows, the December light bled weak and diffuse. The house was dark, silent. Late one Friday, Rory came home from partying—four thirty in the morning. He was supposed to have been grounded. I heard him at the back door, softly clapping his Doc Martens together to knock off the snow. He crept up the stairs in his socks. I lay there, waiting for it. He reached those last two steps, hesitated, went on. *Creak, creak.* Downstairs, Dad stirred in his room and let out a single, short grunt.

At dinner the next evening—beef casserole, mash, and swede—Rory spread the food around his plate but hardly ate. Neither he nor Dad looked up from their meals. Finally, Rory put down his fork, wiped his mouth, and said, "Tyler's picking me up at nine." Now they met eyes. Something passed between them, I'd been away too long to know exactly what. Dad got up from the table, went to the stove, served himself more casserole, tore a hunk off the French loaf laid out in its crumbs on the cutting board.

"There's clothes in the dryer that need folding."

"I'll get to them tomorrow," Rory said.

"No need." Dad started on his second helping standing at the counter, his back half-turned on us. "No, never mind. I'm doing the ironing tomorrow. I'll do the folding as well. Do you want a crease in your jeans?"

"I never like them like that," Rory said.

"I've got some work shirts that need doing," I put in.

"There's ice at the bottom of the drive," Dad went on. "I'll get up early and chip it up. What do you want for breakfast?"

"Nothing," Rory said, "I'll make it myself."

"Just leave the dishes, then. I'll do them after working all day."

"Dad, quit it."

"If you're here for dinner tomorrow, we're having steaks."

"I don't know what I'm doing yet."

"I'm supposed to go up to Madison tomorrow night," I said, uselessly. "I need one of the cars." They didn't even seem to hear me.

"Do what you like." Dad turned on the tap to rinse the dishes, then just stood there letting the water run. "You always do."

"I don't know what I'm doing tomorrow," Rory said again. "Cut it out, okay?"

"Just do what you like."

Rory shook his head and smiled a thin, livid smile. "Dad, you're being stupid." *Stupid.* It was a kid word, but a hard, barbed thing for a son to say to his father. Dad clattered a dish into the drying rack.

"Scrape your plate in the bin if you're not going to eat. I don't know why I waste my time," he muttered. Then he played, and at the same time withdrew, the card he must have been saving since the night before. "If your mother could see you, she'd—" He took up a Brillo Pad and started furiously scrubbing the casserole dish.

"Bullshit," Rory said under his breath. "That's just total, fucking—" He stopped himself, too. Maybe they would've gone on; it would've flared into a shouting match. But they didn't want to fight in front of me. I was no longer inside their close—stiflingly close—circle. Dad put his head down, clenched his jaw, and started noisily fishing for knives and forks in the dishwater. Rory got up from the table and tipped his half-eaten meal into the garbage.

It was just after seven. Rory went up to his room. Dad left the dishes and went to his. I was still sitting at the kitchen table trying to think of something to say, staring at my dim reflection in the scratched, cloudy Formica.

I went upstairs. Rory stood before his closet, trying on different shirts and inspecting himself in the mirror. He had his Zippo in his pocket and kept flicking its top up and down, the chime of it ringing out every few moments. I leaned in the doorway, trying to look cool, collected, trying to sound reasonable.

"He only wants what's best for you."

"Then why's he on my fucking case all the time?"

I told Rory that Dad was hurting, too. We all had to pull together, help each other through. Grief and loss seemed like something we had to get through alone, I said, but really we all shared it. Getting angry was okay. We had to let it all out somehow. "You and Dad are on the same team," I said. "That's what you have to remember." It was another of my lectures. The difference was Rory wasn't listening anymore.

"Okay," he said, stomping his Docs on. "Sounds good. Sounds fantastic." He buttoned up his Ralph Lauren shirt and carefully smoothed out the collar.

That weekend, I called my friends in Madison and canceled. I somehow knew not to leave. I sat up late listening to Neil Young and Jimmy Smith on headphones, finished *Huck Finn* for the fourth time, practiced my bongo technique. I loved Rory, and I thought he was choosing badly, fucking up wherever he could. I saw Dad's desperate attempts to reform him and knew there was nothing he could do to make Rory change. But Rory couldn't stay at home forever. Sooner or later, he'd have to go out on his own, and then he'd start to learn the virtues of responsibility. Things would right themselves, I told myself. After a day or two the strangling urgency of that night slid away into routine. For lack of anything better to do, I started reading ahead for my winter classes.

The next week Rory and I only crossed paths as I went to work at the SuperSaver and he went off for another night of partying. We traded off the keys to the second family car, a '94 Dodge Spirit bought to replace the Lumina. It was the wine red color of an old lady's lipstick with a gray interior worn to fuzz. The hood was pocked with hail marks, and on the inside corner of the windshield Dad had put a sticker (which Rory had all but picked away) of a cartoon frog pursing its lips and saying, "Kiss me, I don't smoke!" We'd bought the Dodge the year before at a used lot in Elkhorn. Rory had tried to talk Dad into a Mazda with a spoiler and sunroof; I'd argued for the Dodge: lower miles, easier to service, cheaper parts. Joyless common sense won Dad over, as I knew it would.

THAT NIGHT I walked to work. Under the fluorescent lights, I worked aisle eight, the dog food aisle, my uniform covered in the coarse brown dust that always leaked from the forty- and eighty-pound sacks. Christmas music murmured giddily over the PA.

When Rory came in, he was wearing his best pair of Tommy Hilfiger jeans, a crisply pressed rugby shirt, and his Docs buffed to a high shine. That image, when I looked up and saw him, is fixed in memory. His long hair swinging across his angular face, the dark circles under his eyes, his impatient smile when he caught my eye. My brother always walked like he was being *seen*, even there at ten at night, in the dog food aisle. He took the keys to the Dodge from his pocket, jingled them. He always hated showing up to parties in that dinged-up piece of crap. Better to arrive in Tyler's Jeep Grand Cherokee.

"What's up?" I said.

"Nothing."

"Where you going?"

"Shit, nowhere." Habit. He thought I'd inform on him to Dad. And then: "Down to Chicago." He looked me up and down. "You smell like beef jerky."

In the summer, when there was a full crew working the night shift, my job was high times, nonstop fucking around: bowling in the aisles with tubes of Pillsbury biscuits as the pins and frozen turkeys as the balls. Flour fights in the back room. Stocking the shelves wearing Depends adult diapers. But during the winter it was lonely, tedious work, and I could feel like a martyr for punching the clock while Rory went off to party.

"Well, it's called working," I said but shook out my shirt and brushed off my trousers. "Better?"

He grinned. "Yeah, you're cool. Tyler's waiting outside." He tossed me the keys. "We gotta pick up Alex."

"Sure," I said. "Peace."

"Yeah, peace."

I drove the Dodge home, a five-minute drive, if that. I heated up one of the containers of split pea soup Dad had put in the freezer, took a shower, brushed my teeth. In bed I took up the book I'd been laboring over since the beginning of winter break, Jacques Derrida, *Of Grammatology*. I was asleep before I even turned the page.

17

ONE OF THE LADS

At the end of the summer of 2005, I packed a twenty-six-foot U-Haul with everything from the house in Fontana and my books, records, and drum set and drove it down through Indiana and Kentucky, up into craggy, lost West Virginia, and out into the grand, rolling hills of Virginia. I was moving to Charlottesville, to take another shot at grad school at the University of Virginia. The week before I'd had a lot of good-bye drinks, taken a last couple of swings at getting with girls I'd had my eye on, and humped around boxes in the swampy heat, brushing dead cicadas off my stuff and swatting them out of the air. On one of my last nights in Bloomington, Zach and I killed four pitchers of PBR at the Video Saloon, and I woke up at a stoplight at a lonely intersection outside of town with my forehead on the steering wheel.

As I came over the crest of the Blue Ridge Mountains, riding the brakes of the moving truck in the dark and the fog, I felt isolated, exhausted, adrift from whatever I thought my life had been. And I felt elated. Now I could start over. No more bisexual girls, no more making out in bars, no more getting shit-canned for secret fiancés back from India. I could remake myself, start exercising more, dressing better. Hell, I could even start talking with an English accent again and people might believe it. They'd only know as much about my life as I told them. Here in this new place—a new home, however temporary—I was determined not to be seen as damaged goods.

I went on dates. They were polite affairs, dinner or cocktails in yuppie nightspots I felt ridiculous being seen in. On first dates, family always comes up: Where do your folks live? What do they do? Sisters, brothers? I had a studied, almost icy reserve in these conversations and kept up a barrage of counterquestions, so I'd hardly have to say a thing about myself. When I went in for a kiss at the end of the night, my date would back away, smile nervously or assume a blank demeanor as if she were being frisked at the airport, and say, "You seem nice, but . . ."

There was one woman, a graphic designer with some really cool tattoos—our second date ended with a quick, frantic fuck on her bed. Afterward, she started shivering. It was chilly, late October; I pulled the blankets over us. Then I saw she was weeping. "What's wrong?" She told me she was thinking about her ex-boyfriend, who'd been murdered (at random, it seemed) on the streets of Philadelphia. She hadn't been with anyone since. "It's okay," I said. "It's okay. Really, I understand." I was secretly thrilled—someone equally damaged. But after that night she didn't return my calls.

THE WEEKEND before Christmas, I went across from Southampton to Brighton on the train. Arthur wasn't at the station to meet me. I called him at home from the platform, and he told me to take a cab. I tried not to sound disappointed. We hadn't seen each other in a year—with my move to Charlottesville, I hadn't been able to come over in the summer—and I'd been expecting a more dramatic reunion. When I got to Treetops, Arthur gave me a hug and a kiss. "Sorry," he said, "just had a bit much to drink tonight." He'd grown his hair out, down to his shoulders in a glossy dark wave. He looked like my dad in disguise.

"Very romantic," I joked.

Arthur laughed, but it sounded strained. "Well, us poofters have to wear it long every now and then."

We went out to eat at a place on the waterfront—Woody's. It was done up like an American diner: bright and loud with movie posters and state license plates on the walls. Arthur ordered a bottle of Australian wine—"cheap and cheerful," he said—and winced as he sipped it.

My move wasn't the only reason I hadn't come over in the summer. For the past several months, I'd been trading letters with Arthur and Harry, reluctantly broaching the question of what to do about my dad's estate. Every other week, it seemed, I got an urgent phone call from the junior partner, warning me that the court wouldn't wait any longer. Another week, month, whatever, and the court would strip me of my personal representative status. And then who knew what would happen? Certainly not my lawyer. He could only inform me about the emotional fallout in other cases he'd worked on. The two sisters who'd stopped speaking to each other over the family silver—he loved to tell that one.

I wrote to Arthur and Harry, tentatively—very tentatively—suggesting we might avoid a trial and settle the estate out of court. I could feel my words sliding down into some kind of euphemistic sludge, heartfelt confession and slimy legalese mixing queasily together. "I don't want to make it seem like I'm trying to buy my way into your family," I wrote. "Brotherhood is the most important thing." If I could just finesse the language, I thought, we might all come away from this unscathed and unashamed. And, of course, there was the money. After going through all the psychic contortions and death throes of my working-class pride, I'd discovered I not only wanted the money but could hardly stand to give any of it away.

My pangs of conscience, however, were far from Arthur's or Harry's primary concern. In his reply, Arthur told me that when he heard his dad had died, he'd assumed there'd be no money left to anyone at all. He'd even thought he might be asked to help pay his dad's debts or the funeral expenses.

When his parents split up, Arthur told me, his father had refused to pay the mortgage on the house. The bank had foreclosed, and he, Harry, and their mum were put into emergency state housing. They moved nine or ten times in as many years, he and Harry being shuffled from one terrible school to another. (Things hadn't been much better when his dad was still around. He remembered his mum cutting up linoleum to slip into his and Harry's shoes when the soles wore out—and his father going out and buying handmade Italian loafers and tailored clothes.) Arthur spent the rest of his childhood, all the way into his twenties and thirties, wondering if his dad even cared about the family. Then, all these years later, he had to learn that, while there was actually a significant amount of money in his father's estate, no consideration whatsoever had been made to him and Harry. It was as if his dad hadn't recognized either of them even existed.

Being told these things made me furious. *My* father had been honest, respected, responsible, beyond scrupulous. He paid his bills the day they arrived, kept every receipt and a zero balance on his credit cards, filed his taxes months before they were due. Tailored clothes? Italian loafers? He had his business suits, sure, but out shopping and even at restaurants he wore his Filtertek shirts and sweatpants. *He* wore his shoes till they had holes in the heels. Was it *my* fault Arthur was so misinformed? Could I help it if his mother had lied to him?

But then I remembered that black-and-white photo Arthur had given me, the young buck posing in his finest Continental duds. I pictured the camel-hair coat that hung in the back of Dad's closet and the hand-stitched shirts, and suddenly I didn't know what to think.

We both had Woody's Hot Rod burger and a plate of cold chips. "At the Hop" kept playing on the jukebox, stuck on repeat. "I'm going over to Southampton tomorrow," Arthur said on the way back to Treetops. "I'll give you a lift to your nan's. Mum's back in hospital."

Just before I flew to England, I'd heard through Harry that their mother had collapsed and had to be taken to Southampton General. Harry had played the news down, or I'd been too distracted to attach much importance to it. (Why is it so hard to see even an inch beyond your own crises?) I thought about asking Arthur if he wanted me to go with him to see his mum. But I was annoyed and a little hurt that this trip to Brighton had been so perfunctory. Besides, I hated hospitals.

CHRISTMAS WAS FINE. It passed anyway. I spent a very quiet New Year's Eve and Day at my nanny's. The next day, Harry came to pick me up. We were going to the football. I wore my Saints jersey, bought as a present to myself one year, over a sweatshirt.

"Won't tell you who we're playing," Harry said, grinning. "A surprise."

On the way to St. Mary's, we stopped for a pint. The pub was jammed with men in white-and-red-striped Southampton jerseys. (I was wearing the blue away strip.) "All right then, mate?" men kept calling out to Harry over the crowd.

"Season pass holders," Harry explained. "See them every match." He took a long drink of beer. "Nice to get out with the lads now and then. Feel like I can be more myself. Nice to get away from Rose and the kids. Much as I love them." He seemed lost in thought. "Anyway, nice to take your mind off things."

Looking around the room at the sea of Saints supporters, some laughing and calling out to each other, some anxiously watching the pregame on TV and putting away their fifth or sixth pint, I didn't feel threatened or out of place as I had on the few occasions I'd wandered into the rough workman's pubs near Nanny's house. All those men in red and white jerseys, red and white scarves, and red and white knit caps and gloves made that small pub a refuge, a place where no one would speak a hard word against you, as long as you were for the right team.

This could've been me, I thought as I looked around. If we'd never left Southampton, I could've been standing in this pub, season pass in my pocket, pint in my hand. I could've felt at home here. It could've been me calling out over the crowd to a tall lad with dark, curly hair, a fellow Saints fanatic I saw almost every week—*All right, then, mate? What'd you think of last week? Rubbish, wasn't it!?*—not knowing we shared a name, that there stood my flesh-and-blood brother.

All at once the place started to empty. Match time. Harry and I finished our pints and went out into the cold, following the crowd streaming toward Saint Mary's. Just before we went in, Harry stopped at the outer wall.

"When Charlie was born, they were just finishing the stadium." Harry pointed to a brick in the wall—CHARLES CARTWRIGHT—

and then leaned over quickly and kissed it. "For good luck." He smiled and seemed embarrassed.

We pushed through the turnstiles and into the stadium. I bought a match program. Now I saw what the surprise was. Southampton was playing Brighton!

"Our new southern rivals now we've been relegated," Harry said.

"Ah, the fearsome Seagulls," I said, pretending I knew what I was talking about.

Under the night lights, the pitch was a beautiful pale green, the sidelines and penalty lines sharp and clean as one of my dad's engineering schematics. In the far corner, a small group of Seagulls supporters, wearing all blue, were cordoned off in the away section.

When the kickoff whistle blew, the crowd leapt up to a roar. The chanting started right away: ten thousand men belting it out in that groaning, barrel-chested way unique to English football. The chants were so loud, and the accents so thick, I could hardly make out a word. "What are they saying?" I asked Harry. He shouted the words in my ear, his breath warm on my face.

> *We love Southampton, we do,*
> *We love Southampton, we do,*
> *We love Southampton, we do,*
> *Oh, Southampton, we love you!*

"This is great!" I started singing along. "It's been too long!"

All my life, starting with those noon recesses in Fontana when I stood at the edge of the playground watching the other kids play, I'd wanted to be part of something like this. Though I'd failed every time I'd tried to sneak my way in, I wanted to be part of the crowd. To the tune of "Auld Lang Syne," more or less, we all sang:

> *Come on you reds,*
> *Come on you reds,*
> *Come on you reds,*
> *Come on!*

I felt my vocal cords roughening up, going hoarse like the rest of the Saints supporters. The quality of the play wasn't exactly blinding. Saints were tentative on the ball, the action hovering uncertainly around midfield, with a few abortive runs up the sidelines. But standing there beside Harry, singing along, I found myself not caring how badly we played, just as long as we won.

> *Oh, when the Saints!*
> *Oh, when the Saints!*
> *Oh, when the Saints go marching in!*

Behind us a very serious middle-aged man in a dark raincoat and a flat cap stood with his hands jammed in his pockets and a folded newspaper clamped under his arm. He tapped Harry on the shoulder and offered his solemn appraisal of the Southampton side: "They've got pace, but they don't communicate."

"It'll come," Harry said. "It'll come. They've got to get used to one another."

Just then one of the Saints halfbacks snuck a ball into the penalty box, and the striker, stumbling but still managing to get a touch, dinked it into the back of the net. We all went crazy. I went crazy. I was screaming at the top of my lungs and couldn't even hear myself, my own voice lost in the roar.

After that first goal, a different set of chants started. The Saints supporters were worked up now. The new chants were lower in pitch but even louder than the others. They had a mocking tone and were directed not at the Saints players but at the Seagulls

and the away section. Ah, I thought, now we were going to gloat
a little. I expected Harry to tell me what everyone was singing,
but he kept quiet and didn't join in.

At halftime, we went down to the concessions, had another
pint, and ate a beef and onion Pukka Pie each.

"I couldn't make out some of those songs."

Harry smiled, tight-lipped. "Oh, well. Lads will be lads."

When we went back out to the stands, the chants started back
up. I thought to ask Harry what the words were again, not wanting to get left out of the fun, but then, as if my ears could suddenly hear another language, I began to understand.

"Up the ass . . . Up the ass . . . Up the ass . . ." went one in a
deep, barely melodic drone. Another was strangely quaint and
childish:

"You've got shit on your willy! You've got shit on your willy!"

They were basically a series of fag jokes. We were playing
Brighton, after all. There was a reprisal of "Auld Lang Syne," but
with different words:

> *Does your boyfriend know you're in?*
> *Does your boyfriend know you're in?*
> *Does he know you're in?*

Without quite getting it, I had to laugh at that one. "Well, this is
all pretty silly," I said to Harry. He nodded but stayed tight-lipped.
Though he sometimes joked about Arthur listening to Diana
Ross records when they were boys, there was perhaps a reason
he'd had to defend his older brother in the schoolyard. Saints
had a good chance, and the crowd leapt up in volume again.
"Up the ass . . . Up the ass . . ." Brighton scored an equalizer,
and then Southampton put in a second goal. Despite myself, I
couldn't help singing along. Saints had a man sent off and played

a dull, defensive game for the rest of the match, but the crowd kept on. I got lost in the frenzy for a while. It was a surprise, and a disappointment, when the ref finally blew three whistles and the match was over, 2–1.

We shuffled out into the night, moving in the broad stream of Saints supporters. It had just started snowing, and all the lads together in the street, laughing and calling out, made a jolly sight. I held on to the feeling of belonging a few more minutes. Harry and I drove back into town. It hadn't been an important match. Seagulls were a weak side, and there'd been little doubt Southampton would win. But we went over the whole thing again in detail. "They're a good young squad," Harry kept saying. "They've got some good young talent." In front of my nanny's, we said our good-byes, hugged, and wished each other a happy 2006, and it wasn't until Harry was gone that I realized we'd gotten through the entire night without talking about the will or his mother.

18

SAD STORIES

Playing in the honky-tonk band in Chicago, I used to dream about meeting a girl. She'd come in one Tuesday night, drawn into the bar by our music, wearing cowgirl boots and her straw-colored hair in pigtails. Tall and fearless, she'd two-step with one of the shriveled old dudes who always sat hunched at the bar. Or she'd stand out on the dance floor by herself, eyes closed, swaying to my train beat, a little drunk, tipping her head up to the ceiling in surrender to the music, then slowly leveling her gaze on me—some girls, the quiet, fierce ones, have a thing for the drummer. After the last set I'd say hey, buy us doubles of Jack with the last of my drink tickets. We'd talk country music—Webb Pierce, Loretta Lynn, Buddy Miller—she'd know all the good stuff. Past closing time and a melancholy calm settled over the bar, the night's work done, the songs still echoing in my skull, the flubbed notes and the fleeting ecstasy, drifting back down to the world—that's when I felt raw and vulnerable, when I wanted to talk to someone. When a band's hitting so hard, so precisely, when you're a part of one perfect machine and the floor and the air are trembling, there's no space to think, let alone remember. But after, it always comes seeping back in. Well, shoot, I'd say to her, I'd better start loading up. She'd want to help. I'd refuse. She'd help anyway. Outside, a light snowfall dusting our hair and coats. Where you living? Logan Square? That's not far out of my way. I'd drive us back into the city on the empty streets, everything muted and winter pristine. Mind if I swing by my place, drop off my stuff? I might go out, look for another beer.

No beer at your place?

Sure, I got beer.

She'd play with one of her pigtails, look down at the floorboard, smile to herself, and in that moment something wondrous would flood in. If home can't be a place, maybe it's a person.

Well, she'd say, in that case, you got two?

HER NAME was Anna. It wasn't every day she wore boots, and I only saw her wear her hair in pigtails a handful of times, but it was enough to spark the imagination. We had a couple of classes together. She was tall, blond, and brash, thought my jokes were dumb but laughed anyway. Her laugh—Jesus, her laugh. Bright, intelligent, sometimes goofily self-parodying—it seemed to strip all my torpor and sadness from me. I'd taken to wandering the tidy neighborhoods of Charlottesville at night, lingering at the ends of manicured lawns, gazing up at lighted windows where families were eating dinner or sitting down to watch TV. Her laugh was the sound of the close, comfortable happy lives behind those bright windows; I went to sleep with it singing in my ears.

Naturally, she had a boyfriend in New York. All the girls in graduate school come with them attached. When she started to express doubts about their future, I was all too happy to listen and offer my advice and carefully considered opinions, as if I, too, were acutely aware of the vagaries, charms, and flaws of the mysterious Kev. I threw a party at my apartment. After everyone else had gone home, she and I stayed up sipping bourbon and talking about him. I gave her my bed to sleep in, said I'd crash on the couch. She was cold; I told her she could wear my pajamas. In the living room, I lay on the shitty little couch, practically frying with desire, and it was all I could do not to get up, creep into my room, and help her change out of them.

THERE'S A PRICE for every injury. I saw a table once, the insurance company's, so much for an eye, a finger, a leg, an arm. After Rory's accident, the police reports and accident reports were filed, the blame spread around equally, a matter for the lawyers. Dad hired the senior partner in the firm that was now handling the will. A settlement was negotiated. The payout from Rory's death now made up more than two-thirds of my dad's estate. (I felt I'd earned that part of it anyway.) I couldn't put off executing the will any longer, so I decided to make Arthur and Harry an offer. The idea of going to trial and having aspersions about my dad's past thrown around, that I couldn't stomach. Besides, I wasn't giving the junior partner a cent more than I already owed him, and I was too far along in the process to make hiring someone else palatable. The question, then, was how much. How do you put a price on having grown up without a father? What exactly were Arthur and Harry owed? Would they still love me after all this ugliness was through? I knew the price for Rory's life. How much, then, for my half brothers?

✻   ✻   ✻

WE WERE LYING on a blanket on the courthouse lawn, underneath a statue of some dead Confederate, stoic astride his bronze stallion. We'd been spending more time together, going for beers in the afternoon or hikes out in Shenandoah. Once, she asked me to go lingerie shopping with her, to help choose "something Kev would like." I backed out, at the last minute, almost but not quite able to torture myself with a joint perusal of the racks of Derriere de Soie. But I saw that I wasn't the only one lonely here—and that New York was beginning to feel very far away. Lying next to her in the warm spring sun, I felt giddy, exultant, stupefied with longing.

Over the last month, I'd started to allude to my family around her. She didn't prod me with questions, just let me talk. As she listened, she'd shake her head, set her jaw, make a low murmur of commiseration. Now I heard myself telling her about Rory, about the funeral, about his friends who, months after the accident, still dropped by the house to say hi to Dad, see how he was doing. Then, without quite meaning to, I was telling her something I'd hardly told anyone. I was telling her about Darren.

Darren was the older brother of Tyler, the other boy who'd died in the accident. I'd met Darren a few times. He was a guy you tried to get out of conversations with quickly. He was in his late twenties and lived with his mom in a condo near the lake. He talked in a halting stutter, his voice pleading and childlike. There was something wrong with him. Manic depression? Mild schizophrenia? No one seemed to know. In the polite, decent Midwest, these were not facts you paraded in front of people. From what Rory said, Darren didn't have friends of his own, but occasionally he tagged along with Tyler's high school buddies and bought them smokes and beer.

"He came to Rory's funeral," I told Anna, "wearing this ridic- ulous getup, linen pants and a jacket with anchors on the but- tons, like he was going yachting or something. He came up to me and started talking about how much he missed Rory, and how it was hard to lose a brother, and how he'd lost a brother, as well. Then he asked if I wanted to hang out sometime, go see a movie, maybe come over to his place, play video games or something." I tried to mimic Darren's voice, still so clear in my memory, but I couldn't quite get the high, wheedling tone, the breathlessness. "I didn't know what to tell him. I just said sure. Okay, fine. Sounds fine."

He started calling me at home. The first couple of times, I made polite excuses, saying I had too much to do, things were a little crazy, Dad and I were still kind of in shock. He seemed to take it well—it was obvious, I thought, that I was snubbing him— but both times, just as I was about to hang up, he went into his routine: We'd both lost our brothers; only we knew how that felt; if I ever wanted to talk about anything, anything at all, I just had to give him a call. It made me sick to hear it—the loneliness, the desperation, his voice seemed about to break from it. The guy just wanted a friend, and the best shot he saw for one was in me, someone he barely knew.

"You've got enough to worry about without him adding to it," Dad told me when I went to him for advice. He was right, but it didn't make me feel better. Dad said he'd start screening my calls, and I was glad for him to do it. Once, Darren actually showed up on our doorstep, and I had a rushed conversation with him where I pretended to be getting ready to leave for Madison, even going so far as to pull on my coat and boots. "You and me got to stay close, buddy," Darren said as I turned him away. "We got to be real close. We both know what it's like to lose our brothers." When he was gone I took off my coat and boots, sat on the couch, and cried.

"That was the last I heard from him," I told Anna, "though I think he called and talked to my dad once or twice. A couple of weeks later, I went back to college. Then after maybe three months, my dad called, told me he had some news . . ."

I paused—the same way I did when I first told Claire about Arthur and Harry.

"My dad told me Darren had been found in a hotel outside of town. He'd holed up there. No one knew where he was. Somehow he strung up a rope or a belt, and I guess he . . ."

I let the silence take over. The bronze Confederate on his frozen steed kept charging eternally toward the horizon.

"Fucking Christ," Anna said, her jaw set.

"I know I shouldn't think it's my fault. But I can't help—"

"Of course it's not your fault. How could it be your fault?"

"I could've tried to be his friend."

"Would that have helped anything?"

"No, I guess not. But what happened to him . . . It could've been . . ."

I felt disgusted with myself. Not because I was seeking absolution from someone who didn't even know the people I was talking about. Or because I felt guilty about Darren's suicide. (Though even now I'm not sure I've made peace with it. I could've hung out with the guy; it wouldn't have done any harm.) No, it was because I knew I'd been rehearsing this moment. Darren had his routine, and now I had mine, my desperate plea.

"I mean, Jesus," Anna said under her breath, "how much can one person take?"

When she said those words, I felt something wriggle up and down my spine. It was a difficult act, being stoic and sensitive, tough but tortured, but I'd finally made someone see me the way I wanted to be seen. How could she help, now, but fall in love?

I'D COME UP with an offer—I could hardly say if it was too much or too little—but couldn't quite take the last step. I wasn't allowed to make these kinds of decisions, not without my dad's say-so. (Then again, what great decisions had he made in life?) Finally, I sent word to Arthur and Harry. I heard back from them both within a week. If I was happy with it, they were happy with it. The lawyers drew up the necessary paperwork. To celebrate I went out and got royally drunk. I was less rich than I might have been, but I was still set up for years to come. At last, I thought, it's time to start enjoying life again.

But somewhere along the way, the final tax return on the estate got tangled up with the IRS, a mountain of paperwork that took two years to sort out. I can hardly say another word about it. The will, the settlement, everything—it was a brutal business, and I taste bile every time I think of it.

ARTHUR WANTED to know about my plans for the summer. I'd been putting off making arrangements to go to England. I knew I couldn't spend *another* summer in Southampton or Salisbury—I'd lose my mind. Brighton seemed cool, I wrote to Arthur. Maybe I could find a place on the outskirts of the city, where the rents were cheaper. "Don't be silly," he wrote back. "Come stay with us. You can have the run of the guest room."

I was nervous about the idea. Three months was a long time to spend with someone you'd only met on a few occasions. But now the estate was settled, maybe it was time to start really being brothers. I'd spend a week with Nanny when I arrived, then I'd go down to Brighton and live with Arthur and Phillip.

Not long after this, Anna broke up with Kev. I didn't see her for over a week. She wouldn't answer any calls. Finally, I got hold of her. She agreed to come out for a drink.

"We can be together now," I told her.

She seemed hurt. "I'm not looking for a boyfriend right now."

"But he was a dope. You didn't even respect him. You told me that enough."

"I did," she said, her jaw held tight. "I did, actually. I was kind of in love."

"Christ, he was a fucking *bellhop*."

"Maybe in a month or so. We can see what happens."

"Well, I'm going to be in England in a month."

"Listen," she said. "I'm not saying no. Just . . . not right now."

In her hesitation I saw an opening, and I pressed it, buying her drinks when we went out, concert tickets, cute little gifts. Things were winding down at the university. She and I went to a party, got drunk and stoned. We danced all night. She let me touch her: her hip, her elbow, the small of her back, an arm around her waist.

"I'm too drunk to drive," she told me.

Halfway to her house, I declared that I, too, was too drunk to drive—she'd better crash at my apartment. "I've got two beers," I said.

"What?"

"Nothing, just come up, all right?"

When we got there, I yanked a foldout mattress out of the closet, went into the kitchen, brought out the High Life. We talked, arguing about something, and then we were rolling around on the mattress. One moment she was laughing and shoving me away, the next she was pulling me to her, kissing me, my chin, my neck, my eyes.

When I woke the next morning, she lay next to me, a knit cap pulled over her eyes. I lay there looking at her, and thought, *Here she is, here's the one. And when everything's over and done here, I'm taking her back to England with me.*

19

BRIGHTON

Most nights we went out. The Melrose, the Grand, Terre à Terre, Hotel Du Vin—oysters and shots of chilled vodka, fresh-caught lobster, goose terrine on buttered toast, game pie, brawn, cocktails, wine, whisky . . . Still, I preferred staying at Treetops, sitting at the kitchen table, watching Arthur cook and listening to Roxy Music, David Sylvian, and old jazz records. The way Arthur came into the kitchen with a heavy but glad sigh after a long day or rubbed his hands together when it was time to get started on the meal or cocked his head to listen for a certain moment in a song, the way he tasted sauces from the end of the wooden spoon, considering, adding more flour, more stock—I recognized it all. In those dark eyes of Arthur's, there was the same distance, the same solemnity my dad always carried with him. When Dad laughed, it came up from a deep place, a hidden place. The kind of joke he liked best was a private joke, the kind we laughed at because only the two of us under-stood it—we were in on the same intimate conspiracy against the world. Yet half the time I never quite knew what was so funny.

On Fridays, I'd go into the city center—through the doors of the brightly lit gallery and then into the back offices, where I'd say hi to Arthur's secretary and go in without knocking. Arthur finished up the day's business, and we'd tumble out to the street for a glass of wine at one of the cafés around the Royal Pavilion. A group of Arthur's friends would join us. He was always the center of attention, his stories the funniest, his gossip the juici-est. When I inserted myself into the conversation and tried to tell some story about America and Americans, I mumbled or got lost in the details; I exaggerated too much, and the exaggeration was never convincing. I wanted to impress Arthur, wanted him to think I was charming and wry, but I could never keep up. I was getting sick of the sound of my own voice, not just my awful American accent but the sarcasm, the disdain in everything I said, trying to sound cool, trying to take the piss, trying so hard to impress my older brother.

When we were alone, Arthur and I talked about Dad. Arthur would smile and nod, taking it all in, these vicarious memories of a man he hadn't known since he was nine. I told him how I used to like driving down to Filtertek to have lunch with my dad. He'd always take me out to a nearby diner. "There'd be other guys from the plant there," I said. "They'd wave him over, tell us to join them. But he always insisted we eat together, just the two of us. He seemed proud having me there, like he was showing me off."

Arthur looked past me for a moment. I thought maybe I was mumbling again.

"Do you think he was lonely?"

"He didn't have many friends at Filtertek. People respected him, but I think he was pretty tough to work with. He used to be good friends with this guy Gary Houston. Then Gary left to start his own company, and we never really saw the Houstons after that. Mom always had lots of friends. After she died Dad just sort of stopped seeing everyone. About the only people he talked to were waitresses and cashiers. And me and Aunty Sarah."

Arthur still seemed distracted. "Did he ever talk about George and Alice? I remember Alice being absolutely stunning. They were beautiful, beautiful people. Of course, they were sleeping around on each other the whole time."

I grinned at this bit of salaciousness. "I only remember his friend Glenn."

"Glenn had this great big mane of blow-dried hair. He worked in the rag trade, a prêt-à-porter on the high street. Dad bought his clothes from him."

For a moment, it didn't make sense that we'd both known his best friend, that Dad's two lives had bled into one another. But, of course, Glenn had been the one who'd pointed Arthur out in that pub in Southampton. *Go over and say hello, Andy.*

"Quite a posh shop," Arthur went on.

"Really? Because, I mean, Dad hardly spent a thing on clothes." I couldn't help sounding irritated. "He went to the Big & Tall twice a year. That was it. He was thrifty. Actually, most of the time he was just cheap."

"Mum did like young men in posh clothes."

It felt as if Arthur and I were having an argument and he wouldn't let me win.

"How's she doing, anyway?"

"They say it's gotten into her lymph system now."

For years I tried to write this story—Mom, Rory, Dad, discovering my half brothers—as fiction. I finally showed the manuscript to a writer friend. If you put all that in, she said, no one will believe it. Life doesn't care if the plot feels clumsy. Here was one more unworkable coincidence: My mom had died of cancer. Now it was killing Arthur and Harry's mother as well.

"Amazing how she's holding up," Arthur said, still staring past me. "But then she's always been tough."

WE WENT to a wedding reception. Earlier that year same-sex civil partnerships became legal in the U.K. Brighton had more bookings for gay weddings that summer than the rest of the country combined. Arthur and Phillip's friend greeted us at the door. Kisses and hugs, and a handshake from me. The catering staff— tanned, athletic young men with acrobatic hair—moved among the guests, serving canapés.

Arthur started making his rounds. Phillip and I stood on the terrace overlooking the marina, sipping champagne in silence. I couldn't unstick my tongue. The simple fact of Phillip made me dumb. I tried to remind myself: Arthur's partner, Arthur's lover.

Someone came up to Phillip, gave him a hug and a kiss on the cheek. It was the groom—or the other groom, anyway. He wore diamond stud earrings and a tux with a purple vest. He was American, from the South, and his twang, not dissimilar to mine, made me feel embarrassed and harangued in that room full of string-quartet accents.

"And how's your big summer in Brighton going?"

"Fine," I said gruffly. "Crappy weather."

Then I just stood there, staring at the marble floor. I could've asked him how he met his husband-to-be. I could've made some simple conversation.

"Sorry," I said, gesturing at the guests and the caterers. "I'm just not used to this kind of thing." I felt the need to explain. "I grew up in a really small town in Wisconsin."

I thought I was saying, I'm not accustomed to this high-society stuff, but the groom heard what I really meant.

"Hon, I grew up in Arkansas," he said. "Believe me, this is better."

I STARTED HAUNTING the clothing boutiques in the Laines, slipping in furtively to finger the sleeves of a few shirts and turn over the price tags, then slipping back out when I saw how much they were. I forced myself to shell out for a couple of new oxfords, a sport coat, and a velvety pair of moleskin trousers. Anna had mentioned once that she thought it was hot when guys dressed up. I'd started talking strategy with Arthur, whether to come on strong over e-mail before I went back to Virginia or just keep it light and bantering. Her birthday was approaching, and I was putting together a package: a few local souvenirs, Brighton Rock, a small stack of mix CDs, and a pair of handcrafted earrings I'd found in the market. "How much were those?" Arthur asked when I showed him the earrings.

"Enough," I said. "Enough that she'll notice."

"Couldn't you just write her a lovely letter?"

"Well, sure, obviously I'm going to do that, too."

"There's something to be said for remaining mysterious."

"Right, of course," I said as I started carefully lettering the annotations for one of the mix CDs. "But not too mysterious."

HE'S ON THE COUCH flipping channels—dragging downstairs at noon, bleary-eyed, hair in matted disarray—a bologna sandwich, an Orange Crush, lunch, breakfast, whatever. He's in a blizzard, packing snowballs, should be shoveling the drive. Whipping through the back forty, flying down the sledding hill, hiding behind the couch, calling to Kismet, playing Super Bomberman till his eyes water. He fumbles with the buttons, his words keep mixing up, he goes over the jump and into weightlessness. He's lying on his back in the snow, looking up at me, eyes bright as coins. He's looking right at me. His life hasn't been cut off, only shunted onto parallel tracks, just out of sight. I bob up into the morning light—for a second, maybe two, the world's been righted, we're together again.

I'm running room to room, a big, empty house. I open a door, his bedroom, and catch him masturbating. I'm running, late for work, going to miss the bus, then I stop—he's across the street, he's sitting on my bed staring up at me, a bright question in his eyes. His presence at the edges of everything, he won't show himself. I throw open another door, the bus pulls away, I'm running through woods, trees thick around me, the roaring of the leaves. Then I hear him speaking, the words coming in a torrent, all at once—I call out to him . . .

I woke to my own voice shouting out into the night, echoing around the room, and I was glad there were two floors between me and the master bedroom in Arthur's tall, narrow house. Then, elated and afraid, I sank back into the thicket of dreams, to search for my brother again.

WE WERE OUT at dinner one night. Arthur and I were talking. Phillip sat patiently, listening and trying not to listen. Arthur had been asking me about Rory. I told him that Dad must have seen a lot of himself in Rory, must have seen him making the same mistakes he had. Mom's death had crippled Dad, I said, but Rory's had destroyed him. Arthur and I were leaning in very close over the table, our heads nearly touching, shutting Phillip out.

"He absolutely adored Harry," Arthur was saying. "I think losing Harry was the hardest part for him."

I poured Arthur and me another glass of wine, forgetting to fill Phillip's.

"He loved Rory so much," I said. "That's why they fought. Dad could hardly bear the thought of letting Rory go, letting him become his own man. He practically murdered himself with grief after the accident. He just didn't know how to—"

I looked at Phillip. He sat fumbling with his glasses, swiping at his eyes with the sleeve of his shirt. At first I thought he was crying because the story I was telling was so sad. He said something through his tears. I couldn't make it out.

"It's all right, sweetheart," Arthur said. "What is it?"

"I shouldn't be here. You two finish your talk. I shouldn't be here. I should go home."

"You're very silly," Arthur said gently. "Of course we want you here."

Arthur's voice, so comforting and calming—but in that moment I felt my heart being strangled. Until I arrived, everyone had been happily carrying on with their lives. It hadn't even occurred to me that I might be intruding on Arthur and Phillip. I was the one who shouldn't have been there.

I could hardly get the words out: "I want you here as well, Phillip."

"Thank you," he said softly. "I'm sorry."

"I'm sorry, too."

"Now don't you start," Arthur said. "Or we'll all be crying."

Later, I asked Phillip how he and Arthur met. Through a classified ad, Phillip told me. They were both living in London at the time. He told me about their first date, how they'd arranged to meet on the steps of St. Paul.

"When you saw Arthur for the first time, did you know he was the one?"

"Oh, well, yes." Phillip smiled to himself. "I did have my suspicions."

20

AMBROSIA

A family day out had been planned. A day with the "new" family. Arthur, Phillip, and I drove across the South Downs and through the New Forest, finally arriving at Reptile World. We parked and sat watching the tops of the trees swaying against the iron gray sky.

Reptile World was a rescue center for abandoned pets. England is full of these little fanciers' havens—owl sanctuaries, model villages, *Doctor Who* museums—stashed away in the countryside or in the depths of crumbling manor houses. We'd been planning to have a picnic in the forest, then take a stroll around the facilities, peering in at the lizards and snakes in their dim enclosures. It had been Sara's idea apparently. She lived ten minutes away, but it was the kind of place you somehow never got around to visiting. Now that she was dying, she finally had an excuse.

Rain started pattering down through the leaves, and then it

opened up, blackening the tree trunks and turning the parking lot to mud. The ticket girl huddled under the eaves of her booth, looking at us dubiously.

A few minutes later, Harry pulled up in the big BMW X5 he borrowed from work. An older woman with shoulder-length auburn hair sat beside him on the passenger side. It was hard to see her face through the rain. Behind her sat Rose and an older man, trim, gaunt even, with a shock of white hair. Neil, Sara's second husband. The kids were in the far back, faces pressed against the window, looking out at the rain. Harry got out and dashed over to us, his jacket tented over his head, the expression on his face harried and questioning.

Arthur rolled down the window. "Think there's room to try the picnic at Mum's?"

"Expect so. If Mum doesn't mind."

We followed the BMW until we came to Marchwood, a village on the edge of the forest. We turned onto a cul-de-sac, parked up on the curb, and ran for the front door, where everyone else was already gathered out of the rain.

Then I was hugging Harry and Rose and kissing my niece and nephew. "On the wips, on the wips," Charlie insisted with his seven-year-old's lisp. I shook hands with Neil. He had a Scots accent. "Hello there, laddie," he actually said. Here, then, was the man Sara had married years after she and my father split up—long enough anyway that Arthur and Harry didn't call him "dad" or even "stepdad."

Sara stood off to the side as we all bustled through the front hallway. I'd prepared myself for a quick peck on the cheek, but when it was time for us to say hello, she stood a few steps away, her handbag held in front of her. "Lovely to meet you finally," she said in a rather proper voice.

Inside, the house was close quarters, not unlike the homes of my great-aunts and -uncles, cozy, if not cramped, sealed off tight from the damp and the cold. Neil drew the curtains, so that we wouldn't have to see the rain bucketing down.

Harry came in dripping wet, carrying the picnic things. We pushed back the coffee table, unfolded the picnic blanket, and laid it in the center of the room for the kids to sit on. Charlie had brought in his football and was having a kick around as we set out the food. We were having a potluck—an "American supper." My contribution was still in the car. I was saving it for dessert, as a surprise.

Rose directed traffic: "Violet, please ask Uncle Phillip for another sausage roll." "Charlie, would you like to eat lunch now and perhaps not play football just at the moment?" "Uncle Will's very quiet today, isn't he?"

I was trying to participate but was in one of my mumbling moods. It was a relief when everyone had full plates and I didn't have to talk, only eat. I found myself glancing at Sara. She sat across the room in an overstuffed armchair, not eating much herself, leaning over every few minutes to keep Violet from spilling her lunch down the front of her pink dress. She seemed composed and elegant, and distant. I only had that old photo Arthur had given me—his mother decked out in a brown and Day-Glo orange sundress, her hair up in a beehive—to compare. Now she wore a coffee-colored skirt and matching jacket and a crisply pressed white blouse. *Six months.* Maybe you dressed up when your time was short, tried to meet each day with poise and dignity. She looked a little drawn. I could see she was handling herself delicately. We met eyes for a moment. She smiled, shyly, I thought, and I looked away.

"This your first time visiting England?" Neil said in his brogue.

I mumbled something about visiting every year, sometimes twice a year. Not quite a Yank, I said, not quite a Brit.

"Citizen of the world, eh?"

". . . guess I'm . . . just confused or . . ."

"Eh?"

"Right, citizen of the world."

The conversation got onto Rose's father and his Angolan wife, and her sister, whom they'd recently brought to the U.K. and adopted as their daughter. "How's that for a family?" Rose said. I followed along, nodding now and then like a guest at a party where I didn't know anyone. I saw Rose whisper something in Charlie's ear. He came over and said, "Could we please try some of your pudding, Uncle Will?"

"Oh, yes," Rose said. "Could we finally see this famous pudding, Uncle Will?"

All that week on the phone, I'd been promising them a surprise and had been, perhaps, a little overenthusiastic about it. I'd wanted to bring something special to the picnic, something truly American, straight from the heartland.

Ambrosia. I'd only tried it on one occasion myself, the first of the several Thanksgivings we spent with the Houstons. Every year they gathered all the relations, Grandma and Grandpa Houston all the way down through second cousins, and served up a big bruiser of a turkey and enough side dishes to fill every inch of countertop in their big kitchen with its double-door fridge and illustrated wallpaper depicting scenes of frontier living. They were generous enough to include us, their adopted family from jolly old England. At the Houstons', I had, for the first time, Tater Tot casserole, candied yams, twice-baked potatoes, and "stained glass" salad. These all seemed blandly exotic to me—half-plastic artifacts from the 1950s better-living-through-chemistry era. I could stomach a forkful or two out of politeness. The ambrosia was a different story.

I remember it sitting there in a huge Pyrex bowl, blindingly white with lumps of canned fruit submerged in it and, here and there, bright red candied cherries floating like buoys on top. I plastered a spoonful to my plate. It was like digging up topsoil, the surface hiding chunked pineapple and pear, sliced bananas, shredded carrot. That one spoonful, which sat practically glowing on my plate, was enough to put me off the entire meal. For any other kid, it was like getting dessert for dinner, enough sugar to set your eyes pulsing. Rory loved the stuff. I figured Charlie and Violet would, too.

But that wasn't the only reason I'd decided to make ambrosia. The truth was I'd been dreading this day out. It was the first time we'd all be together, the first time I'd get to see my place in the family, if I even had a place at all. More than that I'd been dreading meeting Sara. It had occurred to me to hate her for what she'd done to my dad—the returned letters and gifts, the unanswered calls, forcing him out of the family—even if she was dying. Now all I wanted was just to get through this little living room picnic. Our potluck was one of the few times, visiting England, that I played up my Americanness rather than scorning it. I'd do anything that afternoon to get a laugh.

The preparation did not go well. I had to go to three different supermarkets to find marshmallows (not a popular item in the U.K.), and then all I could get was the miniature, multicolored variety you put in hot cocoa. When I started to blend them, they turned an odd grayish pink, the color of spray insulation. I plopped in the pineapple, banana, carrot, and sour cream and gave it another go with the hand mixer. There wasn't enough time to let the stuff sit in the fridge and set properly, so I slapped the lid on the bowl and stuck it in the freezer for an hour. As we were hurrying out the door to get to Reptile World, I took a peek. The marshmallows had turned to a half-frozen sludge. A hunk of banana poked above the surface like the prow of a wrecked ship.

I dipped a finger in and took a taste. It wasn't terrible, actually, just incredibly sweet.

"Wait a minute," I said to Rose. "I'll go grab it."

When I came back in, I took the lid off the bowl. Everyone leaned in to look.

"I don't know, Uncle Will," Rose said. "Is this what you have for your pudding in America?"

"It's a traditional dish," I explained. "It's really more for the kids."

Charlie came up and peered into the bowl. He seemed uncertain. Here was something sweet—practically radiating sweetness, in fact—but it looked like something you'd use to fix a crack in a wall. I spooned out a dollop for him. He sat cross-legged on the picnic blanket, contemplating. He took a small taste, held it in his mouth, swallowed it with a quick gulp.

"What do you think, Charlie?" Rose said.

He smiled a pained smile.

"Well, son, what's it taste like?" Harry prompted.

Charlie gave us a tiny, almost imperceptible shake of his head, as if, for the sake of appearances, declining to answer.

"Would you try another bite for Mummy?"

"No, thank you," he said tentatively, unsure exactly how he should be behaving. He shook his head again, his whole torso swaying with his head this time.

It was Violet's turn now.

"Come on, Vi," Harry said. "Uncle Will made it just for you."

Violet stood on tiptoe to look into the bowl. "No!" She was following her older brother's example, not understanding exactly what she was refusing but sure she didn't want to know. "No!" Her face was lit with mischief.

I sat there smiling, trying to show that it didn't bother me. I'd made the ambrosia as a joke—still, I'd wanted it to go over well.

The bowl sat at my feet, sweating down its sides, its contents already getting a little soupy. Neil started picking up the plates and silverware. Everyone settled back into their chairs, stuffed and sleepy. I sat staring into the bowl.

"Excuse me, Charlie," Sara said from across the room. "Charlie, would you pass the pudding, please?"

Charlie looked at her in disbelieving awe. He picked up the bowl, holding it at arm's length, and took it over to her. She spooned a quivering lump onto her plate. Her first bite was dainty, but she swallowed without apparent effort, then cocked her head slightly as she considered. "Quite nice, actually." Her expression remained thoughtful, serious even. "Quite nice," she pronounced again. "Quite unique." She finished what was on her plate and even took another small serving.

Charlie and Violet crowded up at her knee, looking on in wonderment. "Here you go, my dear," Sara said and popped a spoonful into Violet's mouth.

Violet chomped away, laughing and swinging her arms around. I don't think it much mattered to Violet what the ambrosia looked or tasted like—she'd eat just about anything—but at least she didn't spit it out. "Chew with your mouth closed, please, sweetheart," Sara said and gave her another spoonful. Now Charlie was interested, too, and took another taste, though he still didn't seem to think much of it.

Sara offered the bowl around the room again, but the adults, myself included, protested that they were full. "Suit yourselves," Sara said and finished what was on her plate. I looked at her. She looked at me. "Thank you," she said. "That was lovely."

Outside, it had stopped raining, and by the time we were done clearing up, the sun had come out. English weather.

21

ARCHAEOLOGY

I thought if I wrote about Rory maybe that would get him out of my dreams. This was later, after I'd finished my degree and was still hanging around Charlottesville. I was renting a house—four months' rent paid up, nothing to do *but* write—from a professor of archaeology away on a dig. She'd promised to have someone come in and clean before I moved in, but there were books and papers piled everywhere, not to mention her Cappadocian artifacts—clay wine pitchers, tiny stone figures dancing and hunting, lyres with fraying gut strings—which gave the place the air of a private museum or an antiques barn. Still, it was a big house for a single person, and I soon colonized my own little area with empty food containers, beer bottles, and scattered manuscript pages—my roman à clef about my family. The archaeologist had told me, "Just use the sheets on the bed, they're fresh." But four or five nights a week, I woke with a start, soaked in sweat. I bought my own sheets.

My novel, I'd decided, would start in the winter of 1999, just as the older brother—studious, reserved, responsible—arrived home from college on break. The younger brother, having barely graduated from high school, had been hanging around town for the last six months, caddying at the golf course through the summer, getting wasted with his buddies whenever they were back home, and warring with the overprotective, paranoid, grief-stricken father. Four nights before Christmas, Rory and his two best friends set off for a party in the Chicago suburbs, an hour and a half's drive away.

I'd told myself I needed to write as honestly, as accurately as I could. The funerals, the candlelight vigil at the high school, the three class photos blown up on the front page of the local paper—I had all that firsthand. But I didn't know the details of the accident.

I drove out to my storage shed, where the contents of our old house in Wisconsin now lived, and picked through boxes: old stuffed animals, the family crystal and china, Mom's stamp albums—Rory's wallet, keys, and Zippo, still sealed in a plastic bag. I found the accident report among Dad's papers, in a file folder he'd marked *Rory's death*. I took a box of stuff back with me. At the archaeologist's dining table, I spread out the pages in the folder. The report itself was brief, the legal correspondence around it endless. Some pages were filled in with a cop's tight handwriting. Others had been typed up, in all caps, by the coroner. There were references to photos of the accident scene, but none had been included. For this, I was secretly relieved.

Here's what happened: At ten thirty on the night of December 21, 1999, Rory, Tyler, and Alex were driving along a county road in Tyler's Jeep Grand Cherokee, doing seventy-five, fifteen over the limit, enough THC and beer in all of their systems to show on the tests. The driver of the grain truck was working late. He was backing his rig across the road, lining it up with the grain silo he meant to unload in—his truck in one lane, headlights shining straight ahead, the trailer jackknifed across the other lane. When the truck driver saw the Jeep coming, he flashed his headlights, but the Jeep didn't slow down. The broadside of the trailer was lit by one red warning light, almost invisible from a distance. Eighty feet from the trailer, Tyler hit the brakes, but at a hundred feet or a hundred and twenty, the result would've been the same. The Jeep "submarined" under the trailer, tearing off the windshield and half of the roof. The cause of death was typed crookedly in its little box: "massive blunt trauma to the head, chest, and abdomen."

I STARTED drafting it, writing in third person, from Rory's perspective, using his name and the names of his friends as stand-ins until I could think of better ones. The scene opened with Alex beating out the rhythm to "Down with Disease," their favorite Phish song, on the back of Rory's headrest—to establish that Rory was in the front and Alex in the back. Rory turned around and stared at Alex with red eyes. "*Dude*, fucking cut it out, okay?" Alex just laughed and kept on. Tyler, who was driving, skipped back to the beginning of the song. The last time they'd seen Phish at Alpine Valley, "Down with Disease" was the final encore, and Rory had been tripping so hard the whole *sky* was pulsing to the bass and drums. A lengthy description of an acid trip followed. (This was pure imagination; I've never tried LSD.) And then back to the beginning of the song, back to Alex beating on Rory's headrest, my clumsy method of ratcheting up the tension.

The setting: a cold, clear night. A two-lane road, down near the state border, fields of dirty snow and chewed-up cornstalks stretching off into the darkness. Rory stared out the passenger-side window, watching the radio tower beacons blinking in the distance. Then, just for an instant, almost too brief to believe, a vision darted into his mind: He saw himself standing out in the middle of a field, shirtless, shivering, goose bumps coming up on his arms and chest as the long, slow wind drifted across the prairie.

Abruptly, he came back to himself. Alex fired away at the headrest again, laughed, said something about the music. But Rory didn't hear. He looked through the windshield, into the lights of an eighteen-wheeler that seemed to have paused in the other lane. A gray shape filled his view, a wall emerging suddenly from the dark, the Jeep's headlights making it flash a pale, mud-spattered white. From its center, a small red eye opened, pulling them toward it, growing larger, glaring at them. A scream rose up in Rory's throat, and then—

I couldn't. On the page, I snatched them away just at the last moment, fixed it so the grain truck hadn't yet started to back into the farmhouse driveway, wasn't blocking the other lane with its trailer. Yes, they made it just in time. A few seconds later, and they would've been—

They sped through the night, Alex and Tyler bullshitting about the party, macking on chicks, the classes they were taking next semester. Tyler got on I-90, exited forty miles later in the northwest suburbs, drove through a subdivision where the houses were all massive split-levels sitting in the middle of perfectly square, snow-covered lawns. When Rory saw the houses, they reminded him of Mom's stamps, each one almost exactly like the next, pasted into neat little rows. He stayed quiet. He didn't know where they were going and didn't really care. As long as there was beer. As long as he didn't have to spend the night at home. The sickly sweet smell of morphine, of soiled sheets and wasting flesh, had bled into the walls.

Tyler found the street and the address, a modest brick ranch at the end of a cul-de-sac. All the lights in the house were out. There were several cars parked discreetly along the blocks they'd passed, the only sign that this was the party. Behind the house, there was a wide stretch of undeveloped land grown over with prairie grass, everything quiet but for the distant clunking of cars hitting spacers on the interstate and the grass rustling and ticking in the breeze.

"Damn," Tyler said. "No one to call the cops out here."

They rang the doorbell, started shedding their coats and hats. Rory tapped one boot against the other, knocking the snow off his Doc Martens. Someone came and let them in, and they followed the guy down into the basement. There was a roomful of kids their age, a pony keg, candles stuck into wine bottles, their flames dancing shadows across the wood-paneled walls. A group of guys standing around the keg were wearing U of C and U of I sweatshirts. Rory felt uncomfortable, tried not to show it. "Here, get down on this," Alex said, bringing out his hip flask. Rory took a long pull. He glanced around, checking out the girls, caught a few of them glancing back. Pink Floyd was playing on a boom box. There were clusters of balloons tied around the room, as if someone were having a birthday, but no cake or presents. Shit, what kind of a party was this?

A girl came up to them. She wore corduroys and a sweater just loose enough at the neck to show one light pink bra strap. Her skin was very pale against it. She seemed nervous, maybe because she didn't know them. Some guy Tyler went to school with had told him about this thing. Rory could smell the sweet, earthy smell of whatever the girl put in her hair. Her parents were out of town, she started explaining. They were both professors at Lake Forest and did lots of traveling, conferences, stuff like that. They didn't know she was having people over. She introduced herself. Her name . . .

"I'm Morning."

"Morning?" Rory said, as if he hadn't heard quite right.

"Yeah, my parents thought they'd get real creative."

"I'm Rory. It's cool if we hang out?"

"Glad you could make it."

She smiled, and he saw that she had small, slightly crooked teeth. She wore clear braces, and on each tooth a little line of saliva glistened.

She went to talk to another girl. Rory slipped in next to the keg, pumped it, poured a beer, looked over at the two of them whispering together. His dusty blond hair hung almost to his shoulders; when he tucked it behind his ears, he seemed bashful, boyish. Yet he was already starting to grow into his adult face, his expression calm and coolly appraising, and in his blue eyes, bright and still, there seemed frozen a perpetual startle, like the moment glass begins to shatter. Girls, it should be said, were not a problem.

What came next? He found Tyler and Alex again. They went upstairs and rolled a joint on the back step. "Hey, Boast," Tyler said, "got your flame?"

Rory brought out his Zippo and sparked up the joint.

"Ride on," Tyler said.

"Ride on," Rory said.

It was a Harley-Davidson Zippo, engraved with the words "Ride On," which had become a kind of joke between the three of them. Rory slid the lighter into his pocket, held it in his palm, the metal cold against his skin. He used to think Harleys were so cool. He'd bought the lighter not long after he started hanging with Tyler and Alex—fifty bucks, everything he had left from caddying, plus a few extra he'd skimmed out of Dad's change jar. He didn't mind working at Tyler's mom's art supply store, liked working with the little kids, but the idea of a job, a real,

forever job, was no big thrill. He took another toke, listened to
Tyler and Alex talking.

"Know that one girl in my poli-sci class?" Alex said. "Going
out with her again when we get back."

"That Jess chick? The one with the legs?" Tyler said. "Shit,
man, ride on."

Rory laughed. It was the lazy, stoned way Tyler said it that Rory
loved. His friends were everything to him, and Dad hated them.
After his sixth or seventh whisky—fucking hypocrite—he'd start
yelling about them, calling them reckless, irresponsible, bums,
losers. Rory tried not to be sad his friends would be away again
soon, off starting their lives. On pot, his feelings seemed to swim
in some other stream, separate from him; he could lean back and
watch them drifting by.

"You gonna rush?" Alex said.

"Hell, no," Tyler said. "I don't got to pay to make friends."

"Been thinking about it. Some of the guys seem like good
guys."

When they went back inside, Rory was high out of his mind.
He sat down on the couch in the basement, tried to maintain,
started another beer. Someone sat down next to him, her leg
brushing his. It was that girl again. Morning.

They talked, or anyway he let her talk. She was drunk and
happy now, less nervous. She was still a senior, she said. Her
parents wanted her to go to either Lake Forest or U of C, but
she wanted to see the world first. Europe, India, Japan, South
America maybe.

"Are you done with your applications?" she said. "Or are you
already—"

"Nah, I'm through with school. Four more years of bullshit?
No way."

"What are you doing, then?"

Across the room, someone popped a balloon. Rory flinched, but the girl didn't even seem to notice.

"Maybe I can get a job at the plant where my dad works."

"How would that be?"

"Fine. Probably pay good."

"Well, what do you want to do? What are you good at?"

He didn't want to talk about this kind of stuff. She sounded like Dad. Like Will.

"I don't know, drawing."

"You could go to art school."

She had pale, silvery blue eyes. He couldn't help his glances lingering too long, blowing his cool. He tried again to shrug off the conversation.

"School sucks. Teachers are morons."

"My parents aren't morons."

"Shit, I didn't mean . . ." He looked around for Tyler and Alex. They were gone, probably smoking somewhere. He changed the subject. "If you go traveling, you should collect stamps from the places you go."

She laughed. "Why, do *you* collect stamps?"

"My mom did." He hesitated. "She had stamps from all over the world. Some of the countries aren't even countries anymore."

The memory of Mom carefully licking the adhesive hinges, patiently lining the stamps up, came back to him. He cradled it for a moment and then let it go.

"I don't know how she got all those countries," he said.

"I think you write to different places, get them to write you back. Maybe you trade for some other ones. It sounds nice, actually. So, why'd she stop?"

Rory scrutinized the girl for a moment.

"I'm sorry, I didn't—"

"Don't worry about it," he said.

"I didn't realize . . ."

"Don't worry about it."

I knew how this conversation ended: awkward apologies, silence. But I steered Rory away. They kept talking, about music. Morning liked Phish as well. Turned out they'd been at the same show at Alpine Valley.

Alex and Tyler came back down into the basement, red-eyed and a little sloppy. Rory got up and went over to them. "You got something going over there, Boast?" Alex said, punching him in the shoulder. "Saw you talking with that chick."

"Shit," Rory said in a lazy drawl, an echo of Tyler. "Just talking."

"Man, get down on that. She's young, high school maybe, all innocent and shit."

Tyler brought out a film canister from his pocket—his weed—and tapped the lid. "How about another smoky smoke?"

Dad didn't need to be jealous of his friends. Rory knew Tyler and Alex were already pulling away from him. He could stay with them now, get high again, crack all their old jokes. But he felt the alcohol coming over him, and he didn't want to smoke and then just pass out.

"Nah, I'm cool," he said. "Pretty messed up already."

The three of them did their shake, one of those elaborate handshakes boys their age love doing.

"Ride on," Tyler and Alex said at the same time, and Rory couldn't help laughing.

And then the night tumbling ahead. He finds himself upstairs with Morning, raiding the fridge, drinking tart box wine right out of the plastic spigot, the music from the basement loud, thrumming through their feet. She leads him down a dark hallway. He sits on the edge of her unmade bed, the sheets warm, damp, and sweet, smelling of overturned earth, like when Mom and Dad used to work together in the garden. Morning sits next to him. He jumps and lands on the bed again, bouncing them both into a pile with the sheets. "How frigging drunk are you?" she cries through a giggle.

"Very, very, very."

They kiss. He looks her in the eyes, those silvery eyes— painful to look at them. There's a rushing in his ears like speeding through a tunnel. He lies with his shirt off. She rests her head on his bare chest. "You should go somewhere," she says. She tells him he should get on a bus, a train, whatever. Just go. If he doesn't have any plans, he should *do* something.

He wrestles her over, holds her down, kisses her again. There's a reason he hasn't left home already, the same reason he can hardly stand to stay: Every time he's at the front door, putting on his Docs to go out for the night, Dad comes out of his room to say good-bye, drunk, a stunned look on his face. A look of loneliness—utter, heartsick loneliness.

They roll and fumble among the sheets, kissing. Falling back on the pillows, they start talking. He tells Morning about Mom, about the last two years, all the fights with Dad.

"He yells at me, but basically I do what I want. I guess we could keep going the same way forever. It's like everything good has come already and from here out it's all just shit."

She drags her finger along one of the delicate curls that have just begun to grow on his chest, pulling it straight.

"Don't say that."

"You're smart. It's different for you. The things you're talking about—Europe, London, whatever—that's what Will's going to do. My brother, he's the brains in the family."

"Older or younger brother?"

"Guess."

"Well, why not do what *you* want to do?"

"I can't. I have to stay."

He feels her fingers moving down his chest, his stomach.

"Don't make excuses."

"It's not an excuse."

She unzips his jeans. In his drunkenness, he hangs for a moment between wanting to be touched and wanting to roll over, curl up, fall into dreamless sleep. Then he reaches up the back of her sweater and undoes her bra in one quick motion.

"Slick. You must get a lot of practice."

He grins at her. She stops, looks at him.

"You're not just telling a sad story to get laid, are you?"

"Fuck you," he says gently. He doesn't care what either of them says now. He lifts up her sweater and starts to kiss her breasts. She rubs his hard-on through his jeans. She doesn't know what she's doing, and, really, neither does he. He's done it maybe half a dozen times, but drunk, furtive, rushed, with voices and music on the other side of the wall and his friends making jokes to him later.

But this time he knows exactly where to touch her, when to unbutton her corduroys, slide a finger under the elastic of her underwear. Her breath is hot against his chest, the smell of earth all around him. She undoes his belt, tugs his jeans past his ankles, the moment endless with anticipation and the clumsiness of undressing, with the slow warmth of their bodies, with need, all other possibilities closing down, nothing but the girl radiating warmth and life beside him. He closes his eyes. His head swims in the darkness. His penis has come out from the slit in his boxers and is hard against her cotton underwear.

"Wait," she whispers.

"What? What is it? Listen, we don't have to . . . If you don't want . . ."

Then he hears the voices. Voices murmuring down the hallway, the back door opening and shutting quietly. Footsteps coming quickly up the stairs. Morning tilts her head, listening, but Rory knows what's happening.

"Cops," he whispers in her ear.

"What do we do?"

"Outside. We scatter."

He searches for his clothes, pulls on his jeans, his socks, his Doc Martens. He can't find his shirt. She eases open a sliding glass door that leads out to her balcony. It's a short drop to the ground.

"What are you doing? Your shirt."

"I'll be okay."

They run across the yard into the tall grass. Around the corner of the house, they see a pair of headlights shining up the driveway. They stop twenty yards into the field.

"I should go talk to them," she says.

They hear whispering all around them, stifled laughter populating the dark. He puts his fingers to his lips, takes her by the hand, leads her farther into the field.

Morning catches up to him, pulls him to her. "You'll freeze."

"I'm fine," he says, but for the first time he shivers.

She pulls him closer. The voices begin to quiet. They're alone now. He sinks to his knees, onto the hard-packed, dirty snow. The skin on his chest begins to prickle. He shivers again, a long, rattling shiver.

"We should go back."

"I can hold on."

He hears only the tall, dry grass rasping against itself. His chest is hollow with cold. His legs and arms twitch and burn, telling him to leap up and rub and slap himself, bring the feeling back. But he stays there, kneeling in the snow. He looks for the headlights of the cop car. They're gone. He turns to speak to Morning. She's gone as well. His breath makes only the most delicate curl as it seeps out into the cold.

Then everything is still. The grass no longer moves but stands strangely upright. He tries to rise, to come up from his knees, but realizes slowly, as if through the passage of hours, that he's on his back. The cold earth presses up against him. He looks up at the stars. There are no stars. There's no sky. He closes his eyes, tries to say the girl's name. His lips part but make no sound.

Then his eyes open. She kneels above him, staring at him with her silvery eyes. She puts her hands on his bare, shivering chest and begins to push.

ONE NIGHT in the archaeologist's house I woke from a heavy sleep. On my way to the bathroom, I stumbled into one of the display shelves lining the hallway. Two of the little Cappadocian figures fell. They survived, having bounced off some papers stacked on the floor. I knelt there, swaying, drunk, studying the figures. They were so very finely made, the stone so old it was almost translucent, their tiny, thin arms flung out, as if to catch something or cast it away.

The photos in the accident report—Dad had thrown them away. "Massive blunt trauma to the head, chest, and abdomen." To have looked once was enough. Or maybe he knew I'd find the folder one day and wanted to spare me. I remembered what he said the night of the accident, when the cops came to our door with the news. Dad and I were in each other's arms, rocking together. Over his shoulder, I saw the headlights of the cop car shining up the driveway. "It never ends, guy," he said to me, choking back a sob. "It never ends." He threw away the photos, but he kept the report itself, just as he'd preserved the clothes hanging in Rory's closet, the sheets on his bed, the loose change on his bedside table. He'd needed to keep the wounds open and bleeding.

I shuffled the two little figures together on the dusty wooden floor and got up clumsily from my knees. Then I went to the door, got one of my shoes, and smashed the things to powder. I hadn't dreamed of Rory in over two weeks.

The next afternoon, in the back garden, under a fading September sun, I dug a hole with a garden trowel and scattered in the remains of the figures. I got the box I'd brought over from my storage shed. The words for a decent burial wouldn't come, and I had to deepen the hole, but eventually I got all four of the stamp albums to fit.

I KEPT WRITING, eighty pages, a hundred, and when I finished, I rewrote, polishing, ordering, trying to make it real. I'm bringing him back, I thought. Here on the page he's alive again. How far could I have gone? Marriage—the girl I'd invented for him, or someone like her—a house, kids? Yes, all of it. For my brother, all of it.

But no matter how I revised that night—the archaeologist was coming home, and I was readying to move again—it still ended the same way:

She presses down, his chest caving under her hands, and the last of his breath rises out of him, just the faintest curl drifting up into the starless, skyless night. Then she lies down, takes him in her arms. No stars, no sky. No grass, no field. Only the girl and the ghost of my brother, their tiny figures huddled together, waiting for the story in which they will be saved.

22

THE FAMILY SEAT

Arthur said he'd take a Friday off, and we'd drive to West Gomeldon—the "family seat," he joked. On their own, ages eight and six, he and Harry used to take the bus all the way there from Southampton. In the mornings, Granddad Boast toured them around the garden, telling them the names of the herbs and veg, pulling weeds and plucking stones from the earth as they moved through the rows. Arthur helped Granny in the kitchen as she prepared Sunday dinner: roast chicken, boiled potatoes, runner beans, marrow, rhubarb crumble and hot custard. After dinner Granddad got his old combat helmets down from the wardrobe and counted off drill as the boys marched up and down the lane, a rake and a spade over their shoulders in place of rifles. Those summer weekends, Arthur said, were some of the happiest he could remember.

So I went along with him. But I was nervous. Over the last

couple of weeks, our conversation had felt labored. We always seemed to be repeating ourselves, and when I went to meet Arthur for lunch, he seemed in a rush to get back to the gallery. Since meeting Sara, I'd become hesitant to talk about Dad. When I saw her, my expertise on the subject of my father suddenly faltered. Everything I said about him now seemed provisional. In fact, *I* seemed provisional. It was odd, unsettling, like back in Wisconsin, when the light turned green and the air went dead, the tornado sirens wailed, and we huddled down in some basement or shelter, suspended between stillness and disaster.

We stopped in Salisbury on the way. Arthur wanted to see Great-aunty Joyce's chocolate factory. When we found the spot, it'd been replaced by a grubby little teashop.

"You know he invented the After Eight mint?" Arthur said.

Oh, God, not that old story. Dad always claimed that, while working for his Aunty Joyce, his first job out of school, he'd come up with the recipe for a thin mint covered in dark chocolate, a flash of culinary inspiration that came to nothing.

"They sold it to Rowntree's," Arthur said. "They must have given away a fortune."

"Well, you know, turns out he wasn't exactly forthcoming with the truth."

"He was very clever, though, wasn't he?"

"He invented the gas release valve for colostomy bags. I believe that one—the fucking fart valve."

"Ah . . ." Arthur said philosophically.

I was being too acidic, pushing too hard, tearing my father down while Arthur searched for any little shard he could recover. We walked through the market square with its cobblestones and striped awnings over the butchers and bakeries. It was strange being here in Salisbury without Aunty Sarah or Uncle Rog. I kept worrying we'd run into them. We turned toward the old city gate, stopping at a redbrick building with white shutters. Bishop Wordsworth's Church of England School for Boys.

"He boxed in school," I said. "Played third-team rugby for Wiltshire when he was fifteen."

Arthur nodded, taking it in. "I used to infuriate the phys ed teacher. He'd hand me a ball and say, 'Run.' And I'd stand there looking at him and say, 'Well, why? Why on earth would I do that?'"

I laughed; Arthur didn't.

We passed through the city gate out onto the cathedral green, and as I always do when I visit Salisbury Cathedral, I felt vertiginous from the scale of the whole hulking, ornate thing, its spire soaring above the frumpy row houses of the town.

"I remember picnics here with Granny and Granddad," Arthur said. "That's a nice memory."

Only then did it occur to me to wonder why Arthur and Harry had spent so much time here in Wiltshire. I came to these old places as a sightseer. For Arthur they were part of the ragged, living past, episodes from the childhood—shuffle the kids off to the grandparents so Mum and Dad can fight in private—he'd spent the last thirty years trying to understand.

On the way back to the car, we stopped in front of the Red Lion Hotel. Arthur led me through a wide arched entryway, built for horses and carriages. We looked inside. In the bar, an old man sat alone with a pint of lager and the newspaper.

"That's where they met," Arthur said. "She was the barmaid. Dad used to come in with his friends, get pie-eyed drunk, and flirt with her. She said he was the most obnoxious of all of them."

IN WEST GOMELDON, we made our first stop at the church. We walked among the graves, but the stones were too old and weather-beaten and mossy to make out family names. In the field behind us, a little stream gurgled. It was a beautiful spot, but I hardly noticed.

"Good day, so far?"

"Yeah, good." I couldn't help sounding sullen. This was Arthur's history we were visiting, not mine. It might have been perfectly natural for him to show me the parts of the family life he knew and I didn't. But I felt we were somehow competing over the memory of our father, and that in bringing me here Arthur had taken the upper hand.

"Everything is very clear to me," he said. When he lost his first tooth and first rode a tricycle. When, at the beach, his father showed him what cockles and whelks and periwinkles were and how to tell the difference. You had to boil them, take a little pin or a sewing needle and pluck out the meat. "He was always explaining little things like that."

"Yeah, he liked being the expert. He lost that in the last few years, just got obsessed with useless little projects around the house." What was I doing? Was I going to undermine every fond memory Arthur possessed? "His world shrank to just those four walls."

We walked down a gravel lane to a row of cottages. Arthur stopped in front of a tall wooden gate with a brass nameplate, *Greenfields*. On either side of the gate stretched a dense hedge. "This was never here," Arthur said, seeming disappointed. You could hardly see the cottage at all. We tried the gate. It was locked. Where the hedge ended, there was a carport crudely built of cinder blocks, covering a red Vauxhall hatchback and a wet-smelling heap of grass clippings.

"Should we shout?" I said. "See if anyone's home?"

Now that we were here, I wanted to see it, the house where my dad grew up. I called out. No answer. From a nearby farm came the bleating of lambs and the reek of manure. In frustration, I kicked a stone across the lane. We stood with our hands in our pockets, the dust settling around us.

"Well," Arthur said wearily. "I think this is all we get."

I TOOK AWAY the tall hedge and the shoddily built carport. In place of the Vauxhall hatchback, I substituted the old Jowett Javelin—spoke wheels, semaphore turn signals—I'd seen Captain Boast standing next to in black-and-white photos. I tried to see the garden stretching out behind the house in its regimented profusion, flowers on one side, vegetables on the other, all the way to the back fence, where the marrows lolled gluttonously on top of the compost heap. In the kitchen: a stringy roast chicken sweating on the counter, the pots on the stove on full boil, and Granny Boast leaning over them, stirring, her thick brown hair, not yet gray, worn up in a bun, her plastic-framed National Health glasses slipping down her nose in the heat.

I pictured Andy, nineteen, arriving home. He gets off the bus in Winterbourne and walks another mile to West Gomeldon, the dust from the gravelly road settling behind him. He comes to the green gate, opens the latch, goes around back where his father is working at the bottom of the garden, forking his compost, wearing a cardigan, a collar and tie, and Wellington boots. Andy waves to him; the old man waves back. They're accustomed to not speaking much. Andy goes inside, kisses his mother on the cheek, puts his duffel in the tiny, cold spare room, and sits down in front of the telly to wait for dinner. He watches snooker. Usually, he dozes off to the balls clicking against each other, the hushed applause. But this evening, he can't stop fidgeting. It's all he can do not to get up and walk right out the door again.

At a quarter to six he hears a faint *ding*. It comes from the bottom of the garden, where Granddad Boast has a bell hung from a rake handle. He rings it when he's ready for his wife to bring him his tea. Every night before dinner, he stands in his garden, drinking his tea, surveying the products of his labor.

At the table, the vegetables sit steaming in their bowls, the color boiled out of them. The exasperated-looking chicken waits to be carved. Finally, his father's footsteps at the back door, the flopping of his Wellies coming off. He comes in, his clothes spotless, not a fleck of dirt, posture straight and stiff, the bearing of a military man. He greets his son in his gruff, deep voice with its elongated vowels—his Welsh accent.

Sunday dinner. As if in protest to all those times during and after the war they had to scrimp and make do, it's too big a meal to finish. The chicken comes from Andy's grandmother's coop. His father's garden—so prodigious, a hymn to self-sufficiency— provides the rest. Andy's mother tells him what they've had on at the Women's Institute: a lecture on Norman churches, a preserve-making demonstration. His father asks him about his work at Dreamland, about his night school courses, and then, almost as an afterthought, about his girlfriend, Sara. Andy is evasive, says everything's good, fine. He already knows how his father will respond to what he's come to tell him.

But he *wants* to tell him—how every morning he wakes up in what feels like a stranger's life, a life in which nothing will ever be easy or simple again, as easy as evenings spent listening to jazz and reading *Private Eye*, ringing up friends to meet at the local for a pint, as going off to work every morning knowing that, if he wants, he can chuck it in anytime. All that is gone now. *I've gotten her in trouble, Dad,* he wants to say. *Put her in the family club. I'm in love, Dad, and I'm terrified.*

Andy's mother brings out the pudding, rhubarb crumble and

hot custard, and afterward they sit down in the living room for a glass of sherry and the end of the snooker match. The BBC has started broadcasting in color, but it's a black-and-white set. The announcer keeps on murmuring, the balls clicking together, and Andy, glancing over at his father, tries to read his mood, every moment about to part his lips and speak.

Captain Boast goes outside to smoke his pipe, and Andy follows. The evening has sunk into its deepest blue, the blue just before black, when just the outlines of things glow: the stones in the footpath, the runner bean frames, the compost heap. Andy leans on the fence next to his father, breathes in his pipe smoke and the sweet smell of manure. They stand in silence, listening to the lambs bleating down the hill. The moon has risen, and still they stand there, frozen, silent.

I'D SET the scene. So why couldn't I get them to *speak*? Did Andy fear his father so much? All my relations remember my grandfather as "a lovely man," charming and gentle. I was bent on portraying Captain Boast as severe and forbidding, with no time and no reassuring words for his younger son, just as I'd imagined Granny Boast sweating in the kitchen to make a meal as unpalatable, as English, as possible. I'd always devoured her cooking when we visited Salisbury.

I'd hoped fiction—my densely realized, closely observed novel—would somehow bring me closer to the truth. But if I wanted, I could make it all go differently: My father explains himself, pours out his heart. Granddad Boast answers him, gravely but tenderly, proffers hard advice, life lessons, the things a father passes on to his son that, heard but not yet understood, might one day show him how to become a man. But I didn't know those words. Everything I put into the mouths of my "characters" seemed to take me away from the truth, or left it in so many pieces I hardly knew how to start putting them back together.

And this was barely half of the story. I was sympathizing with my father, with his youth and confusion. What about Sara? Nothing would be simple or easy for her, to say the least. How could I begin to understand her story? Was it even mine to tell?

WE WERE HALFWAY back to Brighton when I asked the question, the one I wish now I'd kept to myself. "So," I said, trying to sound casual, "what did finally end the marriage?"

Arthur looked at me, hesitated.

The marriage ended, he said, because his dad was a drinker, because he stayed out all night with his friends and some weeks they hardly saw him. It ended because he spent all his money on clothes and beer, while the family went without. It ended because sometimes he came home and knocked their mum about, and on a few occasions he'd threatened him and Harry, as well. But, finally, it was the girlfriends that did it. Dad was sleeping around, and eventually he grew so bold that he started bringing his women home. "Mum got to be friends with a few of them," Arthur said, laughing ruefully. "And they ended up ganging up on him."

"Oh," I said, "the swingin' sixties, huh?"

And then I laughed, too. It seemed so absurd I didn't know what else to do but laugh. Arthur didn't elaborate on this last item, about the girlfriends, or on any of the others, and I didn't ask any more questions.

23

BURIED

t was August, the one month in Brighton that actually feels like full summer, and the beach was mobbed. Rose and I sat together watching Harry and the kids try to fly a kite. They'd come over to Brighton for the weekend; I was headed back to the States in a couple of days. There'd been talk of Sara and Neil coming as well, but Sara had just had another round of radiation and was too weak to make the trip. As we watched, the kite's strings kept tangling, and it kept nose-diving into the stony beach.

"You're very quiet, William," Rose said. "Arthur says you've had a bit of a disappointment."

"Yeah, I got my ass dumped."

I'd gotten an e-mail from Anna. She'd thanked me for her birthday package and told me, in a funny, apologetic way, that she really couldn't accept the earrings. She went on about summer in Charlottesville, about dog sitting, house sitting,

swimming in the pool. Then she let it drop: She'd met someone. I went out that night along the seafront promenade, crying,
pulling my hair, shouting at the grumbling sea. I lingered in
front of the dance clubs, staring icily at the people pressing
to get inside, hating their bright laughter and their flirting. It
started to lightly rain, not much more than a mist. I turned my
coat collar up, hunched inside it, and started cursing under
my breath, doing everything I could to keep up a tragic act. A
prop that had held me up for a very long time had crumbled:
No one was going to love me just because I'd suffered. Had I
really thought that she would save me, that she could redeem
everything? On my visits home with Claire, Dad would often
start unfurling his old schoolboy stories. I'd groan and protest,
but Claire ate it up. Sometimes she'd get him going just to see
the exasperated look on my face. We all knew our parts in the
routine, and I played the put-upon son with relish. Had I really
thought Anna could bring even that back?

"Shit, dumped isn't even the right word for it," I told Rose. "I
was never even going out with her. Fucking pathetic."

"Oh, William, I'm sorry. She probably wasn't right for you
anyway."

"Probably not," I said bitterly.

"You'll know when you meet the right one," Rose said, sounding a little defeated. I wasn't making it any easier for her to comfort me. "You won't have to work at it," she told me. "It'll just feel
right."

"Some things are worth working for though, right?"

"Well, maybe not everything," she said cautiously.

"I give up," I said, practically spitting out the words. "I just
fucking give up."

Harry and Charlie were kneeling over the kite, untangling its
strings. They got it up in the air and let Violet have a go flying

it. It crashed down again, but Violet and Charlie were all giggles anyway. A happy family. It felt like a taunt to me. Rose caught Harry's eye, and that thing passed between them, their unspoken communication.

"Why don't you all go swimming?" Rose called out. "William?"

"It's too cold."

"Nonsense!" she said, affecting a high, mock-posh accent. "Utter poppycock!"

Charlie and Violet splashed around in the shallows while Harry and I went out about thirty feet and treaded water.

"Everything all right?" Harry asked me.

"I give up. I give up on women."

"It can be hard. I remember how hard it can be."

"You met Rose when you were nineteen."

"God, I was lucky there." We were both breathing heavily keeping ourselves above the surface. Harry dunked his head and came up with the water streaming off him. "Jesus, that's cold."

"The sunny south," I said sarcastically.

"You're heading back early, then."

I'd called British Airways and moved my flight up. I had some frantic plan to win Anna back, though now I can hardly say what it was. I thought maybe just my presence, my dramatic return, would be enough.

"Back to regularly scheduled life."

"It's been nice having you so nearby."

"It has been nice," I said, and then I apologized for not getting to Southampton to visit more often.

"Don't worry," Harry said. "There'll be plenty of time."

As we bobbed up and down with the waves, I could see Rose playing with Violet and Charlie, pushing up piles of stones on the beach. Now Phillip and Arthur came down to join them.

Together, they were all laughing and talking, but I couldn't hear them over the waves.

"Everything's so fucked up. The past, now, everything. I mean, how the hell did we all get here?"

I looked to Harry for an answer. He didn't say *Things will get better.* Or *Look on the bright side.* I was grateful to him for that. "Well, here we are anyway," he said.

"I wish Rory could have met you."

"I would've liked that, too."

We came up the beach shivering. I laid out my towel. The stones were warm, and I lay there thinking about Anna and hating myself for thinking about her. Everything that had happened, everything I'd come to learn, all of the confusion and contradiction, and *this* was undoing me?

Charlie and Violet's giggling roused me. I pushed myself up on my elbows to see. They were pouring handfuls of pebbles on Arthur. "Oh, you rotten lot!" he said, pretending to be angry. They started with his belly. The little mound of stones began to spill over his sides and spread across his legs and chest.

"All right, all right, that's enough!" Arthur said, rising up, stones sliding off him in a cascade. Charlie could hardly hold back another fit of giggles.

"All right, William," Rose said, "your turn."

I squinted at her doubtfully.

"Sorry," she said, "no choice."

Charlie was already scooping up pebbles and pouring them over me. Fine, I said to myself, if it keeps the kids occupied.

The first stones were warm from the sun and felt good on my bare, wet stomach. But as Charlie dug deeper, they were wet and cold. Now Violet got in on the act, too, and then Rose and Harry. After a few minutes, my legs were completely covered. Arthur and Phillip joined in as well.

"Don't wriggle, Uncle Will!" Charlie scolded me.

"Well, it's cold." I couldn't help shuddering. Stones spilled off me, opening a little crack at my belly button. Charlie dumped a fistful of pebbles right on that spot. "Charlie," I warned. But my protests only encouraged everyone to work harder.

I tried to lie still, hoping that would get it over quicker. My arms were covered. I tested the weight of the stones and found it difficult to move. I squirmed, felt for air, but my fingers touched only dry stones. My skin prickled, a heat building that made me almost insane with rage. I had to hold my tongue to keep from saying something violent. I was up to my neck now, with only my face uncovered, and they kept going, the kids' shouts and laughter muted by the stones filling in around my ears.

24

HOME

I parked the Dodge in the driveway, then sat listening to the engine tick down till I could see my breath on the frigid December air. I'd driven eight hours to get from Indiana to Wisconsin. My back was sore. I was hungry, thirsty. Still, I couldn't bring myself to go inside. The night before I'd called him to say I'd be getting home around six. Now it was nearly eight, and by this point in the evening, he'd usually had at least four or five drinks.

But he was bright-eyed, all smiles. "There you are, guy. Always keeping me waiting." He was happy to see me, excited that we were going to spend these few days over Christmas together. Apart from sporadic visits from Rory's friends and Connie, the woman he'd recently hired to clean, he was always alone in that house. I carefully knocked the snow off my boots. We shook hands.

In the kitchen, he put a pan on the range to fry up the sweet-breads he was doing for hors d'oeuvres. By now he counted on me being late and knew to time the meal accordingly. "I thought something Continental for Christmas Eve," he said as the pale yellow sweetbreads sizzled in the oil, "then the old traditional roast for the big day."

I closed my eyes and yawned, luxuriating for a moment in the fleeting contentment, the wholeness, that comes with arriving home. That feeling would pass quickly enough. If Dad hadn't started drinking yet, tonight might go okay. He was a large man, and it took time for him to get really stewed.

We had the sweetbreads, a few dollops of caviar and sour cream on cocktail rye, and then filet mignon with cornichons and *pommes frites* for our dinner. Dad had even bought a half bottle of champagne for the occasion. Still, even in this meal, he'd satisfied his thrift: The sweetbreads, he said, had been cheap as chips.

After dinner we watched *Under Siege*, a cheesy action flick, which, inexplicably, he claimed to be his favorite movie. No, I knew why he liked it: the scene in which a big-breasted pinup model pops out of a cake, a moment he never failed to comment on, though he so rarely talked about sex, or even women. I knew that he'd quickly become infatuated with Connie. He talked about her often enough, anyway. Still, his interest in her seemed wholly innocent to me, an innocuous cliché—the widower's suppressed longing for the maid. There was also a woman at Filtertek who'd been bothering him. With his salary, his English accent, and his reserved, sometimes courtly manners, I could see how he might appeal to this woman. But she was way off the mark. Her advances were repugnant to him, either because he was loyal to Mom or because he found this woman hideous. Probably both.

After the credits rolled on *Under Siege*, we put on *Fawlty Towers*. We knew most of the lines by heart and sat mouthing them as John Cleese worked himself into a froth. Dad went out to the kitchen and got us each a Newcastle. "There you are, guy. Real English ale." We had a couple of beers each and then some cheese and biscuits. I was getting a little rosy-cheeked and felt as if I might be having a good time. This happened sometimes: These rituals could make us feel that we were close, that we were communicating, without either of us having to cast so much as a ripple over the silence that floated between us. We retired to the back room. Dad put Bill Evans on the stereo. When "Waltz for Debby" came on, I looked over and saw a tear running down his cheek.

"Christmas tomorrow," he said just as I was going upstairs to bed.

I turned and looked down at him.

He gave me a pained smile. "I know it's not a very happy time of year for us . . ."

"Right," I said, "I know."

I just wanted to go to bed having had a pleasant, somewhat dull evening with him. I just wanted to get through the next three days and then escape to Madison to get fucked up with my buddies for New Year's.

"We've got to pull together, guy. This time of year especially, we've got to keep the family together."

I felt an almost adolescent exasperation with him. We'd had a good night together. Why did he have to ruin it by getting all soppy? I nodded meaningfully, grimaced. "Yeah, we've got to stay together." Then I yawned conspicuously and put a foot on the second-to-last step, which creaked under my weight.

"Night, guy." I could hear it in his voice—the last thing he wanted now was to go to bed. He wanted to talk. Even if it took all night, he wanted to talk. But it wasn't like him to impose. "Sleep tight," he said and released me to the privacy of my room.

I lay awake in the dark, my feet hanging off the end of my childhood bed, listening to my father tossing and turning and groaning in his own bed, remembering that night four years before. The knock on the door had come just after midnight. I went down in my pajamas without my glasses on, squinted out from the stairwell at two police officers in dark blue jackets and turtlenecks, a man and a woman, their faces pink from the cold. Dad stood in his dressing gown, wearing just one slipper. I paused on the stairs, looking at the future, waiting on the edge of it. I already knew. Of course I knew. We all understand how these things go. First they tell you something's happened—an accident, they say where and when—and then they tell you the impossible.

I remember reeling around in tears. Fast, hard, disbelieving tears that came heaving up, then stopped abruptly, time enough to stammer out another question and even to apologize for making such a scene—then it came shuddering through again and I could hardly stand. I found myself in Dad's arms. The officers stood by silently. They weren't strangers. Fontana didn't have many of those. (Connie was the ex-wife of the male cop. Dad was always reminding me of this.) They had information, numbers to call, business cards. I wiped at my tears with the sleeve of my pajamas, trying to remember everything they were telling us, trying to keep my knees from buckling.

After the police left, we made a pot of coffee. By the time we thought to drink it, it was cold. I slept in Dad's bed that night. There was no other way to weather it. I felt the bulk of him next to me, the heat of him. In the dark, I turned and turned, orbiting my father's body. When he wept, I wept. Then, exhausted, we fell into fitful sleep. This went on for hours, until I couldn't tell his heavy, spluttering snores from his sobs. In the middle of the night, I woke. My father was rolled over on his side, away from me. I could hear him breathing but couldn't tell if he was awake as well. I lay there thinking: Rory is dead, Rory is dead. And as the enormity of that idea began to gather, the terror roared back in, breaking all the floodgates—all the voices screaming at once, everything all at once—and for maybe four or five minutes, I knew everything. I understood everything. The sound of my dad's breathing quieted; I could hear only the screaming. I lay very still, so that I wouldn't forget any of it, and I felt unutterably, horribly alive.

After Rory's accident, things seemed to continue as before. I went back to school and graduated. I thought about traveling, maybe bumming around Europe, but knew Dad wanted me close to home. So I moved to Chicago. Once a month, Claire came up to visit, and we'd spend long weekends making love and exploring the city. Every other visit, she and I drove up to Fontana. Dad would take us out to Friday night fish fry at the Big Foot Inn, or we'd go to the Milwaukee Zoo to see the penguin that Mom had adopted as a sixteenth-birthday present to Rory. When Claire was around, he hardly touched a drink, and when he mentioned Rory or Mom, it was always a fond memory, unsullied by guilt and regret.

One morning I woke to the phone ringing. "Turn on the TV, guy," Dad said. "We're at war." In my pajamas, hungover and unshaven, I watched the second of the Twin Towers fall. When I called Dad back, he told me to come back to Wisconsin. It was too dangerous to be in the big city, he said. No telling what the next target would be.

I told him, in a roundabout way, that I'd take my chances. He called me every morning for almost two weeks. To make sure I got to work on time, he said, but I knew better. Now I understood: For him, I could never be close enough to home.

The following summer, I moved to Indiana and, a month

later, broke up with Claire. The first time I made the drive from Bloomington to Fontana alone, I knew what I'd done. Eight hours. It was hardly worth coming home for the weekend. That same Sunday I left again at eight in the morning. Dad insisted I leave early—he didn't want me driving in the dark—but just as I was gathering my things, he disappeared into his room, complaining of an upset stomach. I said good-bye to him from behind a closed door.

He'd tried to hide it, but I'd seen the look on his face just before he fled to his room. I'd been home not much longer than a day, and already I was leaving again and wouldn't return for another two months. For me, two months of friends, parties, writing, drumming. For him, two months of solitude and desolation.

I WOKE on Christmas morning and lay there waiting for his call. *Hands off cocks, on with socks.* When I went downstairs, he wasn't up yet. I knocked on his door, put my head in. He was still in bed, the sheets kicked to the side. He stirred, looked up at me. He was drenched in sweat. He looked confused and exhausted. It had been a hard night. Even now, midmorning, his nightmares hadn't let him go.

When he got up, he made me an omelet and a cup of black coffee but had nothing himself. He worked at the stove, starting on Christmas dinner. He truly loved food. He should've been born and lived somewhere in the French countryside, running a bistro serving simple, rich, heavy fare. *Chez Andy*—we still joked about it sometimes. Toward the end his stomach pains were constant. Where once he would devour a meal, now he picked at much of what he made, saying he'd burned it or that the potatoes were practically raw, the whole thing inedible.

We opened presents. From me: a Nina Simone CD and *Miles*, the autobiography. He thanked me, effusively. I don't remember now what he'd bought me. Probably a couple of records or books I'd asked for. And a wallet, I think.

He was restless. He kept getting up to check the turkey, then stood at the front window staring out at the snow. I put on the Modern Jazz Quartet. He told me to turn it off, he had a splitting headache. But then he put the TV on, the volume so loud it rattled the TV's speaker. Around two o'clock, he went into his room. To take a nap, he said. He kept the bottle of Seagram's tucked behind the bedside table. There was always a wet ring from the tumbler he left on the cover of whatever Frederick Forsyth paperback he was rereading.

When he came out an hour later, it was with a heavy tread. He put on the gravy and vegetables and stood sweating over the stove. I helped dish up the meal. He'd put together quite a feast, all the familiar trimmings: stuffing, bread sauce, stump, roast potatoes, roast parsnips. But after a few mouthfuls he pushed his plate away with a low, dissatisfied grunt. His face was flushed, his glasses fogged from standing over the stove.

"Don't eat it, guy," he muttered. "It's ruined."

"It's good, Dad." I'd been eating greedily. A good meal was one of the few pleasures I had in coming home.

"The turkey's bone dry. Just throw it away."

"You don't have to be such a perfectionist."

"Just leave it."

The clawing in his stomach, the slow, agonizing burn of the ulcer—in his worst moments, and there were many of them, he must have welcomed the pain. How much more time alone could he bear? How many more evenings spent staring out the window, hurting, and waiting? Retirement, relaxation, hobbies— those things no longer held any appeal for him. He knew that, at some point, I'd want to move even farther away, that I'd leave the Midwest, that I'd been wanting to for years. He could see that I dreaded coming home and was always relieved to be gone again. (I could've shouldered the burden gratefully. But I was too impatient. I wanted to start *my* life.) For my father, there was no point looking to the future, and the present was just something to be endured. He kept a diary of sorts. I found it when I was going back through the contents of his desk. In the complimentary day planners he got every year from Filtertek's suppliers, the only dates he marked were "Nancy died" and "Rory died." The only daily entries he made were what he'd had for dinner—coq au vin or split pea soup or egg curry—with sometimes a little note saying "good," "awful," or "leftovers again." It made no difference what he ate; nothing stopped the burning in his stomach, the searing pain that reached down into his bowels and twisted him up like rope. He could no longer concentrate long enough to enjoy music. He left the TV blaring in the other room, filling the house with disembodied voices and laughter.

We both sat there, Dad looking down at his plate, me trying to look anywhere but at him. I finished my meal, even helped myself to seconds, trying to show how much I was enjoying it and also, we both understood, defying him. He rose from the table with another grunt, went into the back room, sank into his armchair. I forced myself to go over and join him. Sweating and dull-eyed, he stared out the window, down the length of the drive, as if I hadn't already arrived.

25

REVISION

My parents met in Dreamland.

So went the joke in our family. Our Dreamland was a light industrial concern on Southampton Water manufacturing electric blankets. Mom worked in personnel. Dad was a foreman on the line, and the dreamiest thing about him, in my mother's eyes anyway, was that he always forgot to take off his hairnet when he came into the office to chat her up. He had a flat in the city center, and they started meeting there to go for drinks or dinner with friends. He'd drive her out to the Concorde Club to see jazz: George Shearing, Acker Bilk, Ken Colyer. She never much cared for the music, but she liked seeing him dressed up. And she liked his laugh, the way it started with a chesty little wheeze and then burst out in his rumbling baritone. A private joke was what he liked best of all. They'd been seeing each other for months, and still he kept coming into payroll, wearing that mint green hairnet, just to get a laugh out of her.

~~This was my parents' history, how they met and came to marry.~~

At least this is the way I once would have told it—the way Mom and Dad had always told it to Rory and me, the details filled in here and there by my aunties and nanny: typical workplace romance; hardworking, elegant bachelor meets obliging office girl.

It wasn't a lie exactly. No one had been actively lying to Rory and me. Until the gaps become chasms, you don't bother scrutinizing your parents' early lives; it's all just prelude to your own arrival. How did Dad vault from dipping chocolates in his Aunty Joyce's shop in his late teens all the way to his early thirties, living in Southampton, and working as the foreman at Dreamland? I'd never asked. His secret had been kept so close I'd never even *thought* to ask.

~~My mother had a white wedding.~~

I'd always pictured a traditional, tasteful ceremony, all my great-aunties and -uncles in attendance, Dad and his best friend, Glenn, decked out in top hats and tails, my pretty young mother swanning down the aisle on her father's arm, crying tears of joy behind her veil while an elderly parishioner pumped away on the Wurlitzer. But I'd never seen a single photo of that perfect day, and, indeed—another discovery—none exists.

Andrew and Nancy were married on 27 March 1979 in the Register Office of Southampton County Council. Nanny and Granddad Snook, whom my parents told about the ceremony just the day before, were the only witnesses. It was done over the lunch hour, and afterward they all went back to work. After his disastrous first go-round with Sara, the last thing my dad wanted, Nanny tells me, was to remarry. And though my grandmother assures me that I was "not yet on the way" when, for some reason, he changed his mind and decided to try it all again, the dates don't lie—that day in the register's office, my mother was already three months pregnant.

I think now of the calculations she must have made. She learned—not long after she started seeing my father—that he'd been married and divorced, that he had two boys from that marriage, and that he hadn't seen them or his ex-wife in years. Whether his own foolishness or his first wife was to blame, he'd stepped out of their lives completely. So, as a husband and as a father, he was a risky bet. What details she didn't know, she might have guessed: There'd been money worries in his first marriage—there usually were. Yes, but now he had a good, steady job: foreman on the line. There'd been drink involved— he *did* like to drink. Well, she liked a few glasses of rosé now and then herself. Infidelity? He was starting to lose his looks. A few years and he'd be bald as an onion. Less danger of him sleeping around. Anyway, he was usually so shattered at the end of the workday he couldn't be bothered to do more than a fry-up dinner and collapse on the settee. Hardly enough energy for one woman.

~~My parents were never really in love~~.

It's easy for me to see their marriage as an accident or an act of duty—that grim, rushed register's office ceremony—and to believe that there was never enough between them to make a contented life together. The separate beds, the fights over piddling sums of money, the long silences that only slid away days later, unaddressed and unforgiven—by the time we got to Wisconsin, anyway, they hardly even seemed to like each other.

But then, truly, what do I know? "When Nancy and Andrew first met," a family friend tells me, "they got on like a house on fire." In photos from that time, Dad looks fit, trim, and happily exhausted. Mom is tanned and freckled from gardening, or maybe from their driving trip across the Alps to San Remo, a memory they trotted out for Rory and me now and then, a drunken revel from what I can infer about it now. I can see what they found in one another, how their contrasting temperaments kept them locked together even when everything else was pulling them apart. A marriage can survive on less. Perhaps it was just the typical story: ~~My father was mysterious, driven, perpetually dissatisfied. My mother pure, open, and uncomplicated~~.

As a girl, she had her share of boyfriends. She was not a stunner but possessed mild, delicate features and a perpetually girlish, inviting expression. In those old snapshots, she always seems to me the very personification of the girl next door: kind, approachable, with some mischief behind those bright blue eyes, but not too much. I know it's almost impossible to be objective about your own mother. Still, she was for me the source of everything gentle and forgiving, everything that abides, all of it inherited from my self-effacing, near-saintly nanny. Whatever turbulence and lack made my father, my mother had always known the restrained hand, the full cupboard, the indulgence and attention of her twelve aunties and uncles. Her childhood, at least, would have made up for some of what life later inflicted on her.

Several years ago I took a closer look at my father's papers. In the folder marked *Marriage/Div*, I found something I couldn't believe I'd missed the first time, another set of divorce papers: *Mom* had been married once before she met Dad. It took me weeks to work up the courage to ask Nanny about it. She'd kept this from me, and I wasn't sure I wanted to know why.

His name was Tommy Barton, Nanny wrote me. He looked like David Essex—meaning, I suppose, feathered seventies-pop-star hair—and my mom's marriage to him hadn't lasted more than a year. Things had ended amicably; they just weren't right for each other. And no, I didn't have anything to worry about. ~~There weren't any more brothers and sisters waiting in the wings for me to meet~~.

Strictly speaking, what my nanny told me was true. She said my mother didn't have any children with Tommy Barton, and that was no lie. It took a few more years for the caveat to come out.

Late in the revision of this book, I got an e-mail out of the blue, a woman informing me that she was doing ancestry research for "a friend." She listed information about my family—birth dates, marriage dates, dates of death—asking me to verify it. For a day or so, I was confused, apprehensive. Who exactly wanted to know all of this? And then I called my Aunty Janet, and it all came out: My mom had given birth to a baby girl when she was fourteen.

Soon after the birth, she and Nanny had gone to what was then—this was 1966—called a mother and daughter's home, a sort of halfway house where the mother could spend a few days with her newborn and decide whether to give it up for adoption or not. It was a time when women who'd "gotten into trouble" were "fallen," little better than prostitutes in the public eye. Many of these homes were essentially convents, and some of the women, those who had no family or were shunned by their family, ended up staying for years, cleaning and working to pay the good sisters for room and board. This, thank God, was not my mother's fate. (Though I wonder now about her distaste for the nuns who taught Rory and me in Ireland.) She went back home and returned to her last year of grammar school, and the whole thing was never spoken of again.

"Oh, dear," Nanny said when I asked her about it. She went quiet for several minutes. "As far as I was concerned, I'd raised two decent girls. I never thought she'd get into anything like that."

It was a boyfriend who'd gotten my mom pregnant.

"He was an intelligent nipper, a couple years older than Nancy. I didn't have anything against him. Of course, it was illegal. We didn't bring any charges. She was at the age when you just had to have a boyfriend. Amber Leah"—that was the name my mom gave her child—"it shows you how old she was. It was a fairy-tale name."

After the birth, the boyfriend wasn't in the picture much longer. Nanny "put the kibosh on that." The Snooks moved house soon after, and that was the end of it.

"Your mum breathed a great sigh of relief when it was all over. She never spoke about it afterward. I didn't think it was my place to tell you." There it was again, the discretion, the absolute devotion to privacy, handed down through the generations. "We never understood why your mum and dad didn't tell you these things."

Mom never spoke about it afterward.

This may well be true. No one else in my extended family, none of my great-aunts and -uncles, knew about the girl Mom gave up. Nor did any of her friends. As far as I've been able to discover, not even my dad knew.

Maybe her choices make more sense to me now. Dad was divorced, so was she. He had children he'd abandoned, she'd had to give up her baby. Maybe, when they met, they felt they'd found a kind of equilibrium in one another, a balance of pain and experience, of trauma and guilt. It must have brought them together, in the beginning anyway. It must have made all the risks easier to take, the moves easier to believe in.

~~We went to America for adventure and opportunity~~.

I once tracked down Dad's old friend Glenn and met up with him in a pub in Dorchester. I told him my dad had died. He was sympathetic and a little upset—he missed Andy. He asked me about my life over in the States. But I'd come to listen to him.

He'd known my dad not only when he'd been with my mother but when he'd been with Sara. Not only did he see Rory and me grow up but Arthur and Harry as well.

"We were rebellious guys," Glenn said, when I finally got him to talk about my dad. "We'd go to the pub after a few matches of badminton, have a few pints, stay up all night listening to Cat Stevens. We had a lot of laughs back then."

I told him some of the things I'd learned from my half brothers about our dad. As soon as I raised these questions—and they were indeed questions, because I surely didn't know the answers—Glenn began to close up. "Sara was older than us. She was more mature. Things could get a bit heated between her and Andy. Sometimes he and I got home a little late. We had some wild times. We were young guys, about your age. You know how it is."

I kept pressing, but Glenn just talked again about badminton and Cat Stevens. He didn't seem to hear the contradictions in the things he said—that my dad could stay out boozing all night and still be a good father and a good husband. (And since when had he ever listened to Cat Stevens?)

"You know," Glenn said as he dropped me at the train station, "the sad thing is that you had the best bit of him. And then you lost it."

It all came out in a rush. "Why'd we leave? Couldn't we have stayed here, in England? We'd have been happy here, right? And safe."

Glenn shrugged, helplessly. What he said next was for the memory of his friend, the same reason, perhaps, that Nanny, Aunty Sarah, and everyone else have tried to soften the hard truths for me.

"Your dad, he was competitive, ferociously competitive. If he was going to play badminton, he was going to be the best. America, plastics—he saw a good opportunity, a way forward, and he thought he'd wipe the slate clean."

And my mother, maybe she wanted that, too. All that heartbreak, all that shame—they were leaving it behind. It could never find them all the way across the ocean. They were going to a place most people back home couldn't even find on a map, the middle of the country, the middle of nowhere. It might be hard, it might even kill them. But it would be a fresh start. Everything would come clean in the wash. And the years piled up, and our lives were sometimes, mostly, comfortable, and if we weren't always happy, at least we had that.

~~MY FATHER cut away his entire past~~.

He turned away from the window and looked at me opaquely, half-erased by his Seagram's Canadian.

"Cheese and biscuits?" I said. But this didn't penetrate his fog. "Well, I think I'll have some. The Stilton maybe."

"Try it on," he said heavily.

"Come on, Dad, not now."

"Go get it and try it on."

I went into his room and pushed aside the work clothes hanging in his closet. Nearly every time I came home he made me do this. I found his dark blue camel-hair coat hanging on the same ancient hanger it always had, draped it over my arm, and took it into the back room. His head was tipped back in the chair. He roused with a snort and a cough when I came in.

"Go ahead, put it on. Cost four hundred quid when I bought it."

Hand-stitched, high-street tailor, no telling what it was worth now . . . He could go on about it. And it *was* beautiful, so well made it'd held its shape for decades. One day, Dad said, he'd make a present of it to me, just like he'd given Rory his shirts.

"Go on, guy."

"Christ, all right."

I slipped it on. The cuffs hung past my wrists, the chest and shoulders were like a tent over a pole, and I looked like what I was, a boy lost in his father's coat. Sitting there in his chair, Dad's eyes shone. A bleary smile came over his face, and I couldn't tell if he was wistful or proud or sad.

Every part of his earlier life, he'd gotten rid of it all. Every photo, every memento, every passing mention, every hint or clue—gone. But he kept his clothes: his bespoke 1960s shirts and that goddamn camel-hair coat. They would never fit him again, hadn't fit him in thirty years, not even close. Was it simple fantasy or wishful thinking—he might one day, magically, be that young buck again? No, they hung there as a reminder, of that glamorous, chaotic time, of the life and the family he'd walked away from, of the young man he'd been and all the mistakes that young man had made.

~~He and I shared the same pain~~.

When I came back in from hanging up the coat and sat down beside him, I saw that he'd been crying. He looked away, into his own reflection floating in the dark outside the window. I steeled myself for it.

"I never trusted him," he mumbled. "His friends . . ."

He'd run down Rory's friends constantly, and then at the funeral, they'd come in droves to show their support for our family. Now he practically lived for their visits.

"I couldn't trust him." The words came with such difficulty it seemed they might tear him apart. "Not even to choose his own friends."

"It's okay." I sat there squirming. "It's okay. Don't worry so much."

He opened his mouth to speak again—I saw him struggling to bring the words forth—and then he gave in and let the alcohol wash over him. He might have gone on. I might have learned something about him if I'd cared to listen. But my silence silenced him. We both sat there, staring out the window. He was so drunk he looked as if he'd been struck.

If we knew each other, it was through our grief. It was in every word we spoke, and in every silence—the taste of it lingering in the meals he cooked, in the sharp bite of his Canadian whisky, the woozy swill of my cheap beer. It was in the movies we watched, again and again, the songs we hummed along to under our breaths. I thought we didn't have to speak because I already knew everything about him. I thought I knew the exact dimensions of his pain.

In those last months and weeks, as the clawing in his stomach became unremitting, he must have thought of his first life more and more. Marrying my mom, having Rory and me, starting over, doing it right this time, putting the past behind him—yes, he'd tried. But the past doesn't let us go so easily, or we don't let it go. Maybe he punished himself in his second life for the wrong he did in his first. Maybe, as he stared out the window, he was remembering everything he'd lost. He was waiting not just for me to come up the driveway and knock on the door but Rory—and Arthur and Harry. It wasn't just one family he was grieving for over those endless winter nights but two.

That night, as he did so many nights, he would heave himself up from his chair and trudge off to bed before seven, to sleep off the booze, and then wake in the middle of the night and pace the house. The next day I would leave for Madison to party with my friends. I told myself there wasn't much point in being home when he was like this. I could've stopped in Fontana again for a night or two on my way back to school, but I lied to him and said I had too much work to do, response papers, that sort of thing. This trip would be the last time I would see him. Six weeks later, he'd pull his Impala to the side of the road, halfway between work and home, decide not to use his car phone to call for help, close his eyes, and let the last of his pain finally ebb away.

Prologue

The news from England came in bits and pieces: Sara was in and out of hospital. She fell and bruised her hip. She was coughing up blood. She thought there were starlings in the house and threw open all the windows and turned all the appliances to high trying to scare them out. The doctors kept revising their prognosis. Somehow she was still hanging on.

I did everything I could to help, which is to say, almost nothing. I could do almost nothing, except be a steady voice on the other end of the phone or write Arthur and Harry long, hopeful e-mails or send flowers to the funeral.

I wrote Sara a letter. I'd been trying to for weeks. I wrote about Wisconsin, about the snow and the cornfields and growing up near the lake, about working at the library with Mom, and Rory and me riding bikes through the back forty and going sledding on the golf course hills. I told her about going away to college and playing music in Chicago, about Virginia and where I thought I might go next—New York? Paris? back to Chicago?—rambling on for pages. But it was done, and it said what I hoped to say: This is my life and my past, tell me about yours. And beneath that, barely concealed, was what I really wanted to know: Who was my father? What kind of man had he really been? Sara was the only person who could tell me these things. She was the only one, now, who could condemn or acquit him.

A couple of weeks later, Arthur told me the letter had arrived. I waited for a response, a powder blue RoyalAir envelope in the mail. None came. I e-mailed Arthur and Harry about coming over to England again for the summer. Better to wait, Arthur said.

Sara went into the hospital again with an infection and while there went into cardiac arrest. They were able to resuscitate her. They even sent her home for several weeks. Then, on another hospital visit, she slipped into a coma for a day and a half. But, again, the doctors brought her around. Arthur was in Southampton almost every weekend—every trip home seemed like the last one. When I spoke to him on the phone, he sounded half awake. She was fading, he said. Some lucid moments but not many. He said again how much she'd enjoyed my letter. She was already too far gone, I understood. There was no chance now of her writing me back.

The last time Arthur mentioned my name to Sara, she looked up at him with questioning eyes, lost in her morphine haze. And then, Arthur told me, she seemed to remember.

"Lovely boy," she said. "Very sweet." She closed her eyes, pursed her lips, slipped away for a moment. "Very sweet," she murmured again. "Really, much too sweet."

It wasn't until later that they realized she wasn't talking about me, but the ambrosia.

* * *

IN JUNE of 2007, I finished at the University of Virginia. What came next, I wasn't sure. I could go pretty much anywhere I wanted while the money I'd inherited held out, and yet there seemed no good reason to go or stay anywhere in particular. (Except for England, that is, but I could no longer make England feel like home.) I went to Paris for a couple of weeks with some tread-worn vision of living in a garret in Saint-Germain-des-Prés. I wandered the museums, applied for a job at the American Library I was wildly unqualified for and didn't get, went back to Charlottesville, and moved into the archaeologist's house.

One day I got a call from one of my best friends from high school. He and his girlfriend of six years had just split up. She was moving out of their apartment in downtown Madison. The place was big, clean, and cheap. Did I want to come take over the second bedroom?

The day I left Charlottesville, driving another twenty-six-foot U-Haul, something came out of the early morning mist and ran straight in front of me. That part of Virginia isn't known for dairy farming, and anyway I was in the middle of a residential neighborhood. But sure enough, it was a Holstein, its black-and-white-spotted haunches swaying with odd grace as it passed before my windshield and disappeared into someone's backyard. I like to think I followed that cow all the way to Wisconsin.

My time there didn't last long, only five months. Shortly after my arrival in Madison, I got news that an application I'd sent off for a fellowship at Stanford had been accepted. Two years to live and write in San Francisco—my friends said they'd kill me if I turned it down.

A week before I left for California, I drove down to Fontana. It was much as I remembered it, only prettier—the willows down at the lake, wildflowers blooming in roadside ditches, the air thick with the fluffy cottonwood seeds that, mid-June, blanket over everything. I turned onto Forest Drive, parked across the street from the house. The new owners had built a garage and cut down the blue spruce that always used to tangle in the power lines. They'd had the deck redone and painted the house itself a cheery cornflower yellow. It looked good. It looked as if someone lived there again. I thought about going up and knocking on the door—thought of the story I'd been told about Arthur coming to Fontana and knocking on our door. The story wasn't true; Arthur had finally put the question to rest—it had never happened. Still, I couldn't get the image out of my head: my brother standing there on the doorstep, waiting for someone to answer, waiting, after all those years, to see his father again. I took a last look at the house, brushed cottonwood seeds off my lap, and started the car.

At the cemetery, a square lot next to the SuperSaver, nearly half of the headstones were topped with little plastic American flags, left over from Memorial Day or in preparation for the Fourth of July. Wandering through the graves, I recognized the family names: Pobursky, Magolski, Gerke, Arneson, Schnitke, Guftason. After a few minutes searching, I found the stone Mom's, Dad's, and Rory's remains were buried under. I'd had Dad cremated, just as he'd done for Mom and Rory. I sat in the grass and looked at my reflection in the polished granite.

Andrew J. Boast—June 30, 1945–February 23, 2004, Nancy P. Boast—October 17, 1951–December 23, 1997, Rory J. Boast—April 17, 1981–December 21, 1999.

It was a simple headstone, the three names engraved next to one another. I'd had the chance to choose a more elaborate memorial after Dad died, but I didn't see the point in splashing out. I was still my father's son, frugal even with the family name. I'd bought flowers on the way down from Madison. I tried to arrange them so they'd look nice, then finally just put them under a flat stone to keep them from blowing away. I kissed the gravestone, then walked across the street, past the Dairy Ripple soft-serve stand and Heyer's Hardware to the bank, where I closed out the savings account I'd started when I was thirteen. The teller handed me $13.23 and thanked me for my business. There was a time when I knew every teller in that bank by name. I knew their families and where they lived. I knew what cars they drove, who their friends were, who they dated. Now the teenage girl behind the counter was a stranger to me, and I was a stranger to her.

IN THE LOWER RIM of my vision, I could see Charlie and Violet working, scooping up stones and spilling them over me. Harry joined in, then Rose, then Phillip and Arthur.

"Right, little bruv," Arthur said, "your turn to put up with it."

They got into it, pushing up piles of stones against my sides, pouring them over my shoulders, covering my hands and feet. I squirmed again. Stones spilled off me and just as quickly were replaced with new ones. Charlie and Violet were giggling their heads off.

I could only just move my neck, enough to catch glimpses of my niece and nephew above me, my two brothers, their two partners. The stones pressed down, but I was weightless, ghost-limbed and hollow. I stared up at the sky, clear and blue for a change, closed my eyes and listened to the laughter around me. Slowly, my anger slipped away. I heard Harry's and Arthur's voices murmuring with the wash of the waves. I heard Charlie faintly: "Uncle Will! Uncle Will!" I kept my eyes closed and floated there, listening to my family. And for a moment I felt surrounded. I felt I was being taken in their arms.

Acknowledgments

My great and enduring gratitude for all of those who read, listened, and helped me along the way:

Molly Antopol, Ann Beattie, Ryan Bieber, Erin Brown, John Casey, Harriet Clark, Jennifer DuBois, Rob Ehle, Deborah Eisenberg, Tom Franklin, Sarah Frisch, Jim Gavin, John Hickey, Skip Horack, Vanessa Hutchinson, Drew Johnson, Ammi Keller, Jason Labbe, John L'Heureux, Ryan McIlvain, Robin Metz, Kim Philley, Kirstin Valdez Quade, Justin St. Germain, Caitlin Satchell, Maggie Shipstead, Stephanie Soileau, Mary Austin Speaker, Elizabeth Tallent, Chris Tilghman, Jesmyn Ward, Gina Welch, and Tobias Wolff.

For all of their careful, intelligent work and guidance in helping bring this book into the world:

Katie Adams, Charlie Brotherstone, Cordelia Calvert, Gail Hochman, Jody Klein, Peter Miller, Max Porter, and Paul Reyes.

For the generous support of these institutions and individuals:

The Bread Loaf Writers' Conference, Martin Pick and the Charles Pick Fellowship, the San Francisco Foundation, Stanford University, the Truman Capote Literary Trust, the University of East Anglia, and the University of Virginia.

Finally, I want to acknowledge the support and love of my friends and family. I'll never be able to thank you enough.